EQUALITY AND RESPONSIBILITY

Equality and Responsibility

CHRISTOPHER LAKE

OXFORD
UNIVERSITY PRESS

OXFORD
UNIVERSITY PRESS

Great Clarendon Street, Oxford OX2 6DP

Oxford University Press is a department of the University of Oxford.
It furthers the University's objective of excellence in research, scholarship,
and education by publishing worldwide in

Oxford New York

Athens Auckland Bangkok Bogotá Buenos Aires Cape Town
Chennai Dar es Salaam Delhi Florence Hong Kong Istanbul Karachi
Kolkata Kuala Lumpur Madrid Melbourne Mexico City Mumbai Nairobi
Paris São Paulo Shanghai Singapore Taipei Tokyo Toronto Warsaw

with associated companies in Berlin Ibadan

Oxford is a registered trade mark of Oxford University Press
in the UK and in certain other countries

Published in the United States
By Oxford University Press Inc., New York

British Library Cataloguing in Publication Data

Data available

Library of Congress Cataloging in Publication Data
Lake, Christopher
Equality and responsibility / Christopher Lake.
p. cm.
Includes bibliographical references and index.
1. Distributive justice. 2. Distribution (Economic theory) 3. Equality. 4. Responsibility.
I. Title.
HB523 .L35 2001 330.1—dc21 2001036385
ISBN 0-19-924174-0

1 3 5 7 9 10 8 6 4 2

Typeset in Minion
by Best-set Typesetter Ltd., Hong Kong
Fine Print (Services) Ltd., Oxford
T.J. International Ltd., Padstow, Cornwall

PREFACE

Before going to university I was a civil servant. Despite, or perhaps because of, being involved in government on the inside I really did not have much idea of what academics in politics departments did all day. It certainly did not occur to me that there might be an entire academic industry, made up of intelligent men and women from all over the world, devoting themselves to something as nebulous as *political theory*. That there was such an industry only became clear to me during my first year as an undergraduate at Newcastle University when I took a course in democratic politics. Having fancied myself as something of a sophisticate when it came to understanding the underlying principles of government and politics, it dawned on me that there existed a whole body of theoretical thinking out there which raised questions that had never occurred to me and supplied answers more advanced than any I had imagined could exist. As a result, I very soon found myself acquiring two prejudices that I am still unable to shake off. One is that the most fundamental, and fundamentally interesting, questions in politics are theoretical. The other is that the very best of those who theorize about these questions are very good indeed.

The thought that it was not only legitimate but in some ways respectable to spend your days theorizing about the world in the way of political theorists led me to try to get as much political theory under my belt as I could in the second and third years of my undergraduate degree course. Looking back, however, I see it was never the case that the subject just sold itself to me or that I peered into it and effortlessly saw its possibilities. The simple truth is that I was very well taught. Both Tim Gray and David George did much to inspire and satisfy my curiosity, whilst the dominant figure in my undergraduate life was Peter Jones, who managed to combine modesty and decency with wonderful intellectual clarity. When I was lucky enough to have the chance to teach undergraduates myself, I wanted to be the kind of teacher that Peter had been to me.

From Newcastle I went to Nuffield College, Oxford, where I was fortunate to have David Miller teaching, supervizing, and otherwise guiding me through graduate life. A good deal of what I learned about political theory in my time at Nuffield I owe to him. I also learned much from other graduate students in Oxford at the time, weekly meetings of whom were convened under the auspices of the Nuffield political theory workshop. Presenting papers in this forum was a stimulating but demanding exercise and certainly not for the fainthearted.

It was in my first year at Nuffield that I began to get interested in questions of equality and individual responsibility. Thomas Nagel's *Equality and Partiality* had just been published and it brought home to me not only how compelling was the combination of arguments about responsibility with those about equality but also how problematic. After spending some time concentrating on what Nagel had to say in these matters, I then went on to explore more general questions involving egalitarianism and responsibility in my doctorate. In this enterprise I was very well supervised by David Miller and, for a term, by Joseph Raz. I owe a debt of gratitude to both, as I do to my friend and erstwhile Nuffield colleague, Daniel Attas, who put me right on issues too numerous to mention. I am also indebted to my examiners, John Horton and Raymond Plant, for their encouragement as well as for their intelligent and thought-provoking comments. More recently, I spent a very happy term on sabbatical at the politics department of the University of Glasgow. Chapter 7 benefited considerably from the observations of Michael Lessnoff, who was generous with his time throughout my stay north of the border. The chapter also benefited from the comments of David Miller and of the person at whose work much of it is directed, Stuart White.

I am very grateful to the three anonymous referees who were good enough to offer detailed and incisive comments on all aspects of the manuscript. Their influence is felt throughout and, in particular, in Chapters 5 and 6. For the rest, I can only say that the book would be unrecognizable were it not for the time, effort, and clear thinking devoted to it by Matt Cavanagh. I owe him special thanks. As befits the subject matter, (liability) responsibility for all errors falls to me and me alone.

There are other debts I should acknowledge. If it was the work of Thomas Nagel that made me think there was something important here to explore, it was the work of G. A. Cohen that pointed me in the direction of what that something might be—so much so that I often had the feeling that I was either responding to or trying to develop Cohen's intuitions in these matters. The thought that I was working within the terms of an existing debate, and that that debate had been conducted to a high level of sophistication, was in part reassuring and in part frustrating. I never felt entirely alone but nor did I always feel confident that I really did have something to tell the world. T. M. Scanlon, for one, has interesting and important things to say about the questions I address here and I readily admit to being much influenced by his work. When in doubt about questions of responsibility, I often found myself referring to and agreeing with Bernard Williams. When confronted by similar doubts in the matter of equality, I looked to the work of Derek Parfit for clarification. All of which is a roundabout way of saying that I owe these thinkers a profound debt. Without them, I would not have known where to begin.

Dominic Byatt has been an exemplary editor at OUP—tough but encouraging, he was as efficient as he was approachable. I could not have asked for more from him.

It so happens that my mother, Rhona, was good enough to read the manuscript and to point to a number of things that I had got wrong. Her intellectual involvement in the book means, happily, that I can include her name in these acknowledgements whilst sparing her the embarrassment of another kind of tribute altogether.

CONTENTS

INTRODUCTION

The chapters that go to make up this book are organized around the theme of equality and responsibility.[1] What draws me to this theme is the belief that much of the contemporary debate about distributive justice—that is, about *who should get what*—centres on the demands that equality and responsibility are thought to make on us. This is true of that debate not only as it is conducted in political circles but also as it is conducted in academic circles. In both arenas it has proved difficult to escape the thought that in deciding how goods should be distributed we are required to defer *in some way* to equality and *in some way* to individual responsibility. Of course, people disagree about how we should interpret these demands just as they disagree about how we might combine or balance them. But the thought that concerns about equality *and* concerns about responsibility will occupy a fundamental place within any plausible distributive theory is one that continues to exert a powerful hold on our political imagination.

This is especially true of those who regard themselves as egalitarians. Egalitarians claim that their distributive schemes succeed where those of their rivals fail. And their schemes succeed, on this view, because they honour the demands of equality and responsibility—singly and taken together—in a uniquely compelling way. This they do through serving the requirements of what I term the egalitarian intuition. According to that intuition, it is objectionable for some to be worse off than others through no fault of their own.

The progenitors of this intuition are *philosophical* egalitarians, an epithet conveying the idea that egalitarians of this kind approach and write about questions of responsibility, equality, and justice from the perspective of academic theoreticians. This is in contrast to what might be termed *political* egalitarians, this being the community of left and centre left political practitioners and thinkers.[2] Their approach to questions of who should get what is less abstract than that of their philosophical counterparts and more attuned to the compromises and exigencies of everyday political life.

I am naive enough to think that the question of how equality and responsibility fit into our thinking about who should get what would be philosophically interesting regardless of the political backdrop against which it was considered. It would be interesting, that is, even if the commitments of political egalitarians, and of the left more generally, were stable and unambiguous. That we are not living in such a time—and that the left is engaged in the business of redefining its commitments and priorities—does nothing to make the question less interesting *philosophically* and a good deal to make it more interesting *politically*. So although the chapters that follow are an exercise in philosophy, they are intended to cover some of the theoretical ground that political egalitarians need to cover as part of the process of examining their fundamental commitments. Indeed, the overlap between the two enterprises is such that I have taken the opportunity in this book to touch upon a broader question of concern to political egalitarians, albeit one that follows directly from arguments about equality and responsibility. This is the question of whether egalitarians should, in the name of an attachment to the notion of reciprocity, insist upon forging a link between work and the claiming of social benefits.

I suppose there would be no call for a book like this were it obvious where the demand to honour the claims of equality and responsibility came from— and indeed where it led; or were it obvious that equality and responsibility lend themselves to being combined in the way that egalitarians want; or obvious what we should and should not hold people responsible for. But none of these questions has an obvious answer—although, of course, many philosophers have tried to supply answers to them. I take some of these philosophical arguments as a starting point but I do not pretend to offer a comprehensive review of the literature on offer. Nor do I pretend to advance or unearth a new theory of justice. What I have tried to do is identify the more important and interesting arguments in circulation, to assess their strengths and weaknesses, and to see what is left standing at the end. My aim in all this is to see where, and how far, the appeal to concerns about responsibility and equality takes us in thinking about who should get what. In this connection, I see there being certain questions that naturally and necessarily occur to us when we think about how these concerns bear upon the issue of how goods should be distributed and it is these concerns that I have written about. In some chapters I concentrate more on the arguments themselves than on what individual thinkers have to say about them. In others—especially where it seems to me that a particular thinker has presented the arguments in a compelling way—the emphasis is somewhat different.

In terms of style, I have tried to write the book, or at least the better part of it, in a way that is accessible to those unfamiliar with the ins and outs of philosophical egalitarianism. In this sense, the work is pitched at two audiences rather than one. And whilst I have tried to stay close to my intuitions throughout, I make no bones about the fact that this is in essence a theoretical exercise rather than a recipe book for actual or aspiring politicians. The approach I adopt, the arguments I draw upon, and the cast of characters to whom I appeal will be a good deal more familiar to those who view political questions from the vantage point of academia than it will be to those who view these questions from the vantage point of practice or, indeed, general interest. The essays do not require prior familiarity with the work of contemporary philosophers such as John Rawls or Thomas Nagel or G. A. Cohen. What they *do* require is a willingness on the reader's part to think about political questions in abstract terms and a certain open-mindedness when it comes to understanding the sorts of debates that preoccupy political philosophers.

As it is, I have been speaking so far as though there were a settled and clearly defined body of thought conveniently labelled *philosophical egalitarianism*. Needless to say, this is misleading. The egalitarianism with which I am concerned is not that of socialist and social democratic thinkers such as Tawney and Laski. It is, instead, the egalitarianism of contemporary liberal thinkers, an egalitarianism that began its life with John Rawls and has largely grown out of responses to, and refinements of, Rawls's work. By this I do not mean that the egalitarian thinkers I focus on are Rawlsians to a man, merely that the debates I address are ones in which Rawls's work occupies a prominent place. In this area of contemporary political philosophy, as in others, it is the work of Rawls that has largely determined the terms of the debate and this influence is reflected in my own treatment of the issues.

So much for the preliminaries. In what remains let me sketch the trajectory that the book follows. The first two chapters pose perhaps the most searching question confronting anyone who recites the equality and responsibility mantra. This is the question of why equality and responsibility *matter* in thinking about who should get what—allowing for the possibility that they should not matter at all, or that they should not matter as much as people think, or that they should matter but not for the reasons people think they should. The issue of equality is dealt with in the first chapter where I ask what, if anything, is objectionable about inequalities. At the heart of this discussion lies the thought that the question of whether inequalities are objectionable is easily confused with the question of whether inequalities give rise to objectionable effects or come about through objectionable means. Identifying what is *distinctively* objectionable about inequalities allows us to consider how arguments about inequalities in general tie in with arguments about individual responsibility in particular.

From there I move on in the second chapter to offer a similar treatment of concerns about responsibility. To this end, I start by pointing to the different senses in which people are said to be *responsible* for things and I then ask why our responsibility for something matters in assessing the claims we advance. As part of this exercise, I review a number of attempts to account for the significance of responsibility in our thinking about who should get what. One such attempt holds responsibility to matter for instrumental reasons—we defer to personal responsibility because doing so is likely to have better effects than not doing so. Another attempt holds responsibility to matter in itself—

we defer to personal responsibility because we owe it to individuals to treat them as rational and choosing beings. Running alongside these two views is a further distinction—a distinction between arguments that focus on claims of responsibility as these apply to individuals considered in isolation from one another and those that focus on claims of responsibility as these apply to the regulation of relations between individuals.

The question of why responsibility matters does bear upon, but is nonetheless distinct from, the question of what people can be held responsible *for* and it is the latter I look at in the third chapter. To this end, I begin by asking whether questions about what people are responsible for can be answered without our becoming embroiled in deeper philosophical questions about determinism and the metaphysics of the will. Armed with the thought that they can, I go on to examine different ways in which we might draw the boundaries of individual responsibility and its preconditions and to express doubt about whether we really do have the materials at present even to stabilize our judgements in this area, still less to pronounce upon them with confidence. From there, I move on, in the fourth chapter, to say something more about the place of claims about individual responsibility in arguments not just about how goods should be distributed but arguments also about what those goods should be. It is under this heading that I take the opportunity to examine an argument that appears to combine claims about what people are responsible for with claims about what they should have equal amounts of. This is the social division of responsibility argument advanced by Rawls.

The fifth chapter tackles the egalitarian intuition itself and points to the difficulties confronting egalitarians in their attempt to combine relational concerns about equality with non-relational concerns about individual responsibility. I claim that egalitarians are often caught between these two concerns and that their commitment to distributing goods on the basis of responsibility is weaker than appearances would suggest. The sixth chapter examines the egalitarian position in the matter of the moral status of natural talents and in particular the claim that the distribution of natural talents is morally arbitrary. Having tested this claim, I then go on to look at the link between the egalitarian position on natural talents and the claims egalitarians make about the standing of markets and market outcomes. The seventh—and last—chapter explores the broader question relating to the egalitarian project that I mentioned before, namely, the question of whether claims of reciprocity should occupy an important role in egalitarian thinking and how such claims bear upon the issue of work and the receipt of social benefits.

Having said that I am not out to supply a novel theory of justice—and, indeed, that my objectives are largely critical rather than constructive—let me end here by indicating what I hope will emerge from the whole project. First and foremost, it seems to me pretty clear that our ideas about why equality and responsibility matter—and about what *kinds* of demands they make on us—are more confusing and more diffuse than we intuitively recognize. This is so even where those ideas are examined in isolation from one another. The attempt to *combine* our ideas about equality with our ideas about individual responsibility does nothing to resolve that confusion and much to heighten it. Indeed, it is for this reason that the attempt to construct a theory of distributive justice out of claims about equality and responsibility runs the risk of incorporating the intuitive pull of neither. I do not mean by this that the enterprise is condemned to failure. But if egalitarianism is to stand up as a compelling distributive scheme then there are a number of questions it must confront. It is these questions, and some possible answers to them, that I try, in what follows, to pinpoint and assess. And even where answers are not forthcoming, I hope that the reader will at least come away from the exercise with a sense of what philosophical egalitarians are arguing *about*—amongst themselves and with their rivals—and of what it is about those arguments that makes them interesting and important.

1

What is objectionable about inequalities?

I want to begin with the question of what, if anything, is objectionable about inequalities. By *objectionable* I mean morally objectionable—objectionable in the sense of being wrong or bad—rather than aesthetically objectionable—objectionable in the sense of being ugly or vulgar. *Inequalities* I interpret broadly to embrace social, or socially induced, inequalities as well as what are sometimes called natural inequalities. The *if anything* part of the question is intended to ensure a certain neutrality in the prosecution of the argument. My starting point is to be agnostic as to whether there is anything objectionable about inequalities at all. Whilst my approach is to test the case against inequalities I might just as easily have approached the question from the other end and tested the case against equalities. In the matter of whether inequalities are or are not objectionable, I have no axe to grind.

In thinking about what is wrong with inequalities three broad kinds of argument are at work. One focuses on the consequences of inequalities. Another focuses on their causes. And a third sees inequalities as objectionable for reasons to do neither with their consequences nor with their causes.[1] The first and second arguments adopt something of a permissive stance on the matter of inequalities. By this I mean that they do not necessarily object to the bare fact of inequality: they do not necessarily hold inequalities to be objectionable regardless of their consequences or regardless of how they have come about. Inequalities are objectionable if, where, or because certain things are true of those inequalities—other than that they *are* inequalities. Were none of these things to be true of inequalities—were we to be confronted by what I have called the bare fact of inequality—then neither argument would necessarily supply grounds for objecting to inequalities. Of course, neither would necessarily supply grounds for *not* objecting to inequalities, but we can leave that complication to one side for the moment.

Whilst the first argument targets the consequences of inequalities and the second their causes, the third holds there to be something objectionable about inequalities as such: bare inequalities are objectionable simply because they

are bare inequalities. This claim gives the impression of being morally primitive and invites an obvious rejoinder: if inequalities do not come about by
objectionable means and if they do not induce objectionable consequences,
what possible objection could there be to them? To which, I think, the primitive, and seemingly compelling, answer comes that inequalities simply *are*
objectionable in the way that injustice simply *is* wrong and pain simply *is* bad.

Before proceeding to the main body of the argument, I ought to say something about how these three arguments relate to one another. The first and
second are not mutually exclusive: we can at one and the same time object to
inequalities because of their causes *and* because of their consequences. Nor
are the two arguments, for the purposes of this discussion at least, incompa-
rable. In assessing whether inequalities are objectionable, we may need to
weigh the claims of causes against the claims of consequences. We may, for
instance, believe inequalities that would otherwise be objectionable by virtue
of their causes are rendered unobjectionable by virtue of their consequences—
and vice versa.[2] A more difficult issue is that of how the third argument—the
argument that objects to the bare fact of inequality—relates to the first two.
Presumably, when we object to *inequalities* by virtue of their causes or their
consequences we are doing more than objecting to the causes or the consequences themselves. What we are objecting to is the *conjunction* of inequalities with certain causes and consequences. After all, were we not already
suspicious of the moral standing of inequalities we would hardly think it
worth investigating them in conjunction with their causes and consequences—or anything else for that matter. And if we are already suspicious of
the moral standing of inequalities, then it seems we are already under the
influence of the third argument I mentioned: we are operating from the
assumption that the bare fact of inequality is objectionable. That being so,
would it not be better to begin by exploring the third argument? Having got
to the bottom of it, we might then go on to examine how the concerns about
bare inequalities it contains tie in with the concerns about causes and consequences contained within the first two arguments.

Tempting though this is, I have opted not to begin with the third argument.
This is for two reasons. First, my guess is that often we do conflate objections
to causes and consequences, regardless of the distributions they issue in or
from, with objections to *inequalities*, thereby attributing to one the sins of the
other. Working our way through the first two arguments will, I hope, help us
to distil such conflations and thereby to identify more clearly the issues at
stake. The second reason is less well grounded in analytical fastidiousness. It
is simply that my own intuitions on these matters seem to be at their most
vivid in the case of causes and consequences. In any event, I am hopeful that
by the time we have worked our way through the first two arguments we will
have a better idea of what the arguments are concerning the third.

Let me begin with the first argument, the argument from *consequences*. Some believe that inequalities give rise to bad consequences. Thus it is sometimes claimed of inequalities that they are demoralizing and divisive and that they corrode the cooperative spirit. Others claim that the bad consequences of inequalities should be understood in terms of inefficiency. They argue that if we are to benefit those who need it most or if we are to maximize aggregate welfare, it may be better to distribute goods more rather than less equally. The argument from consequences can, however, be expressed in two quite different ways. According to the weak version, inequalities *would be* objectionable were they to have the relevant bad consequences. Were inequalities not to have the relevant bad consequences, there would be no objection to them, on the grounds of their consequences at least. Indeed, were it to be shown that the bad consequences commonly attributed to inequalities ought properly to be attributed to equalities, then, on the grounds of consequences, we would be committed to objecting to equalities instead. In practice, it may be that neither form of distribution is without its bad consequences and that neither is without its good consequences. As such, we may have to balance the relevant consequences against one another according to the circumstances of the case. We may, for instance, have to trade claims about the desirability of giving people incentives against claims about the undesirability of undermining the cooperative ethos. Only where the balance of consequences is more favourable to equalities than to inequalities will we be disposed to favour the former over the latter.

There is, however, a strong version of the argument from consequences. Whereas the weak version leaves open the question of whether inequalities have bad consequences, the strong version holds bad consequences to follow unavoidably from inequalities. Some will think this stronger claim vulnerable to empirical challenge. They will say that whether inequalities have bad consequences is an empirical matter: it cannot plausibly be accorded the status of an a priori truth. This objection is a powerful one if our concern is with the sorts of consequences I have been examining so far and the sorts of relation between distributive patterns and consequences I have implicitly been holding to obtain. But note *what* I have been assuming so far. I have assumed there to exist a relation between an inequality and that which is not an inequality (a consequence) and a consequence and that which is not a consequence (an inequality). Imagine now that we abandon these relational boundaries and, with them, the claim that inequalities *have* or *give rise to* bad consequences. Imagine we put in place of that claim the claim that inequalities simply *are* bad consequences.[3] Thus it might be said that it is bad for people to be on the receiving end of inequalities in the same way as it is bad for people to be on the receiving end of pain. Just as we do not have to answer the question of why pain is bad (pain being pain simply *is* bad) so we do not have to answer the question of why inequalities are bad (inequalities being inequalities simply *are* bad). On this view, inequalities, like pain, are bad in and of themselves in the sense that what is bad about them is not derivative of some other bad consequence.

Why might we be drawn to this view? Motivating us to see inequalities as bad consequences in themselves might be a belief that it is better for people to be equal in whatever we are concerned with than for them to be unequal in that thing. We might believe, that is, that equal states of affairs are better *qua* states of affairs than unequal ones. As Derek Parfit has pointed out, however, to sign up to this view of inequalities is to commit oneself to a counter-intuitive position. Most obviously, there is what Parfit calls the *levelling down objection*.[4] Imagine that A has more units of pleasure to his name than B. If we think that inequalities are bad in and of themselves, we will think it better for A and B to be equal in the amount of pleasure to their name even if this can be secured only at the cost of reducing A to the level of B and, *in extremis*, of reducing both A and B to nothing. Something else follows from the levelling down objection. Imagine that A has more units of *pain* to his name than B—would we want to say in this case that it is better for A and B to be equal in the amount of pain they experience, even if this can be secured only at the cost of increasing the amount of pain B experiences and, *in extremis*, of seeing to it that A and B both experience agony? I think not.

The levelling down objection does not, however, conclude the issue, for there appears to be a reply to it. That reply runs as follows. In the examples I used above—featuring A and B and the levels of pleasure or pain each enjoyed—it would seem that I conflated two quite different versions of the claim that equal states of affairs are better, *qua* states of affairs, than unequal ones. According to the strong version of that claim, it is true *all things considered* that equal states of affairs are better than unequal ones.[5] According to the weak version, it is true *ceteris paribus* that equal states of affairs are better than unequal ones. The examples I drew on—examples where, in the name of equality, A is deprived of pleasure or B condemned to pain—certainly seem to tell against the strong version. But they do not seem to tell against the weak one. If we subscribe to the weak version, we can allow that the bad consequences of permitting inequalities to stand need to be weighed against the possibly worse consequences of pursuing equalities regardless of the effect of such equalities upon the amount of pleasure or pain in the world. In this way, we can preserve the idea—as we cannot if we subscribe to the strong version of the argument—that inequalities are indeed bad in and of themselves, without signing up to the intuitively implausible idea that inequalities are the *only* thing in the world that is bad, or that in all cases we must forego any

amount of pleasure and pain in the name of equality. From the fact that equality has intrinsic value it certainly does not follow that it has unconditional
value.[6]

Having, however, attempted to rescue the claim that inequalities are bad
consequences in and of themselves—the claim that there is something about
states of affairs being unequal that makes them worse, *qua* states of affairs,
than equal states of affairs—I must now cast further doubt on that claim.
Imagine you have a toothache and others do not. What would improve that
state of affairs? If you believe equality to have independent value, then you
will believe it would be better—in some sense and to some extent—for others
to have a toothache as well. But for whom would this be better? Certainly not
for you: your toothache does not become less bad by virtue of being experienced by others nor more bad through not being experienced by others. From
your perspective, there is nothing bad about your toothache over and above
the fact that it is *your toothache*. Indeed, it would be mysterious to say of your
toothache: 'It's too bad that you happen to have a toothache at a time when
others don't, but things may yet improve, for others may have a toothache
tomorrow'. If others having a toothache is not better for you, then is it better
for them? Clearly not. So now we confront two claims that pull in different
directions. On the one hand, stands the claim that a world in which everyone
has a toothache is in some sense better than one in which some have a
toothache and others do not. On the other hand, stands the claim that there
is no one *for whom* it is better. In fact, the second proposition is really an objection to the first, what Parfit calls the *person affecting objection*.[7] That objection, in turn, appears telling.[8]

How have we got ourselves into this position? The answer is that we have
been distracted. From the observation that improvements in states of affairs
sometimes involve a move from an unequal distribution of a thing to an equal
one we have been drawn into thinking that the move from inequality to
equality is in and of itself an improvement in a state of affairs. Return to
my example of a world in which some suffer from toothache and others do
not. Of course, it would be better were *no one* in the world to suffer from
toothache. But it would not be better because there would be less inequality
in the world. It would be better because there would be less pain in the world.[9]
It is true that in eliminating pain from the world we would thereby eliminate
inequalities in pain. But from the fact that the demand to eliminate pain may
push in the same direction as the demand to eliminate inequality, it is quite
wrong to infer that inequality *per se* is bad in the way that pain *per se* is bad.

Recall that my concern in this section has been to examine the relation
between inequalities and consequences. I began by considering the claim
that inequalities tend to give rise to bad consequences—that they tend, for
instance, to be demoralizing and divisive or that they tend to be inefficient. I

suggested that even if we accept this as so, the argument points to no more
than an empirical tendency. As *a tendency*, it remains vulnerable to empirical
challenge—not to say refutation. But that is not the most important observation to make about the argument. The most important observation is that it
tells against inequalities only *in so far as* they produce the relevant bad consequences. Only through conflating inequalities with the contingent, and contentious, fact of their putatively bad consequences can we mount an attack on
inequalities. In this sense, the attack on inequalities here is essentially polemical: it uses inequalities as a shorthand for (certain) bad consequences. Having
examined the claim that inequalities are objectionable by virtue of giving rise
to bad consequences, I then examined the thought that inequalities *are* bad
consequences. This claim I found unpersuasive and, for the time being, I reject
it. I say *for the time being*, however, because I will return to it shortly.

Consider now the second kind of argument I mentioned at the outset. The
test this argument applies to inequalities is not that of whether they give rise
to good or bad consequences. Instead, the argument I have in mind holds that
whether an inequality is objectionable or not turns on how that inequality
came about: here, our concern is not with the consequences of inequalities
but with their *causes*. One such argument claims that if an inequality came
about as a result of *wrongdoing* on the part of some agent or agency, then that
inequality is objectionable. And indeed there seems to be something to this
thought—no one, surely, would want to defend the case where some come to
have more than others through lying, cheating, or stealing. Again, however,
we must take care not to be distracted. From the thought that lying and the
rest are indefensible it certainly does not follow that there is something peculiarly indefensible about these things when they are associated with inequalities. In the case in question, the mischief at which our intuitions are directed
seems to be one concerning the presence of wrongdoing not the absence of
equality. An *equal* distribution brought about by wrongdoing would, seemingly, be no less objectionable on this view than an unequal distribution
brought about wrongdoing. It is the issue of wrongdoing, rather than that of
equality and inequality, that is driving this argument along.[10]

The argument from wrongdoing is one kind of argument about the causes
of distributions and the relevance of those causes to our moral assessment of
such distributions. It holds distributions to be objectionable where they have
come about as a result of identifiable individuals *doing* something wrong. But
there is another argument about the causes of distributions. This refrains from
asking whether determinate agents have done anything wrong. It also appears
to be tied more closely than is the wrongdoing argument to the issue of
inequality with which I am principally concerned. The argument I have in
mind here is the argument from *responsibility*. To avoid any confusion about
this argument, however, let me make something clear. Arguments about

wrongdoing do not occupy one compartment and those about responsibility an altogether separate one. To say of someone that he is guilty of wrongdoing is to say something also about his responsibility for what he did—you cannot *do* wrong by accident, however bad or regrettable what you do might be. In this sense, the purpose of distinguishing between the argument from wrongdoing and that from responsibility is not to show that one engages concerns about responsibility and the other does not. The purpose of the distinction is to show that not all claims about responsibility engage concerns about wrongdoing. From the fact that I am not responsible for my circumstances it does not follow that others have been guilty of wrongdoing. I may be poor through no fault of my own even though no one has stolen from me or cheated me and it is to these kinds of cases that the argument from responsibility appeals. In fact, the specific argument I am concerned with is one associated with egalitarian thinkers and it holds the following: it is objectionable for some to be worse off than others through no fault of their own. This is what I referred to in the Introduction as the *egalitarian intuition*. Whereas the wrongdoing argument is indifferent to whether a distribution is equal or unequal, the egalitarian intuition suggests that inequalities brought about under certain conditions are objectionable in a way that equalities brought about under identical conditions would not be. We do not, after all, find egalitarians claiming it to be objectionable that people are *equally* well off through no fault of their own.

But there is something puzzling about the egalitarian intuition. Is it the absence of responsibility that triggers a concern with equality? Or is it the absence of equality that triggers a concern with responsibility? If the issue of responsibility is a matter of indifference where holdings are equal, why is it a matter of importance where they are unequal? Let me try to run the intuition in two different ways—one placing emphasis on the responsibility component, the other on the equality component—in order to identify where the concerns of its proponents might lie. If we begin by emphasizing the responsibility component, then the argument might look something like this. Our condition in life—whether we are rich or poor, whether we are happy or miserable—should stem from factors for which we are responsible or over which we have significant control or both. If we are not responsible for our condition in life then this is prima facie regrettable—it is something we should be looking to put right or to change, if we can and if what is lost in the attempt to put it right does not outweigh what is gained. (Leaving aside the paradoxes and logical restrictions that would attend any attempt to secure total control over our lives, most of us would probably recoil from the sterility, the sheer lack of wonder, that a world over which we had total control would present. Moreover, many think that to subordinate the world to our will, such that the world ceased to confront us as something independent and inexorable, would

be to deprive ourselves of any realm in which moral action and moral relations could be transacted—points I shall simply have to leave standing as they
are.) This intuition seems, in turn, to be at its most vivid where what we are
not responsible for is bad or disadvantageous in some way, such as poverty or
unhappiness. Perhaps there is some sense in which it would be better if everyone were happy and healthy as a result of decisions and actions of theirs rather
than as a result of a collective stroke of good fortune. These are not, however,
the cases that seem to engage our concerns about responsibility at the intuitive level. Intuitively, there seems to be something peculiarly objectionable
about an absence of personal responsibility sitting alongside a presence of
disadvantage. I do not say that there is nothing more to the argument nor that
the intuitions in question do not admit of refinement. But we are at the preliminary stage of proceedings here and, for the time being, it would be as well
to stick with the cases in which our intuitions are at their strongest before
moving on to those cases where our intuitions are less clear-cut. At the heart
of those intuitions lies, then, the thought that it is objectionable for someone
to suffer a harm or loss through no fault of their own. Call this the *responsibility principle*. The responsibility principle captures and gives expression to a
certain kind of objectionable circumstance, namely, the sort we would take to
be present in the punishment of an innocent man. What is objectionable in
such cases is not the mere application of a loss or harm. After all, few object
to the punishment of the guilty. What is objectionable is the application of a
harm or loss to those who did nothing to bring it upon themselves or who
could not have avoided it.

In view of its close association with retributive justice it might be thought
that the responsibility principle falls at the first hurdle, that it cannot, with
conceptual propriety, be applied to the distributive realm. I do not accept this
argument, however, because it seems clear that the principle is one that
attaches itself to justice *per se*, in its retributive and distributive forms alike.
There is no reason to think that transferring the principle from one realm to
the other drains it of its force. Nonetheless, there remain objections to putting
too much weight on the parallel between the distributive and retributive cases.
Most obviously, punishment is an *unequivocal* loss or harm. No sensible
person could dispute that punishment was indeed harmful to an individual,
on any plausible account of what it is for something to be harmful and a punishment. Indeed, many think that punishment would not *be* punishment were
it not to involve harm or loss of some kind. In order to establish an analogy
between the distributive and the retributive cases we would need to show that
there existed harms or losses in the realm of the former analogous to those in
the realm of the latter such that it could plausibly be claimed that the two
were in some sense on a par in their status as harms or losses. This would then
allow us to speak of its being *as* objectionable for someone to suffer a harm

or loss in the distributive sphere through no fault of their own as it was for them to suffer a punishment through no fault of their own.

Again, however, this presents no real difficulty. To claim that all punishments are disadvantages is not, of course, to claim that all disadvantages are punishments. It is clear enough that pain, frustration, ignorance, and malnourishment qualify to be regarded as disadvantages of the kind to which the responsibility principle might legitimately be applied. That is, it accords with ordinary thinking in matters of justice to hold it objectionable for someone to suffer any or all of pain, frustration, and the rest through no fault of their own.

It is time to recall that my concerns do not begin and end with personal cum individual responsibility. I introduced the issue of responsibility into the discussion because I wanted to establish how that issue meshed with the issue of equality. Specifically, I wanted to examine those cases where an absence of responsibility appears to trigger a concern with equality and to arouse our suspicion in the matter of inequalities: I wanted to see what sorts of concerns the egalitarian intuition explicates. The responsibility principle appears to supply us with the materials necessary to our understanding the relation between responsibility and inequality and thus to our understanding the nature of the egalitarian intuition itself. If—as the responsibility principle claims—it is objectionable for some to suffer a harm or loss through no fault of their own, then it follows—as the egalitarian intuition claims—that it is objectionable for them to suffer an inequality through no fault of their own.

Or, rather, it *would* follow provided we could show that inequalities were indeed harms and losses of the relevant kind. But the case for regarding inequalities as analogous to punishment, or pain, or frustration, or ignorance, or malnourishment is one I have examined already and found wanting. Return to my claim that the allegedly bad consequences of inequalities can be regarded either as contingent features of inequalities or as necessary features. Begin with the first case, that in which inequalities contingently give rise to bad consequences. According to the responsibility principle, there might indeed be a case for holding it to be objectionable that someone should suffer such inequality induced bad consequences through no fault of their own. But the important relation here is between the absence of responsibility and the presence of bad consequences, not between the absence of responsibility and the presence of inequality. We have no more reason to object to someone suffering, through no fault of their own, bad consequences induced by inequalities than we do to objecting to their suffering, again through no fault of their own, bad consequences induced by *equalities*. In this case, inequality has no independent relevance: it is relevant to the responsibility principle only if and to the extent that it gives rise to the sorts of harms and losses with which that principle is concerned. In and of itself, inequality is neither a loss nor a harm and one would simply be confusing the unobjectionable bare fact of inequality with the objectionable fact of its bad consequences in claiming that it was objectionable for someone to suffer an *inequality* through no fault of their own.

Turn now to the second case. If you believe that inequalities give rise to bad consequences—more vividly still, if you believe that inequalities *are* bad consequences—then inequalities, *qua* inequalities, come within the ambit of the responsibility principle. By appealing to that principle, we can show, directly, why it is objectionable for someone to suffer an inequality through no fault of their own. But whilst this approach scores well in analytical neatness, it suffers from an obvious drawback. It presupposes what I have still successfully to demonstrate, namely, that inequalities *are* bad consequences—that they are harms and losses—of the relevant kind.

I said before that there were two views about the relation between responsibility and equality. The first view is the one I have just been examining. On that view, it is the absence of responsibility that triggers a concern with inequality. Where individuals are responsible for the holdings to their name we are indifferent to how those holdings are distributed as between them. On the second view, it is the absence of equality that triggers a concern with responsibility. Where individuals are equal in their holdings we are indifferent as to their responsibility for them. But this argument too is puzzling. It seems to rest on the idea that equalities are self-justifying or, even, that it is sufficient for a distribution to be legitimate that it is an equal distribution, yet these are the ideas we are seeking to test not the ones we are entitled to assume. At this point, some egalitarians will seek refuge in the principle of presumptive equality. They will say that it simply *is* a fixed point of our judgements about justice that individuals should be treated equally (meaning here that they should be given equal amounts of the thing in question) unless there are relevant reasons for treating them unequally (meaning here giving them unequal amounts of the thing in question).[11] They might also say that for a reason to be *relevant*, it is not enough that it not be irrelevant. There must be a positive relevant reason for departing from the position of equality that the presumptive principle prescribes and reasons of personal responsibility meet this test.

It might still be objected, however, that this does not advance the argument very far. To say that there is a presumption in favour of equality leaves open the question of what kind of argument would be necessary to overcome that presumption and indeed the question of why it is that the move from a position of equality to one of inequality should be thought of as *the sort of thing* for which supporting moral reasons must be supplied. Are we not back to the question of whether inequalities are in and of themselves objectionable, disadvantageous, or harmful, and is this not the question to which I have still to supply a satisfactory answer? At which point I think we should confront an argument I have neglected up until now and which many will think resolves some of the puzzles surrounding the notion of inequality. In my earlier discussion I cast doubt on whether it was plausible to think of inequality as analogous to punishment, pain, and ignorance in its status as a disadvantage or harm. I suggested that there was nothing inherently disadvantageous or harmful in some having more or less of a thing than others. In an obvious sense, however, this is quite untrue. If I have more of something good—or less of something bad—than you, then clearly I am in a position of advantage or disadvantage *relative to you*: in this sense there *is* something *inherently* advantageous or disadvantageous in some having more or less of a thing than others. All that my earlier argument establishes is that there are certain things—pain, ignorance, malnourishment—that can be regarded as disadvantageous or harmful to an individual regardless of whether other individuals suffer them. That is, it establishes that disadvantages and harms *need* not, in all cases, be interpersonal. It certainly does not establish that disadvantages and harms *are* not, in some cases, interpersonal. In short, it overlooks the possibility that there exists a compelling account of what should count as an advantage or disadvantage—and, by extension, what should count as a benefit or loss—that is *essentially* interpersonal. Writing of the work of Rawls, Thomas Nagel expresses this point with typical clarity:

Rawls's conception of justice as fairness [is] a moral theory of interpersonal *relations*—specifically, a theory of the acceptable forms of interdependence among the lives and fates of persons engaged in a cooperative social enterprise. The moral nerve . . . of Rawls's conception of justice is the idea of a benefit or loss resulting from certain unacceptable relations to others. It is an essentially causal rather than merely distributive idea. If someone gets a larger or smaller share of the goods of social cooperation, as an effect of the wrong kind of causes—causes that are morally arbitrary and confer no justification on their results—then he stands in a relation of unfair advantage or disadvantage to his fellow men, and he as well as others should want things to be different *for that reason*. If we have a sense of justice, we will, according to Rawls, want neither to gain nor to lose from certain kinds of relations with others, and a well-ordered society should try to create a form of life that avoids such relations.[12]

Recall that my concern in this part of the chapter is with an argument that seeks to connect concerns about inequality with concerns about individual responsibility. Having examined, earlier on, an argument in which concerns about inequality are triggered by an absence of responsibility, my focus now is on an argument in which concerns about responsibility are triggered by an absence of equality. According to this latter argument, as I have suggested, we start—as Nagel appears to do on Rawls's behalf—from the position that departures from equality generate—by which I mean *necessarily* generate—benefits (or advantages) for some and losses (or disadvantages) for others.

From there, we move on to the claim that it is objectionable for some to be in a position of advantage or disadvantage *relative to others* where this is caused by the operation of arbitrary factors. If an unequal distribution is contaminated by the operation of such factors, then it is objectionable. In the name of justice and the integrity of interpersonal relations we should rule it out—unless there are strong reasons, grounded in considerations of *consequences* and of the kind, perhaps, that Rawls's Difference Principle embodies, for allowing such an inequality to stand.[13]

My worry about this argument is not that it is incoherent: to believe that it is objectionable for some to be worse off than others through no fault of their own is not like believing that it is objectionable for circles not to be square. My worry is that the argument moves between concerns about inequality and concerns about responsibility without deciding quite what its target is.[14] If there really is something offensive to our sense of justice and interpersonal integrity in allowing distributions to be contaminated by the operation of arbitrary factors, then presumably this should apply to *all* distributions and not just to *unequal* ones. As I suggested before, it does seem peculiar that concerns about responsibility and arbitrariness are a matter of all-consuming importance in one context but of indifference in another. If an *equal* distribution has come about through the operation of arbitrary factors, then on the grounds of arbitrariness and responsibility, it seems that we would have no less reason for questioning the interpersonal integrity of that distribution than any other. To see this, imagine that A has 15 units of a (desired) thing to B's 10. Through a stroke of bad luck—a change in the weather perhaps—A's holdings fall to 10. It cannot plausibly be claimed that A has not suffered a *loss* of some kind. Nor can it plausibly by claimed that the distributive relation between A and B is not now contaminated by precisely the arbitrary factors that Nagel and others claim corrupt interpersonal relations. And yet, neither the loss nor the contamination can, seemingly, be reckoned upon by egalitarian principles of the kind Nagel advances.[15]

To which the reply is obvious. Whether it is concerns about responsibility that trigger our interest in inequality or concerns about inequality that trigger our interest in responsibility, the fact is that support for the responsibility principle lies in the idea that it is objectionable for an agent to suffer a *disadvantage* through no fault of their own. *Ex hypothesi* agents do not suffer disadvantages—by which is meant *relative* disadvantages—under equal distributions. Therefore there can be no objection to such distributions on the grounds of arbitrariness and responsibility and their corruption of interpersonal distributive integrity.

What is going wrong here, I think, is that we have been presented, by Nagel and others, with an account of what it is for something to *be* an advantage or disadvantage (or a benefit or loss) that leads us into thinking that these things are either necessarily relational or, at least, that they lend themselves to being cast—or *recast*—in relational terms. But what emerges from our analysis seems to be that advantages and disadvantages come in two broad kinds. Some are in essence *intrapersonal*: their advantageous or disadvantageous properties are essentially non-relational. Included in a list of these would be pain and pleasure, frustration, and malnourishment. From the perspective of any given experiencing agent, pleasure does not become better nor pain worse depending on whether *other* agents experience these things: pleasure and pain would be good or bad for me even if there were no others is the world with whom to compare my position. The responsibility principle—that it is objectionable for individuals to suffer disadvantages through no fault of their own—may indeed be applied to disadvantages of this intrapersonal kind. What we cannot sensibly do is both apply it to such disadvantages and *at the same time* extend it into the relational sphere in the way the egalitarian intuition seeks to. Indeed, we would be misunderstanding the nature of the disadvantages in question were we to couch our objections to them in relational terms. In the matter of intrapersonal disadvantages, what worries us is not that some have more or less of these things *than others* or that some suffer whilst others do not.[16] What worries us is that some suffer, full stop.

Not all advantages and disadvantages, however, are of this intrapersonal kind. Some are in essence *interpersonal*: their advantageous or disadvantageous properties are essentially relational. Put another way, they are things of a kind that we cannot judge as advantageous or disadvantageous—or as beneficial or harmful—without viewing them in the context of a plurality of individuals between whom such judgements of (relative) advantage and disadvantage can be made. Let me illustrate what I have in mind. Imagine we think of human life not as an exercise in cooperation but as a competition for scarce resources according to which we are engaged in a fierce bidding war with one another for a fixed stock of goods. Not *all* goods form part of this fixed stock. In principle, there is nothing to prevent each and every person in the world owning a video recorder or going to bed at night with a full stomach. Not everyone, however, can live in the central districts of London or New York, or be sure of a parking space at night, or get tickets for the Cup Final. These goods are *auction* goods and they go to the highest bidder. The greater the gap between your resources and mine the further ahead you are in your competition with me to secure these desired and desirable things. What prevents me from securing these things for myself is not that the absolute level of my resources is too low. In a bidding contest it is not the absolute positions of the parties involved that determines who secures the desired good but the positions of the parties relative to one another. Increasing my holdings in absolute terms does not thereby make all goods more accessible to me than they were before. The obvious—perhaps banal—truth in all of this is that, in respect of certain kinds of goods at least, the purchasing power of *my* resources expands or diminishes according to the size of *your* resource bundle. The bare fact of your having more than me restricts my room for manoeuvre and places you in a position of advantage relative to me when it comes to purchasing the sort of auction goods I have been describing. This means that not only do the better off have more purchasing power *than* the worse off. It means that the better off also have purchasing power *over* the worse off: the superior competitive position of the former allows them to shape, restrict, and otherwise frustrate the ambitions and purposes of the latter, even if the better off do not do this intentionally.[17]

In this respect, there is an analogue between the economic and the political spheres. One of the most compelling arguments for giving each adult a vote is that of self-determination: my having a vote gives me a certain power and control over the collective rules and decisions applying to me. It is pretty obvious that how much power and control my vote gives me will depend on how many others there are in my community and how many votes each of them has. The more others there are, and the more votes each of them has, the more my self-determination is diminished. In short, my say in influencing the affairs of my community increases or diminishes according to how much say others have: the scope of my influence is context dependent. This is quite unlike my experience of pleasure and pain, which does not increase or diminish according to how many others experience these things: the scope of my experience is context independent. The danger is that of moving between these two ideas and of assuming that if something is valuable—in fact, if *anything* is valuable—then it must be better for there to be more of it in the world rather than less, regardless of how it is distributed. Indeed, it is precisely this thought that the levelling down objection trades on in highlighting the fact that nothing is *improved* when we surrender some quantity of a good in the name of apportioning it more evenly. Where the valuable thing in question is food or medicine, the thought seems unimpeachable. But its intuitive appeal is less obvious if we shift from the example of food and medicine to that of votes. Whilst there is a sense in which votes resemble food and medicine in being valuable—and a sense also in which it is better for more people to have the vote rather than fewer—there is quite clearly an improvement of sorts when votes are surrendered by a privileged few in the name of the apportioning them more evenly. In the case of votes, it is not irrational to insist that some should give up something valuable. Indeed, it may be reprehensible not to insist that they should do so.[18]

Interpersonal advantages and disadvantages differ, then, from intrapersonal ones in that they appear to become more or less advantageous and disadvantageous to the individuals concerned depending on how they are distributed within a population. That being so, we would be misunderstanding the nature of these disadvantages in particular if we were to couch our objections to them *wholly* in non-relational terms. In the matter of interpersonal advantages and disadvantages, it appears misguided to claim that the bare fact of inequality is in all cases unobjectionable and (therefore) similarly misguided to think that there really is nothing objectionable about some being worse off than others, especially, perhaps, where the relevant test of individual responsibility fails.

My claim here is not that we can neatly compartmentalize conceptions of advantage and disadvantage into the intrapersonal and the interpersonal: pure examples of either kind are hard to come by. Nor is my claim that there is some merit in sitting on the fence. That there appears to be no hard and fast answer to the question of whether inequalities *really* are objectionable or unobjectionable comes to me, at least, as a disappointment. The claim I have been advancing in the latter part of this chapter is that the stance we adopt towards equalities and inequalities will be shaped by the nature of the advantages and disadvantages with whose distribution we are concerned. In this connection, it strikes me as no coincidence that those sceptical as to the objectionable nature of inequalities—not least Joseph Raz[19]—are prone to make their case by invoking examples involving *intrapersonal* disadvantages such as hunger. The trouble with this strategy, however, is that it runs the risk of tautology: it is not clear what general conclusions about equality we can draw from the thought that non-relational advantages are important to us for non-relational reasons. Similarly, it may be no coincidence that certain egalitarians are at their most enthusiastic about equality when concerning themselves with the essentially *interpersonal* advantages of equal liberty and citizenship. All of which may suggest that the impulse to conceive of advantages and disadvantages in the most abstract terms possible may be misconceived—there may no conception of these things, in the abstract, that is biased towards neither the intrapersonal nor the interpersonal view.

Let me recap. I began this chapter by pointing out that objections to inequalities are of three broad kinds: objections to their causes, objections to their consequences, and objections to the bare fact of inequality. The last of these has been the most baffling to analyse and my account of that objection, unlike my account of the first two, has emerged *sotto voce*. It seems to me that the starting point for the bare inequality objection must be the thought that, tautologies aside, it is regrettable, in some broad sense of that notion, for individuals to suffer harm and it assumes that there exists an intimate—perhaps (even) a logical—relation between an individual suffering a harm and his having less of something than someone else. In a number of cases, this relation does not hold good and it becomes clear that what motivates our concerns has little or nothing to do with how the thing in question is distributed—a point that the levelling down objection makes well. Indeed, it may well be that the pursuit of equality in such cases would, all things considered, serve to make things worse. Tautologies again aside, I am not persuaded, however, that there is *never* a relation between disadvantage and inequality and I think that certain rights of (equal) citizenship and status serve to bear out this thought. Of course, such examples seem rather flimsy and wishy-washy when set against powerful anti-egalitarian examples involving pain, hunger, or punishment. But again I think that we are being distracted by the nature of the advantages and disadvantages in question into drawing conclusions about the distribution of advantages and disadvantages *per se*. Having said this, I am conscious that the distraction may work the other way. After all, if the intrapersonal conception distracts us away from concerns about equality, then presumably the interpersonal conception of advantage distracts us towards such concerns. In other words, the interpersonal conception distracts us into thinking that we care about equality *per se* when in fact we do not.

As I have suggested, the objection to inequalities on the basis of their *consequences* seems vulnerable to attack from two directions. If the claim is that inequalities are objectionable only *in so far* as they generate bad consequences, then we can dispense with all mention of inequalities and say simply that bad consequences are objectionable however they come about. We can get around this, of course, by claiming that inequalities are bad consequences in and of themselves—but then we will run up against the levelling down objection in particular. Only by appealing to an interpersonal conception of advantage and disadvantage can we plausibly tie an objection to bad consequences directly to an objection to inequalities. From which it follows, of course, that if the interpersonal conception fails, so too does the rest of the argument.

The objection to inequalities on the basis of their causes is also vulnerable to challenge. To show that it is objectionable for some to be worse off *than others* due to the presence of wrongdoing or the absence of personal responsibility we have to do more than point to the peculiar moral standing of wrongdoing and responsibility and their relevance to issues of distribution. We have to tie concerns about wrongdoing and responsibility to the issue of inequality in particular—if we do not, then we have no more reason, under this heading, to concern ourselves with inequalities than we do to concern ourselves with equalities. Again, an appeal to a conception of interpersonal advantage and disadvantage will bring the arguments together in the relevant way. But again, the success or failure of the objection to inequalities depends upon the extent to which the interpersonal conception can be sustained.

2

Responsibility and justice

In the first chapter I examined the claim that inequalities are objectionable and I did so by considering three lines of argument, one focusing on the consequences of inequalities, one on their causes, and the third on the bare fact of inequality. Under the heading of causes, I said that egalitarian objections to inequalities were often linked to arguments about *responsibility*. What I called the egalitarian intuition—the intuition that it is objectionable for some to be worse off than others through no fault of their own—is one formulation of this idea. I have pointed already to some of the ambiguities this formulation contains and I shall have more to say about these ambiguities as the argument develops. In the meantime, let me stick with the thought that in constructing, or defending, a theory of justice, concerns about individual responsibility should occupy centre stage—a thought, incidentally, that has proved as attractive to political egalitarians as it has to their philosophical counterparts.

The difficulty with this thought is that it can soon start to run away from us. And it can run away from us because the temptation is to talk as though it were obvious what *sort* of responsibility we have in mind when we say that concerns about responsibility ought to feature prominently in an account of who should get what. But in fact it is not obvious. Do we have in mind the sort of responsibility underlying the claim that causes are responsible for their effects or is it the sort underlying the claim that doctors are responsible for their patients? Or do we have in mind a sort of responsibility quite different from either two? Given the scope for confusion and misunderstanding in the nomenclature of our enquiry, the first task, it seems to me, is to identify the particular *sense* of responsibility we might be drawn to in our thinking about justice.[1]

Identifying the sense of responsibility with which we are concerned will, however, take us only so far. Imagine we have distinguished the different senses of responsibility on offer. Imagine also we have shown that those who appeal to responsibility in arguments about distributive justice favour one sense of responsibility over others. So what? We will still have to show why responsibility *matters*—we will still have to show, that is, why a distributive theory is enriched by the presence of concerns about responsibility and impoverished by their absence. This is because there seem to be on offer some perfectly respectable theories of who should get what that say little or nothing about responsibility. Those who claim, for instance, that goods should be distributed in such a way as to minimize the amount of suffering in the world do not generally see themselves as bound to pronounce upon whether particular individuals are *responsible* for their suffering. So, as well as saying something about the senses of responsibility with which we are concerned, we must say something about the *significance* of responsibility in and to arguments about justice.

But we cannot get away only with examining senses and significances. There is a further question we must explore. This is the question of the *preconditions* of responsibility. Here, we need to ask about the circumstances under which we attribute responsibility to an individual for doing, or being, or having something and indeed about the circumstances under which we deny such responsibility. These circumstances might belong either in the realm of the everyday—such as when we ask whether duress, accident, or mistake undermine responsibility. Or they might belong in the realm of metaphysics—such as when we ask whether attributing responsibility to individuals is compatible with universal determinism, namely, the view that everything about the character of events in the world, including human actions, intentions, and thoughts, is fixed by prior causes.[2] Questions about preconditions are addressed in Chapter 3.

In separating these three questions my purpose is not to come up with distinctions for distinction's sake. Nor is it to suggest that the issue of responsibility lends itself to being neatly compartmentalized. The three questions feed naturally into one another—they are separate but inseparable. In the discussion that follows, my thought is simply this: we cannot hope to advance our understanding of how concerns about responsibility tie in with arguments about justice unless we make sure to disentangle the different threads of the problem.

Let me begin with the first question—the question of the sense of responsibility we are concerned with. Sometimes the notion of responsibility we appeal to is *causal*. When we say that X is responsible for b what we mean is that X caused b. The X in question might be a human agent or agency—such as the infant who is responsible for breaking a vase. Or it might be a non-human entity such as a feature of the natural world—thus I might speak of the weather being responsible for my bad mood. On other occasions, our concern is with questions of what H. L. A. Hart calls *role responsibility*.[3] When we say that X is responsible for b in this sense we are saying that, by virtue of some role or position he occupies, X owes certain obligations or duties to b. Thus we might speak of doctors being responsible for their patients or of parents being responsible for their children. On other occasions still, we appeal to what Hart calls *capacity responsibility*.[4] To attribute responsibility to X in respect of b in this sense is to say something about X's condition in doing, being, or having b. It is to claim that, in doing, being, or having b, X possessed the capacities relevant to being regarded as a responsible agent. Thus if I was in full control of my faculties when I backed my car into your garden fence, I am not just causally responsible for knocking it over—I also satisfied the conditions for being a responsible agent. If, however, I had suffered a sudden spasm in my arm, I would still have been causally responsible for knocking over the fence—but I would not have satisfied the conditions for being a responsible agent.

Important though these three senses of responsibility are, I think it is a fourth sense, Hart's *liability responsibility*, that people have in mind when considering the relevance of responsibility to the question of who should get what.[5] If I attribute liability responsibility to you I am doing something more than describing a bare fact about you. I am making a judgement about you and offering an accompanying prescription: I am evaluating your moral status in respect of a thing and your eligibility for certain kinds of appraisal or treatment. Liability responsibility, in other words, is the sort of responsibility we associate with attributions of innocence and guilt, credit and fault, praise and blame. It is the sort of responsibility we invoke in deciding whether to reward or whether to punish. Thus to claim of X that he has liability responsibility for b is not (merely) to offer a causal account of the relation between X and b, for we can attribute causal responsibility to individuals in cases where no questions or appraisal or treatment arise. When we say of an infant that he was responsible for breaking a vase we might be doing no more than describing a causal sequence of which he was a part. We are not necessarily committing ourselves to any view about the infant's blameworthiness or his liability to punishment. Similarly when we attribute liability responsibility to the careless driver for an accident we are not *merely* describing a causal sequence of which he was a part. Instead, we are endowing his role within that causal sequence with a particular moral or legal significance.

Being judgements rather than bare descriptions, liability responsibilities are not reducible to causal responsibilities. But nor are they merely role responsibilities by another name. True enough, the question of how I should be treated—whether I should receive a benefit or have it withheld from me, or whether I should be praised or blamed—may sometimes turn on a judgement about whether, or how well, I discharged the duties attaching to me by virtue of the relevant legal or more rules. Take the case of the legal duty I am under not to assault others. If I violate that duty without excuse or mitigating circumstance then I am responsible for my conduct and liable to be sent to prison. But not all claims about responsibility and liability are activated by duties of this kind nor couched in the language of such duties. If I lose all my money because of a string of rash investments and in the knowledge that the state will not bail me out, there is an obvious sense in which I am both responsible for my straightened circumstances and liable to remain in poverty until or unless I can get myself out of it. But the liability and responsibility in question do not attach to me by virtue of some duty I am under not to make rash investments or not to be poor. The obvious truth here is this—not all rules place duties upon us. Sometimes they just indicate what it is that follows from acting one way rather than another: if you do a, b follows but if you do c, d follows. In other words, the imperatives from which attributions of responsibility spring may be hypothetical in character as well as categorical: we do not have to invoke claims about guilt, wrongdoing, and duty in order to attribute liability responsibility to individuals. In this sense, role responsibilities are better viewed as potential rather than actual liabilities. They are liabilities that usually become actual where certain other conditions are met. Thus, establishing that the relevant role responsibilities apply to you may sometimes be a necessary condition of attributing liability responsibility to you but that is not to say it is sufficient to do so.

Nor is liability responsibility reducible to capacity responsibility. Questions of capacity responsibility, it is true, commonly arise in cases where we are considering the liability of individuals to certain forms of treatment or appraisal. But that does not mean that X's having capacity responsibility for b thereby entails that X is to be treated or assessed in a particular way in respect of b. As with causal responsibility, I may attribute or deny capacity responsibility to you in circumstances where no questions of assessment or treatment arise. Indeed, I might do so in circumstances where we have reason to think that no such questions will ever arise. From the fact that you were in full control of your faculties when you picked your nose, nothing very interesting seems to follow in terms of the treatment you are owed by others.

In separating out these different senses of responsibility I am not out to suggest that they are applied independently of one another. When it comes to assessing whether you bear liability responsibility for a thing, I will likely want to know whether this is the sort of thing in respect of which liabilities arise (role responsibility), what kind of causal relation you have or had with the thing in question (causal responsibility), and what your state of mind and intentions were at the relevant time or over the relevant period (capacity responsibility). Viewed in these terms, role responsibilities often serve to map out the *area* within which liabilities, in principle, arise, whilst causal and capacity responsibilities help us decide what it is within those areas— which *events*—individuals are responsible for. Of course, as I have made clear already, the area of enquiry is not demarcated by role responsibilities alone—

claims about liability responsibility operate within the context of different kinds of demands and expectations.

Drawing these distinctions does no more than nudge the argument forward, however. We still have to establish what might underlie the thought that individual responsibility should be our guide in deciding who should get what. What, in short, is the *significance* of responsibility? I am going to try to answer this question in two stages. In the first, I ask what we would be looking for in a distributive theory that would allow us to say of one theory that it did take claims of responsibility seriously and of another that it did not. In the second, I ask why we should want to privilege individual responsibility at all. With these two questions in mind, let me begin by noting that ideas of responsibility can enter arguments about justice in a variety of ways. Imagine, for instance, we are presented with an account of justice telling us that the state has certain responsibilities towards its citizens and citizens' reciprocal responsibilities towards the state. From the fact that claims about *responsibilities* features prominently it is tempting to form the impression that concerns about individual responsibility are doing important work at the heart of the account on offer. But I hope to show at greater length that impressions are misleading here: the requirements attaching to citizen and state might be described in the language of jurisdictions just as easily as they are described in the language of responsibility. Given that it is in the nature of theories of justice, of whatever kind, to pronounce upon the jurisdictions of citizen and state there is a sense in which it is in the nature of such theories to pronounce upon responsibilities also. Whatever else this might tell us, it certainly does not tell us what it would mean for claims about individual responsibility to occupy a *distinctive* place in our thinking about who should get what. All it tells us is that an account of the *role responsibilities* of citizens and state will feature—and feature unavoidably—in whatever rules of justice we might care to devise.

In other cases, the question of whether concerns about individual responsibility are being privileged is less clear cut. To see this, recall that in my discussion of liability responsibility I said that to hold X responsible for b *in this sense* is to claim something about the moral status of X's claims in respect of b. Bearing this in mind, imagine now that I am rich and you are poor and that you approach me for a handout in order to pay off your debts. On the one hand, I might be happy enough to turn you down by way of an appeal to my ownership rights and nothing more. I might say that my money is *mine*—for me to dispose of as I see fit—and it so happens that I do not feel like giving any of it to you. On the other hand, I might be of a more squeamish disposition and think there to be something distasteful about turning down your request by way of a brute assertion of my ownership rights. My squeamishness in this matter might be tempered, however, if I could somehow claim that

I was *responsible* for being rich or that you were *responsible* for being poor—
or indeed both. After all, if I am responsible for being rich this would
seem to insulate me, in some sense, from claims others may make upon me.
Similarly, if you are responsible for being poor this would seem to undermine,
in some sense, the claims you may make upon others. Of course, if you are
not responsible for being poor, or if I am not responsible for being rich, the
position changes: my claims start to appear weaker and yours stronger.

The thought here is that arguments about what we do, and what we do not,
have a claim to seem to be strengthened or weakened according to how far
they lend themselves to being couched in the language of responsibility. It is
one thing to rebuff your request for money on the grounds that I am entitled
to keep what I have. It is quite another to rebuff it on the grounds that I am
responsible for having what I do. The appeal to entitlement smacks of a certain
sectarianism—what our entitlements are and whether claims of entitlement
exhaust the terrain of justice are matters of controversy. The appeal to responsibility, in contrast, appears to be capable of commanding assent from those
who would otherwise disagree as to the demands of justice—claims about
responsibility seem to be of a different order from ordinary claims in the
matter of who should get what. The danger in all this is obvious. If claiming
of X that he is *responsible* for b in some sense concludes the issue of how X
ought to be treated in respect of b, then we will start thinking that any moral
claims we want to advance in respect of X and b must be couched in terms of
X's *responsibility* for b. And the temptation will then be to redescribe our
claims about X and b in the language of responsibility and thereby to use
ascriptions of responsibility as a polemical device.

Return to the example of me, you, and your request for a handout. Imagine
that I am not of a squeamish disposition when it comes to turning you down.
Imagine I think it enough for me to be justified in refusing your request that
my money is mine according to the relevant property rules in force. If that
is what I think, then I shall take the fact of my having title to my money as
insulating my claims to it and excluding yours. In other words, I shall take my
claims of entitlement to be indistinguishable in their normative force from
the claims of liability responsibility that I was describing before. Indeed, I shall
think that if being responsible for a thing means having a compelling claim
in respect of it, then there is indeed an obvious sense, on my reckoning at
least, in which I am *responsible* for having the money that I do.

So, if claiming of you that you are responsible for a thing simply is another
way of saying that you have a compelling claim to that thing *according to
whatever rules of justice happen to be in force*, it would seem to follow that all
accounts of justice incorporate claims about individual responsibility. Indeed,
it is a short step from here to the thought that all accounts of justice are, at
root, accounts of what individuals are and are not responsible for. If that

thought is right, then it makes for some curious inclusions in the list of theories of justice that honour the demands of individual responsibility. Imagine, for instance, that I believe that individuals own their talents and that there is a morally conclusive case for their keeping the full product of their talents. I might want to express this commitment by saying that I am *responsible* for my talents: I am responsible for my talents in the sense that liability for (the product of) their talents attaches to me and me only. Of course, in this example the important work is being done by the principle of self-ownership. Self-owners are responsible for (the product of) their talents in the sense that those talents constitute a legitimate basis of reward given the force of the principle of self-ownership. Whether self-owners are responsible for their talents in some further sense—for instance in the sense that their having the talents they do was in some way within their control—is not an issue this argument addresses.

It seems, then, to be in the nature of claims of justice—whatever their content and demands—that they lend themselves to being cast and recast in the language of individual responsibility. Nor is this surprising. As I said before, both kinds of claim involve making *judgements* about individuals. Both address themselves to the question of what individuals are owed. This being so, pointing to the overlap between the two does not so much *resolve* the argument at hand as push it back a stage. Indeed, it should be recalled that my aim is not to identify whether there is some formal sense in which claims about responsibility might make an appearance in all accounts of justice. My aim is to identify what it would mean to *privilege* concerns about individual responsibility in an account of justice such as to render that account more attractive, in terms of its fidelity to the demands of responsibility, than another.

Bearing this aim in mind, I want to insist that concerns about individual responsibility are significant—they exercise a distinctive pull upon us in our thinking about justice—by virtue of being tied to claims about certain capacities we attribute to individuals. (As will become obvious, the sorts of capacities I have in mind have to them an *active* character: whilst there is a sense in which we have the capacity to incur needs or to experience pleasure and pain, these are not the sorts of capacities I shall be concentrating on.) For individual responsibility to *matter* to us we have to think that what people receive by way of burdens and benefits should be related in some sense to the existence, exercise, or development of the relevant capacities. From which it follows, seemingly, that if we think that what people receive should have no necessary connection to these capacities then individual responsibility as such does not play a significant part in our thinking about justice.

I recognize that, stated in these terms, this view raises more questions than it answers. To being with, there would seem to be several levels at which we might privilege responsibility and the capacities that go to make people *responsible* for some things but not for others.[6] We might privilege responsibility by attempting to derive rules of justice from claims about what, in terms of capacities and control, individuals are responsible for. Or we might privilege responsibility by incorporating into those rules certain assumptions about what, in terms of capacities and control, individuals are responsible for. Or indeed we might hold that these rules should be applied and interpreted taking account of what, in terms of capacities and control, individuals are responsible for. As it is, I am pretty confident that we can indeed privilege concerns about responsibility in the way I have in mind whilst stopping short of any attempt to *derive* substantive conclusions about the sorts of conduct that should be rewarded and those that should be penalized on the basis of an appeal to ideas of responsibility considered in the abstract. In short, we can allow that concerns about responsibility enter the picture after we have specified why it is that some kinds of conduct are to be rewarded, others penalized, and others still ignored without draining claims about individual responsibility of independent weight. When we attribute liability responsibility to individuals we generally do so in respect of those things that we have *already* taken to be of moral concern. No argument couched wholly in terms of capacities can explain why harming others is of moral concern but picking one's nose is not.

But to acknowledge the *limits* of responsibility, so to speak, is not thereby to commit oneself to the view that concerns about individual responsibility have no distinctive force. It may be true that no argument couched in terms of concerns about responsibility alone can tell us why, say, murder is wrong. But an appeal to considerations of responsibility enables us to account for the moral importance of distinguishing between murder and accidental killing. Indeed, in the field of rectificatory justice, our concern in deciding whether to act is with the *conjunction* of harm and responsibility. Neither of these two facts is to be understood in terms of the other and both seem to carry independent weight in our deliberations.

All of which suggests that the question of whether I ought to receive a benefit by virtue of being *responsible* for it is distinct from the general question of whether I ought to receive a benefit, and distinct again from the specific question of whether I ought to receive a benefit by virtue of complying with the relevant background rules of justice. My thought is not that claims about individual responsibility—by which I mean individual *liability* responsibility—are, in some sense, unbounded by background rules of this kind. Indeed, the fact that such claims address themselves to the liabilities we incur through conducting ourselves one way rather than another seems to presuppose a context of some kind, be it one of informal social norms or formal rules, privileges, and demands. My thought instead is that bare conformity with a set of rules—the sort of conformity that might arise without reflection or choice—might be enough to establish my entitlement to a benefit but it is not enough to establish my *responsibility* for it. In order to establish that I ought to have a benefit by virtue of being responsible for it we would need to *look behind* the conduct in question and to show that conformity to the rule placed certain demands upon me—the sorts of demands that would engage the capacities I described before—or that the rule was such as to afford me some sort of discretion in the matter of whether, and in what way, I engaged those capacities. In short, if bare conformity is not enough to establish my responsibility for a thing, conscientious conformity might be, sometimes if not always.

In the next chapter, I shall have more to say about the nature of the capacities in question and the difficult issue of what individuals should be held responsible for. For the time being, what I have to say about these capacities is deliberately vague. The important thing to note at this stage in the argument is that for an account of justice to *privilege* the claims of individual responsibility it is not enough that it lends itself to being *recast* in the language of responsibility. To hold that it privileges responsibility an account of justice must take seriously the sorts of capacities I have been alluding to and tie the receipt of burdens and benefits to those capacities in some way. That is, it must make some kind of *essential reference* to these capacities. A rule to the effect that all pensioners should receive a Christmas bonus makes no (essential) reference to the sorts of capacities I have in mind: indeed, it is indifferent to whether those concerned possess or exercise them. In contrast, a rule to the effect that medical treatment for pensioners will be rationed according to whether they have chosen to lead healthy or unhealthy lifestyles *does* make (essential) reference to these capacities.

Thus, *if* individual responsibility matters in determining who should get what, it matters because the capacities that are essential to the exercise of our responsible agency themselves matter from the standpoint of justice. Note that I say *if* responsibility matters in determining who should get what. All I have done so far is show why certain capacities should matter to our thinking about individual responsibility. I have not shown why individual responsibility should matter to our thinking about justice. As I suggested before, some argue that responsibility *does not* matter when thinking about questions of justice or, at least, that it *need not* matter. And indeed nothing I have said so far seems to tells us *why* we should be led to make the connection between distributive justice and individual responsibility to begin with. Why should we not ignore questions of responsibility altogether? To which one response is that the question answers itself—it is part of the *very idea* of justice that burdens and benefits should be dispensed on the basis of judgements about what individuals are responsible for.[7] In short, the relation between justice and individual responsibility is a logical one. As such, we do not need to go further in accounting for the significance of responsibility in deciding who should get what.

The worry again, however, is that we are being distracted by the superficial resemblance between claims of justice and those of individual responsibility into thinking that there exists a deep affinity between the two. True enough, both sorts of claim involve making *judgements* about individuals rather than offering bare descriptions. But judgements about individuals, in order to be such, do not have to address themselves to the sorts of capacities that I have indicated are integral to our responsible agency. We can, after all, make fine-grained judgements about individual *needs* that make no reference to such capacities and I cannot see that an account of who should get what that rested on such judgements would fail to qualify *as* an account of justice—a judgement about what my needs are is, seemingly, no less a judgement about me than is a judgement about what I am responsible for. Nor should we be distracted by the resemblance between claims of justice and those of individual responsibility arising from the fact that both concern themselves with what individuals are owed. Again, this resemblance draws us, unwittingly, towards the idea that there is some deeper or more substantial relation between the two sorts of claim.

All of which suggests that we should resist any attempt to define the problem away and thereby to account for the significance of responsibility to arguments about justice by way of a conceptual analysis of the idea of justice itself. It is simply not clear to me that there exists a straightforward *logical* relation between the two in the way that certain thinkers suggest. If we are to account for the significance of concerns about individual responsibility we must say more about the attractions of incorporating such concerns into schemes of justice and the drawbacks of ignoring them.

To this end, let me return here to what in the previous chapter I termed the responsibility principle—the principle that it is objectionable for someone to suffer a harm or loss through no fault of their own. What is objectionable about my suffering a harm or loss *through no fault of my own* that is not objectionable about the bare fact of my suffering a harm or loss? It is no answer to this to say that one is fair and the other unfair because that is to rehearse the concerns of the question rather than to supply an answer to it. The claim that one is objectionable by virtue of being unfair and the other unobjectionable by virtue of being not unfair will very soon collapse into the claim that one is objectionable by virtue of being objectionable and the other unobjectionable by virtue of being unobjectionable. Nor will it take us very far to claim that it is simply in the nature of the terms 'objectionable', 'loss', and 'fault' that they, in some sense, belong together. In other words, just as the identification of justice with individual responsibility draws us into a tight analytical circle, so too does any claim holding the force of the responsibility principle to be self-evident. Of course, we must start the argument *somewhere*: I am not out to disdain premises. It does seem to me, however, that between, on the one hand, the attempt to tie, *logically*, concerns about justice to concerns about responsibility, and, on the other hand, the claim that it is objectionable to suffer a loss through no fault of one's own there is *something missing* or, at least, something that requires elucidation.

If there is something objectionable about my suffering a loss through no fault of my own, it does not seem to be related to the nature of loss. Self-induced losses are, seemingly, no more or less *losses* for being self-induced. My losing a hundred pounds on a horse is no less *a loss of a hundred pounds* that my having a hundred pounds stolen from me—we can only distinguish between the two *qua* losses by incorporating into our notion of loss precisely the concerns about responsibility that it is important for us to keep separate from that notion. This being so, I do not think it can plausibly be argued that losses vary in their standing *as* losses according to the responsibility of those on the receiving end of them. It may be, of course, that there is a peculiar kind of frustration in suffering an *unavoidable* loss. But bringing a loss upon yourself has its own kind of frustration—after all, you have only *yourself* to blame. In any event, to claim that responsibility is relevant to loss only in so far as it affects the magnitude or intensity of loss is to make the relevance of responsibility contingent and circumstantial. Indeed, it is a short step from here to precisely the idea I said we should avoid, namely that (the absence of) responsibility is an *ingredient* of loss and that the responsibility principle is undergirded by the claim that it is better—less objectionable—for there to be less loss in the world rather than more. The same objection might be applied also to any claim that losses that are no fault of the parties concerned are objectionable by virtue of being in some sense unnecessary—the claim, that is, that the losses in question need not have occurred and indeed might not have occurred had the agent been differently placed in respect of those losses.

As it happens, I do not think many are drawn to the view that the absence of responsibility for a given loss expands the magnitude of that loss, or heightens the intensity with which it is felt, or (thereby) adds loss to the world. Nor are many drawn to the view that the absence of responsibility for a given benefit necessarily diminishes that benefit in the terms described. I do not mean by this that consequentialist arguments are *incapable* of accounting for the significance of individual responsibility to the question of who should get what.[8] In the field of rectificatory justice, for instance, most of us are familiar with the argument that it would in some sense be counter-productive not to tie punishment to individual responsibility. The thought here is not that an individual can only *deserve* to be punished if he is responsible for what he has done. Instead, the thought is that it would be *inefficient* to punish individuals where the relevant test of responsibility was not met. And it would be inefficient because punishments serve as an instrument of social control: they deter rational actors (which, in this context, means choosing and calculating actors) from breaking the relevant rules. Punishing individuals for conduct they could do nothing about—for conduct, that is, lying outside the arc of choice and calculation altogether—would not deter anyone, on this view at least, and there would therefore be no reason to do it.

When it comes not to dispensing punishments but to distributing rewards, it might indeed be argued that we ought to respect individual responsibility because doing so will tend to produce greater tangible benefits, or fewer tangible losses, than ignoring it. Thus it is sometimes claimed that individuals should stand or fall by their own decisions because they are generally better placed than third parties to judge what their wants or interests are, or to advance those wants and interests, or both. In other words, the demand to honour the claims of individual responsibility is part of a more general consequentialist argument against paternalism and in favour of individual self-direction. Related to this is the thought that the more we broaden and secure the realm of self-direction the more we bring stability and predictability to our lives—and the more we reduce the chances of individuals suffering the sort of frustration I mentioned earlier that comes with thwarted expectations. More generally, it is said that a commitment to individual responsibility as a determinant of distributive reward brings with it beneficial consequences to the population as a whole, such as the putatively beneficial consequences of enterprise and prudence, whilst at the same time discouraging waste and slothfulness (these protestant virtues and vices being judged desirable or undesirable purely in consequentialist terms).

But, as I have suggested, few go so far as to say that honouring the claims of individual responsibility *necessarily* has good consequences nor that disavowing the claims of individual responsibility *necessarily* has bad consequences. And even were such a necessary relation between responsibility and consequences to be established, it would remain to be shown that consequentialist considerations were not relevant to the issue of responsibility in other ways and indeed that the claims of consequences might not pull in different directions in any given case.

The argument from consequences provides one kind of defence of personal responsibility. But it is not the only defence on offer. Indeed, many think that the significance of responsibility lies not in the idea that it is *efficient* to respect responsibility but in the idea that respecting responsibility is something we *owe* individuals—by which I mean something we owe individuals regardless of any claims about consequences and efficiency. It is at this point that one might legitimately ask why it matters which defence of responsibility is appealed to. What difference does it make whether we defend individual responsibility in terms of claims about consequences or claims about the treatment individuals are owed? I think that there are two answers to this. In part, the distinction matters in itself—it matters because the two sorts of defences seem to feed off different conceptions of the human individual and different conceptions also of the kinds of rules that should govern interactions between such individuals. In part also, it matters because what we want concerns about individual responsibility to *do* for us, and where exactly we want them to fit into our moral economy, may well have a bearing on how deep the preconditions of responsibility need to go—a point I pursue further in the chapter that follows.

In very broad terms, the different conceptions at work are these. On the one hand, the idea that individual responsibility matters to us for reasons of efficacy seems to sit comfortably alongside a somewhat unedifying view of human beings, one in which we are seen as eligible for regulation in whatever way is conducive to minimizing collisions between us. In case this sounds far-fetched, pause for a moment to think of the vision of human individuals and human life that underlies the deterrent account of punishment. According to this vision, is it not perfectly in order to control and manipulate individuals through threat and sanctions in much the same way as we might control and manipulate portions of the world? And if it is in order to do this, does not the vision present us with a conception of human individuals as things akin to objects rather than as *persons*? Clearly enough, the deterrent view does not altogether diminish the human individual. It holds that whether individuals should be punished depends, amongst other things, on their state of mind at the time, their intentions, and so on. For many, however, this view pays only lip service to concerns about individual responsibility: it treats individuals as objects rather as moral subjects. Thus opponents of the consequentialist defence of responsibility will say it is not enough that concerns about responsibility should *appear somewhere* in an account of what individuals are owed. These concerns must, rather, appear in the right way and for the right reasons.

Standing opposed, then, to the argument from efficiency—however parodied my presentation of that argument might appear—stands the thought that human beings should not be regarded as objects at all and that it is not in order to regulate collisions between them that we live by rules of *justice* and honour in those rules claims about individual responsibility. It is not a test of efficiency that accounts for the link between claims about responsibility and claims about who should get what but, instead, a view about how we should think and deal with one another in our collective life. Rather than dealing with one another as objects we should deal with one another as moral subjects.[9] Seen in this light, individual responsibility is one element of the conceptual apparatus by which we treat and respond to one another, not as objects drifting in the world but as subjects who owe one another respect and who are expected to justify their conduct to one another. The language of individual responsibility is, in this sense, the language of moral dialogue. To disclaim the language of responsibility is to remove oneself from the moral dialogue itself: it is to resort to the exchange of descriptions and predictions rather than judgements and reasons for actions.

Let me concede here that the dividing line between these two underlying conceptions of where concerns about individual responsibility fit into our moral thinking is more nuanced and less stark than I have presented it. I certainly do not want to say that consequentialist concerns have no place in our thinking about who should get what any more than I want to say it is improper to defend the importance of individual responsibility on the grounds of such concerns. What I *do* want to say is that arguments about efficiency are not the kinds of argument that draw most of us to individual responsibility most of the time. What does draw us is the sort of argument I have just outlined—one in which claims about agency and the moral subject occupy centre stage. On this view, individuals are owed certain kinds of treatment by social institutions because to deprive them of such treatment is to dishonour their status as agents. Thus, my status as an agent is inextricably bound up with my capacity to make decisions and choices about my life. This being so, my status as an agent cannot be respected unless my capacity to choose and decide is respected. Respecting my capacity to choose and decide means, in turn, not denying me the opportunity to make choices and decisions and to live by those choices and decisions. To deny me this opportunity is to fail to take me seriously as a choosing and deciding being. Indeed, it is to treat me as a thing rather than a person, an object rather than a subject, and, as such, an instrument of the purposive agency of others and a tool to their advancement.

In some cases this argument is associated with an appeal not to the *consequentialist* value of self-direction but to its intrinsic, or, at least, non-instrumental, value. Thus there is argued to be value in individuals shaping the course of their own lives according to choices and decisions that are *theirs*, rather than anyone else's, a value that has nothing to do with any desirable consequences that might flow to the individual from this. In other cases, the claim that we should respect persons as such is thought to require that each be given a reasonable opportunity to avoid losses. Here again, the thought is one about taking people seriously: you do not take me seriously if you deny me the opportunity to navigate my way through the world as best as I can and instead turn the world against me, rendering it something that happens to me rather than something upon which I impose myself and my purposes. To require of me that I do the impossible is to fail to treat me in good faith, as someone who could in principle fulfil the demands being placed upon him.

This may, however, serve to reinforce the impression that claims about responsibility have to them a curmudgeonly, not to say niggardly, tone. Certainly, appeal is often made to individual responsibility as a distributive criterion when our thoughts turn to the matter of how human life should be regulated and restricted and human action checked and kept in order. Indeed, it is common enough for claims about responsibility to be invoked where something has gone wrong or some bad state of affairs has arisen. But claims about responsibility do not *have* to assume this negative tone. As I have said, we might want to affirm the importance of individual responsibility not only in response to something undesirable—such as that the guilty have been let off whilst the innocent have been punished—but in the service of a vision of what makes for a full, rich, and worthwhile human life. Seen in this light, the claim that individuals should stand or fall according to decisions and actions for which they are responsible is bound up with the view of human beings that I described before, one that privileges their status as sources of intentions, decisions, and actions[10] and that attributes to them what T. M. Scanlon describes as 'the capacity for critically reflective, rational self-governance'.[11] According to this view, individuals should, so far as possible, be authors of their lives. Thus we might want to think of individual responsibility not as something we impose upon people but as something we foster and encourage, something we do our best to draw out of individuals and to prevent others from undermining.

Indeed, it may be that the impulse to put claims about individual responsibility at the heart of claims about justice draws its vigour from a deeper impulse to put claims about intentionality, reflection, and control at the heart of our social arrangements and organization *in toto*. After all, the thought that advantages and disadvantages should be dispensed on the basis of our rational agency is one that sits neatly alongside the thought that the workings of the social order, in all its complexity, should be intelligible to us as rational agents. Jeremy Waldron expresses this idea wonderfully well in describing a view of the social world to which he thinks liberals in particular will be sympathetic:

Society should be a *transparent* order, in the sense that its workings and principles should be well-known and available for public apprehension and scrutiny. People should know and understand the reasons for the basic distribution of wealth, power, authority and freedom. Society should not be shrouded in mystery, and its workings should not have to depend on mythology, mystification, or a 'noble lie'.[12]

At the risk of stretching the point, I would like to suggest that the impulse to tie claims about who should get what to claims about individual responsibility might draw its force from the same source as the impulse to tie claims about the justification of political authority to claims about consent. In other words, the attachment to individual responsibility and to personal consent derive from a broader attachment to the role of voluntariness in political cum philosophical argument and justification. If I am right about this, then some of what is said in support of consent as a basis of legitimate authority might equally be said in support of individual responsibility as a basis of legitimate distribution.[13]

All of which has taken me a long way from my starting point in this chapter—that being the thought that egalitarian objections to inequalities are often linked to arguments about individual responsibility. Having said something about the general reasons we have for thinking that responsibility matters in deciding who should get what, the time has come to start thinking about what is distinctive about the *egalitarian* position in the matter of when and why responsibility matters. Most obviously, egalitarians are in the business of applying certain general claims about personal responsibility to the specific case of relations between individuals. And, indeed, one articulation of this idea has proved especially appealing to egalitarian thinkers. This is the *expensive tastes* argument.[14] According to this argument, it offends against egalitarian justice to transfer resources from those whose tastes are expensive to those whose tastes are cheap, where what distinguishes expensive tastes from cheap ones is that the former cost more to pursue, and (therefore) to derive satisfaction from, than the latter. To understand the force of this argument, imagine that we two are of modest means and modest tastes. On the resources we have available to us we are able to satisfy, in the same way and to the same extent, our taste for cable television and hamburgers. One day, I decide to cultivate a taste for fine wine and sports cars, a taste I cannot possibly satisfy on the modest resources that have hitherto proved sufficient for my needs. Should resources be transferred from you, with your modest tastes, to me, with my expensive tastes, in the name of seeing to it that each of us is able to satisfy their tastes to the same extent or, at least, to derive the same level of satisfaction from those tastes? One might answer no to this question on the grounds that the example points to the folly of making *tastes* and their satisfaction the object of distributive concern, regardless of the responsibility, or otherwise, of the parties concerned. Or one might worry that such transfers will in some sense be inefficient. These are not, however, the arguments I am concerned with here. The argument I am concerned with also answers no to the question posed—but it does so pointing to the significance of my having *cultivated* the expensive taste in question. With cultivation comes responsibility. I am responsible for having the expensive taste that I do and it would be objectionable for you to be required to subsidize me in my pursuit of that taste and the satisfactions it brings.

It might be thought that this objection to redistributing resources from you to me derives its force from the argument I examined earlier, namely, the argument that agents as such are owed certain kinds of treatment by social institutions. Recall that, on this view, social institutions treat me as an agent only where I stand or fall according to that for which I am responsible. If we apply this requirement to the example of me and my expensive tastes, then it seems that the reason why resources ought not to be redistributed from you to me is that doing so would manifest a lack of respect for my status as an agent, that is as one who should pay the price for, and secure the benefits of, his decisions and choices. This would, incidentally, also bear out the thought I canvassed earlier, namely, that in the service of such respect we should attend not only to those who suffer losses through an absence of responsibility but also those who, as in this case, stand to secure benefits. Moreover, it is not just *my* status as an agent—albeit a profligate agent—that social institutions would fail to honour in redistributing resources from you to me. It is also *your* status as an agent—a prudent agent as it happens—that social institutions would fail to honour were they to carry out the redistributions in question. And they would fail to honour *your* status as an agent because they would violate the dictum that each should stand or fall according to *his* decisions and choices.

But even viewing the issue in this way does not quite capture what is *unfair* about the redistribution we are considering. What this view captures is the idea that agents are owed certain treatment by social *institutions*—its focus is on the vertical relation between citizens and state. What it fails to capture is that citizens owe certain treatment *to one another*—it does not say enough about the horizontal relation between citizen and citizen. If it is unfair to redistribute from the profligate to the prudent, that is presumably because agents cum citizens owe *one another* a certain respect, a respect that is incompatible with their seeking to displace the costs of their choices on to others and to have others subsidize their lifestyles. The fact that social institutions serve to enforce the relevant principles of mutual respect ought not to distract from us recognizing these principles to operate primarily between one individual and the next rather than between each individual and the state.

On the view I have been describing, individuals are seen as bound together in a complex web of relations of mutual respect. Each is left free to stand or fall according to the decisions and choices for which he can be held responsible, and no one may displace the costs of his (responsible) decisions and choices upon others nor expect others to do so to him. Each must bear the cost of his bad decisions and choices and each may secure the benefits of his good ones. What marks this arrangement out from *laissez-faire* is the primacy it attaches to determining where individual responsibility begins and where it ends—and of judging the claims of each against the other accordingly. In this, it seeks to apply to social interaction as a whole the intuitions captured by the expensive tastes argument—at least as I presented that argument earlier on—according to which it is objectionable for those whose tastes are cheap to subsidize those responsible for having tastes that are expensive.

In fact, more may be packed in to the intuition about expensive tastes than first appearances suggest. In part, the objection to one person subsidizing another may be connected to the value we attach to self-direction—my being called upon to subsidize you restricts the realm within which I am free to pursue the projects of my choosing and to live according to choices made by me. In part also, the expensive tastes objection may be connected not so much to a claim about justice as to one about *exploitation*—allowing for the fact that these two kinds of claim are not synonymous even if they do seem to have more in common with one another than either has with claims couched in the language of efficiency. On this view, my subsidizing your lifestyle is tantamount to my being used by you and to your treating me as an instrument to your advancement. Beyond this stands the thought that free-riding upsets the hypothetical balance of burdens and benefits that we are required, in the name of justice, to maintain across the population. Support for this latter thought comes in turn from the idea that taking responsibility for a thing is inherently burdensome and shirking responsibility for it is inherently beneficial—and indeed from the claim ventured by some that there is something inherently advantageous in flouting rules that others observe.

One way or another, many think that the expensive tastes objection tells us something important about who should get what and that that something is bound up with the idea that the prudent should secure the benefits of their prudence and the profligate should face up to the cost of their profligacy. Some of these arguments, however, are less persuasive than at first they appear. Indeed, it really is important to establish whether your calling upon me to subsidize expensive tastes for which you are responsible is objectionable because it manifests a lack of respect on your part for me or because such a subsidy would divert resources from my legitimate pursuit of my own, more modest, tastes. If the worry is about diverting resources—from cheap tastes to expensive ones—then it seems to be targeted at the satisfaction of expensive tastes *per se*, regardless of our *responsibility* for those tastes. This is because satisfying expensive tastes for which one is responsible would be no less demanding of the resources of others than satisfying expensive tastes for which one is not responsible: the subsidy called for is the same in each case. If, however, it is not the diverting of resources *per se* that is of concern—if, that is, there would be no objection *in principle* to subsidizing my taste for fine wine and sports cars—then the argument would seem to be motivated by a claim about the respect we owe one another. Perhaps the thought is that fecklessness as such is incompatible with showing others the respect they merit and that it ought therefore not to attract benefit. If that is the thought, however, then enforcing the protestant virtues in this way does appear an odd mission for a supposedly *egalitarian* account of justice, particularly given the traditional hostility of egalitarians to all forms of desert theory.

This may suggest that the underlying concern here is not one about fecklessness as such but about the mischiefs that arise out of fecklessness. Seen in this light, our aim is not to eradicate vice but to safeguard self-direction or to guard against exploitation. Thus, fecklessness comes to be objectionable because pandering to it on behalf of one person will require us to invade the realm within which the choices of another person should otherwise be sovereign or indeed because pandering to it would be tantamount to allowing some to exploit others. It strikes me, however, these arguments may appear convincing primarily because to talk about *tastes* is to conjure up the image of something that is frippery, free-floating, and indulgent to the senses—an image borne out by the example I have been using of someone who has a taste for fine wine and fast cars. Not all tastes, however, need be of this kind. I may, for instance, have a taste for nineteenth-century romantic fiction. In itself, this taste is not only more than a mere whim or sensory indulgence, it may also be one element of a grander project in which I am engaged. Imagine, for instance, that I am engaged in the project of producing sublime romantic fiction of my own, a project I can complete only I am able to satisfy my tastes, such as the taste for romantic fiction from an earlier age, one at a time. Quite where a set of tastes ends and a *project* begins, I am not sure. But I do not need to resolve that question in order to cast doubt on the thought that I show a lack of respect for you—still more that I *exploit* you—through cultivating tastes that are part and parcel of projects whose pursuit is are worthwhile, projects that add value to the world according to some generally recognized standard of what it is for these things to be true of such projects. It may be that pursuing these projects will sometimes require resources to be diverted from you, and others like you, to me. But the benefits of these projects are shared by all and certainly do not accrue to me alone. Indeed, the language of tastes may distract us into thinking of me, the budding novelist, wholly as a consumer of value and not at all as a producer of it. In looking to you to subsidize my projects, however, I am not out to impose some *selfish* purpose of mine upon you any more than do taxes directed towards the funding of good causes impose selfish purposes upon taxpayers. What is going on here is not the subordination of one person to another but the marshalling of a plurality of individuals in the name of something worthwhile. Indeed, to say that the *projects* I pursue merit greater resources than those you pursue in virtue of their superior worth is not at all the same thing as saying that *I* merit greater resources than you in virtue of *my* superior worth.

Nor should we be persuaded by the claim that free-riding upsets a hypothetical balance of burdens and benefits. That claim, as I said before, trades on the idea that taking responsibility for a thing is inherently burdensome and shirking responsibility inherently beneficial. But the argument smacks of stipulation and is often no more than a reworking of the claim that free-riding is objectionable rather than an independent defence of that claim. Moreover, from the fact that securing a certain good was more burdensome for you than it was for me—in terms, for instance, of the effort and self-control required of each of us—it certainly does not follow that you have subsidized me or that I have been a free-rider upon you. Indeed, it does not follow that there has been any kind of *relation* between us at all: it may just be that I got lucky rather than that you were called upon to do anything on my behalf.

Let me end by retracing the argument of this chapter. Having begun by identifying the different senses of responsibility that are on offer, I went on to examine the significance of individual responsibility to our thinking about who should get what. Under this heading I said that there were different kinds of argument to which we might appeal. One kind recommends that we defer to individual responsibility on the basis of calculations about the tangible losses and benefits that a respect for responsibility produces. I do not believe that such arguments should be either dismissed or ignored. What I do believe, however, is that these are not the kinds of arguments to which we are commonly drawn in thinking about responsibility, most of the time at least. The motivation to incorporate concerns about responsibility into claims about distributive justice stems primarily from the idea that individuals are owed certain kinds of treatment as *agents* and that the treatment in question is such as to require that how each person fares in life should be related to their decisions and choices, good or bad. I suggested that the injunction to treat individuals with the respect their (responsible) agency demands is one that is applied not only to the relation between state and citizen but between citizen and citizen. From there, I pointed to some of the difficulties to which this view gives rise.

Before leaving these questions, and turning in the next chapter to the difficult issue of what individuals can be held responsible *for*, I want to add two things on the issue of responsibility. The first is that it is always open to us to account for the importance of responsibility other than by appealing to concerns about fairness or the treatment that is owed to agents as such—or, indeed, by appealing to ordinary consequentialist arguments. We might, for instance, account for the importance of responsibility by appealing to the idea that the state ought to refrain from the direct promotion of outcomes. On this view, there exists pervasive disagreement in contemporary societies as to what outcomes are, and are not, worthwhile to pursue. For the state to promote one outcome, or set of outcomes, over others would be for it to violate the requirements of public endorsement, given the nature of contemporary societies and the constraints imposed by what Rawls calls 'the fact of pluralism'.[15] Of course, this argument is essentially negative in character: its emphases rest less on the value of respecting responsibility as on the disvalue of promoting outcomes. This, then, is the argument from public justifiability.

My second point is this. To claim of individual responsibility that it *matters* in determining who should get what is not thereby to claim—still less is it to *establish*—that it is the only thing that matters nor indeed that it is what matters more than anything else. Most of us think that our commitments to one another go beyond exhibiting a respect for one another's responsible agency and extend, for instance, into relieving suffering regardless of how those concerned have come to suffer in the first place.[16] All of which suggests one of two things. *Either* we need to find a place in our theory of justice for concerns that are not linked directly to the responsibility of the parties concerned. *Or* we need to recognize that the question of who should get what, incorporating as it should concerns that are not tied directly to responsibility, is broader than the question of what individuals are owed in the name of justice, which may indeed confine itself to concerns tied directly to responsibility.

3

What we are responsible for

In the previous chapter I began to look at how arguments about individual responsibility bear upon the issue of who should get what. To this end, I said that three questions in particular needed to be addressed. The first concerned the senses of responsibility that are relevant to the enquiry and the second the significance of responsibility so identified. It is the third question that I pursue here—the question of what, if anything, individuals are responsible *for*. Of course, there is a certain artificiality in maintaining a hard and fast separation between these three questions. Indeed, it was pretty obvious that my discussion of the second question (concerning the significance of responsibility) often traded on assumptions in the matter of the third (concerning the preconditions of responsibility). This suggests that I may have got the argument the wrong way round. Instead of working backwards from the question of why responsibility matters to the question of what we are responsible for, perhaps I should have worked forwards from the question of what we are responsible for to the question of why responsibility matters. After all, establishing that we are not responsible for anything would presumably resolve the question of why individual responsibility matters: it would resolve it by showing it to be redundant. This sort of completeness is not, however, available to us if we work the argument the other way: resolving that individual responsibility, if such a thing there be, matters to us for this reason rather than that would not, of itself, establish anything about what we are responsible for.

All of which seems to bear out the thought that the right place to start the argument is with an investigation into how far, in principle, individual responsibility extends. If we find that it does not extend anywhere—if we find that there is not such a thing *as* individual responsibility—then we can call a halt to the argument there and then. The problem with this approach, however, is that it assumes we agree on what would have to be true in order for someone to *be* responsible for something. It assumes that, in principle, we know *what* the preconditions for attributing responsibility to an individual are and that such disputes as take place centre on how to interpret these preconditions and their demands. In a very general sense, I suppose that we *do* agree about these preconditions. We agree, as I have suggested already, that my being responsible for a thing is bound up in some way with claims about voluntariness, or control, or intentionality, or critical self-reflection, or foreseeability, or some combination of these. Moreover, we agree on the sorts of things that might compromise my responsibility, such as coercion and brainwashing. The agreement about these preconditions is, however, as I described it—very general. We do not agree whether voluntariness requires free will still less whether it makes sense to speak of their *being* free will. Moreover, we do not agree whether individual responsibility would still matter to us if it could somehow be shown that there were no such thing as free will. In short, the question of what the preconditions of responsibility are is inseparable from the question of where we think claims about individual responsibility fit into our moral economy: claims about the significance of responsibility tell us what to look for in claims about its preconditions. The further we move away from arguments about what is required, in the name of efficiency, towards arguments about what is required, in the name of individual desert, the deeper the demands of individual responsibility appear to become. Imagine, for instance, that we want to establish a standard of responsibility by which to distinguish those who set out to break the law from those who break it by accident. In this case, the preconditions for attributing responsibility to individuals will be suitably shallow. Certainly, they will not address themselves to metaphysical arguments concerning free will and determinism. To see this we need only imagine how bizarre it would be for a man accused of stealing chickens to plead diminished responsibility on the grounds that his actions were fixed by prior sufficient causes. Appeal to these sorts of deep preconditions is not, however, bizarre in all cases where mention is being made of individual responsibility. It is not bizarre where claiming of someone that he is *responsible* for something is bound up with an assessment of the quality of his will— mysterious though that claim might be to some. If I say of someone that he is evil or saintly I am not passing any old judgement on him. I take myself to be saying something deep about *him*, something that clearly goes beyond ordinary judgements of credit and fault.

My purpose at this stage is not to try to resolve these questions, merely to illustrate that what we take the preconditions of responsibility to be will depend on the work we want claims about responsibility to do for us. Two things, I think, follow from this. One is that it is often not clear which way round the argument about significance and preconditions should be conducted. The other is that attributions of responsibility are not all of a kind: the standard we appeal to in respect of stealing chickens seems to be very different from the standard we appeal to in respect of the kind of deep moral judgement I described earlier. The trick is to work out where claims about individual responsibility, as these relate to the question of who should get what, fit into all this. Are these claims deep, shallow, or something in between? Are we advancing claims about the quality of will of the distributees or are the claims we advance more prosaic?

So, in thinking about what individuals are responsible for—in the context of claims about distributive justice—the first difficulty we face concerns the nature of the enquiry itself. We have to work out what *kind* of question are we asking and what kind of answer are we seeking to elicit. As I have suggested already, some believe that claims about responsibility, being the kind of *deep* claims about individuals that they are, are unavoidably bound up with arguments about the metaphysics of the will. Under this heading, it is commonly thought that the notion of individual responsibility is vulnerable to attack from two directions. One is from the doctrine of universal determinism— where universal determinism, as I described it earlier, is the view that everything about the character of events in the world, including human actions, intentions, and thoughts, is fixed by prior causes. Why should universal determinism be thought threatening to individual responsibility? In rough and ready terms the answer is this: if my thoughts and actions are the only possible effect of prior causes, there would seem to be only one trajectory those thoughts and actions can follow. So whereas I might like to believe that I have a free hand in deciding how to act or what to think—I might like to believe, that is, that it is something of an open question whether I act or think one way rather than another in any given case—universal determinism seems to deny me this sort of freedom. If there really is only one trajectory my thoughts and actions can follow, then I cannot think and act other than as I do. And if I cannot think and act other than as I do, then it is not clear how I can possibly be held *responsible* for what I am and what I do.

In short, the worry is that universal determinism, if true, is *incompatible* with holding individuals responsible for things. Of course, there are several ways in which philosophers have sought to dispose of this concern. Some, for instance, agree that determinism, if true, would be incompatible with traditional notions of responsibility—but they hold determinism to be false. Others deny that determinism, if true, engenders the incompatibility I have been describing—they see the truth of determinism as being compatible with holding individuals responsible for things. Others still think that *only* if determinism is true does it make sense to hold anyone responsible for anything.

My brief at this stage is not to pick and choose between these arguments— even though, as will become obvious, my sympathies lie with the compatibilists. My brief instead is to point to the complexities we confront once we entertain the possibility that claims about universal determinism might have a bearing upon attributions of responsibility—specifically, lest we forget, attributions of responsibility as these relate to questions of who should get what.

As I said earlier, however, it is not only the doctrine of universal determinism that poses a challenge to claims about responsibility. A challenge comes also from the belief that responsibility is undermined by luck. What is claimed here is that, regardless of the truth of falsity of universal determinism, the world is suffused by what are, *from the agent's point of view*, chance events the operation of which fundamentally affects human life. On this view, the pertinent feature that chance events share with caused events is that they are beyond the individual's control. Since chance events are beyond the individual's control it follows, on this view, that it would be impermissible to attribute responsibility to individuals for the characteristics or conduct affected by them. In a sense, the arguments about luck track the arguments about determinism. To begin with, there are disputes about the extent to which human life is conditioned by luck. Some believe luck to infect all aspects of human life: in this way the luck argument comes to be as all-embracing as the argument from universal determinism. Others deny this. They claim that the luck argument admits of degrees: some aspects of human life are (wholly) the product of luck whilst others are not. Moreover, it is not just over the facts about luck that dispute is centred. It is centred also over the bearing of these facts upon claims about individual responsibility and, in particular, over whether the presence of luck, however small, is sufficient to undermine attributions of responsibility.

It should be obvious from what I have said so far that if claims about responsibility really are deep claims about individuals, then the task of identifying what people are responsible for will embroil us in the seemingly intractable philosophical disputes surrounding universal determinism and the pervasiveness of luck. I float this unpalatable prospect in the knowledge that nothing I have said so far establishes that claims about individual responsibility, as these make an appearance in questions of who should get what, are in fact *deep* claims after all. Indeed, the possibility remains that we can side-step the metaphysical disputes altogether. How? Perhaps we should direct our attention away from the thought that claims about what people are responsible for are the product of a potentially seamless philosophical—let alone *metaphysical*—position and towards the thought that our judgements about responsibility issue from and form part of a *social* practice.[1] Viewed in this way, rules of responsibility occupy a philosophical status analogous to certain conventional rules. Whilst these kinds of rules admit of philosophical analysis—and, being generally beneficial, philosophical *justification*—they are not grounded in nor do they explicate deep philosophical premises. The essence of these rules is that social interaction as we know it would be impossible without them. Attributions of responsibility are, in short, components of a formal system that is self-contained and conventional. They bestow upon our common life richness and texture and they serve as a prism through which we view and construct our social world. Thus, in investigating whether I am responsible for one thing but not for another, what we are really investigating is what sort of judgement the social *conventions* according to which we attribute responsibility direct us to make in respect of me and the things in question. To be sure, these arguments will make some sort of appeal to claims about control and voluntariness. But the answers to these questions are internal to the social practice and its immanent principles.

As it is, my guess is that those who think responsibility *matters* as a distributive criterion would not do so were they to think also that attributions of responsibility were true or false according *only* to their fidelity to conventional practice. Those who hold the responsibility of an individual for a thing to be of fundamental importance in determining how he should be assessed in respect of that thing do not, standardly, think that our investigations into what makes individuals responsible for some things but not for others begin and end with bare convention. They think that there is some fact of the matter and that it is this fact of the matter that gives claims about individual responsibility their distinctive moral force. Mere interpretation of conventional practice is not enough—the investigation of responsibility is an effort at truth.

If the appeal to convention cannot do the work we need it to in understanding what individuals are responsible for in the context of who should get what, does this not mean that we are forced back into investigating the metaphysics of the will? I want now to explore the possibility that we are not and to do so by examining a different kind of argument altogether. This argument overlaps with the conventional approach I have just been describing in that it too directs our thinking about responsibility away from concerns about the metaphysics of the will. But whilst the conventional approach does this by playing down the philosophical status of claims about responsibility, the argument I have in mind preserves that status at the same time as holding that arguments about who should get what appeal to a distinctively *political* conception of responsibility. Whilst the distinction between the political and the metaphysical is one most closely associated with Rawls, the distinction I am exploring here differs from that of Rawls.[2] A political conception of responsibility, as I construe it, is not simply one that is invoked in the context of political questions, that is questions about how rights and duties, opportunities and resources, should be apportioned in a society. A political conception of responsibility is, or would be, one that operates independently of deep metaphysical premises. It is a conception of responsibility whose force as *a conception of responsibility*, there to regulate our dealings with one another in our common political life, can be acknowledged by individuals whatever metaphysical position they happen to subscribe to. On this view, the metaphysical debate about the preconditions of individual responsibility just does not operate on the same plane and draw on the same vocabulary as the political (and perhaps *ethical*) debate. Those who sign up to the political conception need not deny that there is a metaphysical argument *to be made* in respect of individual responsibility. Nor are they committed, by default, to the conventional view. The position they will want to defend is that the capacities relevant to responsibility, politically construed, have some sort of independent standing: they are not mere creatures of convention even if they stop short of enjoying a deep metaphysical status. Political ethics, in short, is regarded as engaging a distinct and distinctive subject matter such that there is nothing philosophically improper in keeping political arguments separate from metaphysical ones.

It strikes me that there is not anything exceptionable in the idea of a political conception of a thing. We do not, after all, need to pronounce upon the metaphysics of the will to hold there to be a politically—or indeed ethically— compelling sense in which Nelson Mandela enjoyed greater liberty after he was released from prison than he did when he was inside. Indeed, we seem able to claim of *political* liberty that it matters normatively without feeling the need to resort to deep metaphysical premises at every turn. The question is whether what is true of claims about liberty is true also of claims about responsibility. On the face of it, the answer is yes. It seems that there are politically compelling senses in which we can talk about people being *responsible* for things that do not embroil us in questions about the underlying operation of the universe.

Nowhere is this more obvious than where our concern is with claims about *role responsibility*—claims, that is, about the respective jurisdictions of citizen and state and about the areas within which liabilities, in principle, arise. Quite clearly, we do not need to get ourselves bogged down in metaphysical argument in order to claim of Smith that she has certain responsibilities to her employees. Indeed, it seems that an appeal to role responsibilities can take us pretty far in working out what individuals are owed before claims about individual capacities of *any kind* enter the frame. Imagine, for instance, we claim of the state that it should assume responsibility for providing its citizens with a fair share of social resources and of citizens that they should in turn assume responsibility for the level of welfare satisfaction they derive from those resources. Imagine further that I am able to derive more welfare satisfaction from my resources than you are from yours. It does not *follow* from the difference in our ability to satisfy our welfare needs that the assumptions contained in the stipulated division of responsibility between state and citizen have been undermined. Nor does it *follow* that it is incumbent upon the state to provide you with the additional resources to bring your welfare satisfaction up to the same level as mine. That would follow only if the role responsibilities in question were intended to overlay or explicate a distinction between what it is—and what it is not—within an agent's *control* to do.

But role responsibilities need not assume this form. Indeed, I suggested as much in the previous chapter when I said that an account of role responsibilities is commonly intended to indicate and set limits on the jurisdiction of the state, limits that need not be established on the basis of an appeal to the capacities of agents. I am guilty of no inconsistency in claiming that your level of welfare satisfaction is not the state's responsibility—by virtue of being outside the state's *jurisdiction*—whilst at the same time allowing that it is not your responsibility either—by virtue of being outside your *control*. It is true that I am invoking the *language* of responsibility to describe the respective positions of the you and the state. But the senses of responsibility are importantly different. In respect of the state, the claim is one concerning jurisdictional or role responsibility. In respect of you, the claim is one concerning capacity responsibility.

If we believe that the realm of jurisdictional responsibility should be coterminous with the realm of capacity responsibility, then we will be troubled by the gap between the state's (jurisdictional) responsibility and your (capacity) responsibility. The gap will not trouble us, however, if we believe that questions of jurisdictional responsibility can be settled separately from questions of capacity responsibility. In the example under discussion, the state will say to you: 'It is true that your shortfall in welfare is not within your control. But, in and of itself, this does not establish that you have a claim on the state for compensation. This is because the state operates upon the principle that it will not compensate individuals for shortfalls in welfare of this kind, whether or not they are within the control of the parties concerned'. Indeed, we might go further. We might say that that which lies outside the jurisdiction of the state thereby lies, *by default*, within the jurisdiction of the individual. Individuals are responsible for shortfalls in their welfare satisfaction in the purely negative—and jurisdictional—sense that no other party has jurisdiction in these matters. Jurisdictional responsibility in such cases falls to the individual and no one else.

At the very least this puts a dent in the idea that an absence or presence of control for a thing is sufficient to establish whether I should be rewarded or penalized in respect of it. Indeed, it draws us back to the thought that, whatever we might say in the matter of individual capacities and their exercise, the merits of my claim to a thing are intimately bound up with the merits of the background rules and conditions against which that claim is advanced. To assess whether I bear liability responsibility for a thing it is not enough to appeal to claims about my entitlements as they are according to whatever rules happen to be in force. Nor is it enough to appeal to claims about the existence and exercise of certain capacities of mine considered in the abstract. To assess my liability responsibility it is necessary to consider whether my claims arise against the background of what Scanlon calls 'good conditions', those being conditions where the state has done as much for me as it could reasonably be expected to do and I have been 'placed in as good a position as [I] could ask for'.[3]

But if good background conditions are a necessary condition of deciding upon questions of individual responsibility, might they also be sufficient? In the name of a distinctively political conception of responsibility can we dispense *altogether* with claims about the existence and exercise of certain capacities in deciding whether I am responsible for a thing? Scanlon, for one, appears to think that we can. He appears to think that we can arrive at a compelling view of what it is for an individual to be responsible for something without invoking claims about the exercise of certain capacities. Thus he writes:

From the fact that a person chose, under good conditions, to take a risk, we may conclude that he alone is responsible for what happens to him as a result. But this conclusion need not be seen as a reflection of the special legitimating force of voluntary action. Rather, the fact that an outcome resulted from a person's choice under good conditions *shows* that he was *given* the choice and provided with good conditions for making it, and it is these facts which make it the case that he alone is responsible. A conscious decision to 'take the risk' is not necessary . . . If enough was done to protect and warn [a person], then this person is responsible for what happens to him and 'cannot complain of it' even though he made no conscious decision to take the risk.[4]

On the face of it, Scanlon seems to be claiming that I am responsible for a thing if and whenever the state has discharged its *responsibilities* towards me in respect of that thing. This is a perfectly respectable view. On my understanding of the issues, however, it is not a view that *privileges* claims of individual responsibility. In essence what it does is offer a description of the jurisdictional boundaries of the state's activity and of my liabilities given those boundaries.

I make these points in the knowledge that claims about capacities of some kind are not in fact absent from Scanlon's account of individual responsibility after all. At the very least, Scanlon's account of what makes me responsible for a thing presupposes that I *possess* certain capacities even if, on his reckoning at least, it does not presuppose that I *exercise* those capacities. Indeed, part of what makes those background conditions *good* conditions— the kind of conditions against which attributions of individual responsibility have force—is that they afford me the opportunity to exercise the capacities in question. If I have a doubt about Scanlon's argument it is not by virtue of its emphasis on the importance of background conditions. On that point, he seems to me absolutely right. Instead, my doubt about the argument is that it appears to assume precisely what Scanlon denies, namely, that our holding people responsible for things is closely tied to the idea of their *exercising* certain capacities. From the fact that I do not consciously take a risk—in the sense of thinking to myself 'I shall take the following risk for the following reasons'—it certainly does not follow that I am *unaware* of what I am doing and of its significance. Indeed, were I to be the sort of person who was oblivious to the world around me—and oblivious therefore to the possibilities and dangers that the world held—then the significance of the background conditions against which I operated would presumably be diminished. Whether there really is much of a gap between choosing consciously to take a risk and being aware of exposing oneself to risk, I am not sure. Both seem to me to presuppose a certain degree of engagement with the world on the part of the agent in question and neither seems consistent with the idea of certain capacities existing but being in some sense dormant or, at least, with their not being exercised on the particular occasion in question.

Either way, it is as well to recall that my concern here is to describe a distinctively *political* account of what makes people responsible for some things but not for others. It is as well to recall also that I have taken a political account of responsibility to be one that operates independently of assumptions about the metaphysics of the will. With this in mind, I have alluded to two ways in which we might construct such an account. One avoids altogether claims about the *capacities* that must exist or be exercised for individuals to be responsible for things and instead couches claims of individual responsibility in terms of the roles and jurisdictions of citizen and state. The other accepts that the existence or exercise of certain capacities is indeed a necessary condition of holding people responsible for things but has it that claims about the capacities in question are in some sense insulated from deeper claims about the will, universal determinism, and the metaphysics of luck. On this latter view, a political conception of responsibility requires at the very least an accompanying *political* conception of human agency, taking this to be the agency of a *citizen* rather than that of a fully formed metaphysical *person*.

I have said all along that the first approach is unable to do the work for us that we need it to. To begin with, I am not convinced that we can in all cases appeal to jurisdictional boundaries without at the same time making *some* assumptions about the human capacities that justify our drawing those boundaries in one place rather than another. My thought here is not that claims about roles and jurisdictions are necessarily *derived* from claims about capacities. My thought instead is that there may on occasion be a close relation between the two, a relation of the kind to be found in the claim that ought implies can. When, for instance, we claim of Smith that she has certain responsibilities as an employer what we seem to be doing is establishing a standard by which her conduct may be judged. We are saying there are certain things that in ordinary circumstances she ought, and ought not, to do in respect of her employees. Thus, if Smith fails to pay her workforce on time, then she is liable to censure. The *in ordinary circumstances* is, however, doing important background work here. Its inclusion suggests that when we attribute role responsibilities to individuals we may sometimes, if not always, be making certain assumptions about what it is reasonable to demand of them in ordinary circumstances—and perhaps unreasonable to demand of them in circumstances that are out of the ordinary.

Thus, in attributing responsibilities to agents and agencies, there are times when we are assuming *something* about the circumstances in which these responsibilities are to be discharged and *something* also about the capacities of the agents and agencies in question. But even if you reject this view, there remains a more important reason why we should opt for the second approach over the first. This is the now familiar one that concerns about individual responsibility exert a pull on our thinking about justice precisely because of their connection to claims about the existence and exercise of certain capacities, capacities that are integral to a particular conception of human agency. My claim here is not that there is something *conceptually* improper in severing the link between responsibility and agency. My claim instead is that severing the link between the two drains claims about responsibility of much of their *normative* force. In short, the challenge that is faced in constructing a political account of responsibility is not to insulate claims about responsibility from claims about agency but to insulate claims about agency from claims about the metaphysics of the will.

So, claims about what, for political purposes, individuals are responsible for must attend to two issues. One is the issue of background conditions. The other is the issue of human capacities. In order for me to be responsible for b—in the sense of being liable to pay the costs or secure the benefits associated with b—it does not seem to be enough that I came to do, be, or have b under generally favourable background conditions. This is because conditions that are *generally* favourable, in the sense of being favourable to the generality of the population according to certain assumptions we make about their capacities and dispositions, may be insufficiently favourable *to me* given *my* particular capacities and dispositions. It is only once we make certain assumptions about the inner dimension of responsibility that we *appear* able to dispense with that inner dimension and to rest our argument on claims about the outer dimension of favourable or unfavourable background conditions. But, as I suggested before, even an avowedly political conception of responsibility cannot avoid altogether an appeal to *some* notion of human agency. By the same token, in order for me to be responsible for b it is not enough that I possessed or exercised the relevant capacities in the course of doing, being, or having b. I might, for instance, have *intended* to do b—for instance, to sell my labour to the local factory owner—at the same time as having formed that intention against the background of unfavourable conditions—for instance, through being born into abject poverty.

As this last example makes clear, the border between conditions and capacities will often be blurred. This is because claims about whether I really did exercise the relevant capacities in any given case, or whether I exercised them to their fullest extent, may often turn on a judgement about the prevailing background conditions. Indeed, what is distinctively political about the conception of responsibility I am concerned with here is precisely this element of *interplay* between conditions and capacities, between, that is, the outer and the inner dimensions of responsibility. Were our concern to be with a metaphysical conception of responsibility, the issue of interplay would not arise and it would not arise because no set of background conditions could free us from the workings of universal determinism. There is no *social* remedy for universal determinism nor any *social* arrangement that could somehow diminish its impact upon our responsibility and freedom.[5]

This stands in contrast to the political conception of responsibility, according to which our responsibility for a thing will indeed be affected by the relevant external conditions and, in particular, by the form in which our social world is constructed. The political conception eschews the atomism that the metaphysical view encourages. On the political conception, it is not determinism that undermines my responsibility for a thing. My responsibility for a thing is undermined instead by unfavourable external conditions, or a corruption of the politically relevant capacities, or indeed both. What makes a set of conditions unfavourable is precisely that they involve the imposition of another's will upon my own or that they frustrate me to an unreasonable extent in the pursuit of my purposes. Indeed, the sorts of factors that impugn my responsibility on a political conception of that notion are precisely those that impugn my freedom construed in similarly political, or political cum ethical, terms. In this respect, Bernard Williams seems to me absolutely right when he claims that

being free stands opposed, above all, to being in someone's power; and the mark of that . . . is that my choices or opportunities are not merely limited . . . but that they are designedly and systematically limited, by another person who is shaping my actions to his intentions. To lack freedom is paradigmatically not simply to be short of choices, but to be subject to the will of another.[6]

Of course, from the fact that my responsibility for a thing is undermined in cases where others impose their will upon me, or deprive me of choices, it does not follow that I am responsible for a thing whenever others do not impose their will upon me or when they do not deprive me of choices. My being responsible for a thing may require something more than the mere absence of imposition. It may require, for instance, background conditions that enable and encourage me to form, and to act upon, desires and dispositions that are distinctively my own. Where it is that I am able to do this, then the necessary background conditions are in place for me to be held responsible for the desires, dispositions, and actions in question on the grounds of their being mine—a view attributed by at least one commentator to John Stuart Mill.[7] On this interpretation of the issue, the causal history of my desires, dispositions, and the rest is indeed relevant to the question of whether I am responsible for them. But it is relevant not because causal laws per se undermine responsibility. It is relevant because the history of how I come to think and act one way rather than another—whether my thoughts and actions have evolved under conditions that are coercive and suffocating or uncoercive and stimulating— bears upon the issue of my responsibility for these things.[8] Just as it does not follow that I ought to do whatever I can do, so it does follow that I am not responsible for everything it was possible for me to do or to avoid doing in whatever circumstances happened to prevail at the time.

Now, however, a further question arises. To accept that a necessary condition of my being responsible for a thing is that I come to do, be, or have that thing under conditions in which others do not impose their will upon me is not to say anything about what those conditions would look like. Would they be conditions of the kind we associate with a minimalist state or with an interventionist one? Clearly enough, this is a question on which libertarians and egalitarians would disagree—a point that Scanlon makes well.[9] Supporters of the libertarian right, for instance, will believe that the question of whether others impose their will upon me—and indeed whether I have sufficient opportunity and choice to live by my own lights–can be resolved merely by asking whether or not I am coerced by others. If I am not coerced, and in particular if my property rights are not violated, then libertarians may well believe that the conditions under which I live are sufficiently favourable to hold me responsible for my station in life. Egalitarians will disagree with this view. They will claim that the question of whether I am coerced, whilst relevant to the question of whether I am free from the impositions of others, does not conclude the matter. On the egalitarian account, others may impose their will upon me in ways that are indirect and unintentional, for instance through tolerating my being in conditions where I am forced to sell my labour at a knock-down price.

On this, my sympathies are with the egalitarians. It is obvious enough that certain prerequisites attach to my being able to develop my own unique desires, dispositions, and actions. Included in these prerequisites would be educational and other kinds of provision we associate with something resembling a welfare state. In the absence of even minimal provision of this kind, it does seem to me wholly disingenuous to claim that the necessary favourable conditions are in place. This said, the language of minimal provision is the language not of equality *per se* but of a principle of sufficiency of the kind advanced by Harry Frankfurt.[10] It may well be, then, that the desired background conditions are not really *egalitarian* after all.

I shall have more to say about these background rules and conditions over the next two chapters. In the meantime, let me concentrate on the issue of capacities. What sorts of capacities will lie at the heart of a distinctively political conception of individual responsibility? The answer to this seems to be that the capacities in question, if they exist at all, will, in terms of their degree if not necessarily their kind, be the exclusive preserve of human beings. They will not be found in natural or man-made phenomena and they will not (therefore) be found in human life in so far as it merely mimics such phenomena. This, however, only takes us so far—it does not tell us enough about what the capacities will be rather than what they will not be. And indeed much of the discussion about individual responsibility has to it this negative bent. Much of it starts with a claim about the sorts of things that undermine responsibility and proceeds by contrast and analogy to identify what it is about those things that is incompatible with attributing responsibility to people for them. Take some examples. Generally speaking, we do not hold people responsible for things they do by accident or under duress or on the basis of inadequate or misleading information. Nor do we hold people responsible for things they do unintentionally, or when the balance of their mind is disturbed, or when they are debilitated in some way. Similarly, we do not hold people responsible for being or having certain things from birth or from before maturity.

What plagues the discussion of preconditions is not any difficulty we face in thinking of examples where responsibility is undermined. What plagues such discussion is the difficulty we face in identifying what precisely those examples have in common and what they tell us about the more general requirements underlying attributions of responsibility—again, to the extent that we can speak of the preconditions of individual responsibility in terms that abstract from claims about its significance. That it makes sense to speak of there *being* general requirements of some kind is, however, something I take for granted: I am assuming that our thinking about responsibility is not so primitive that it comprises little more than a loose federation of disparate intuitions. Having said this, the attempt to construct an account of responsibility out of negatives and exceptions can often be a frustrating one—we seem to end up circling around a target rather than attacking it head-on. That being so, a more promising strategy might be to ask what the ingredients of responsibility are, as these relate to questions of political justice, and how these coalesce within the responsible agent.

I have already made gestures in the direction of such a description—but let me now embellish it. The human individual I have in mind possesses reason and the capacity for critical reflection. He forms intentions, takes decisions, and acts upon them, taking account of the restrictions and opportunities present in the world around him. Sometimes things work out well, at other times badly. He has a sense of what others expect of him and of how they will react if he does one thing rather than another. He has a sense also of himself, of what it is for him to act in character, and of what it is for him to fall short of the standards he sets himself. His life is not something he observes with cold detachment but something he is caught up in, something whose distinctive character has arisen from the decisions, good and bad, he has made along the way. Whilst his life is not an effortless ascent towards truth and self-discovery, it is at the same time something more than an accumulation of unconnected events—a view that, whatever else it does, cautions us against any attempt to segment individual life and to consider whether individuals are *responsible* for each segment considered in isolation from other segments. On the view I am describing, contained within individual life are certain patterns, unities, and continuities which, taken together, form part of an unfolding narrative and it is by virtue of the continuities present within that narrative that individuals are able to engage in an *ongoing* moral dialogue with one another.

Within the terms of this view, it really is important to separate out claims about the specific acts and omissions we are responsible for from claims about how far we are responsible for our more general state of being. Where our concern is with acts and omissions, it seems that claims about individual responsibility usually make reference to some notion of *control*. Nor is this surprising. Either I am a reflecting, intending, and acting being, capable of justifying my conduct to others. Or I am a being to whom things happen that are beyond my control, capable of doing no more than describing and predicting my conduct. I cannot be both.[11] You may regret my scratching your brand new Ferrari when the brakes on my car develop an unexpected fault, but you would hardly claim that I was responsible for driving badly by virtue of some intention I had formed or decision I had taken.

The question is how far an appeal to claims about control and intentionality can take us in marking out the line between what we are and what we are not responsible for in a more general sense. It was not within my control, for instance, that I was brought up to speak English rather than French. As it is, however, I am happy enough that English is my first language and I would not want to speak any other, even if I could. Does this mean that I am *responsible* for being an English speaker? If the test we apply is one of control, then the answer seems to be no. I seem to be no more in control of being an English speaker than I am in control of my car as it collides with your Ferrari, and since I am not responsible for colliding with your Ferrari, it follows, on this view, that I am not responsible also for being an English speaker.

Of course, in order to reach this conclusion we have to assume that the arguments about control, intentionality, and responsibility bear upon one case in the same way as they bear upon the other. This assumption may, however, be unwarranted. On the one hand, it may be that I really *do* have more control over whether I am an English speaker than I do over whether my faulty car behaves itself. On the other, it may be that what might make me *responsible* for being an English speaker but not for driving a faulty car is not really to do with a claim about control after all. Here again, I want to emphasize the importance of distinguishing claims about responsibility as they apply to acts and omissions and claims about responsibility as they apply to states of being. Indeed, it may be that we get confused about which preconditions of responsibility we should take as definitive precisely because we move between these two cases. Where our concern is with acts and omissions, claims about control appear to have a peculiar salience. As I said before, I cannot be responsible for *doing* a thing—such as colliding with your Ferrari—if there was little or no sense in which my doing that thing was within my control. Where, however, our concern is with states of being, claims about control appear to matter less. Seemingly, I can be responsible for *being* or *having* a thing—such as being an English speaker or having a chip on my shoulder—even if there was little or no sense in which my being or having that thing was within my control, to begin with at least. In the matter of being and having—as opposed to doing— what appears to be important is whether I endorse the trait in question as my own. Provided that I do endorse or affirm that trait—provided that it forms part of a more or less settled set of dispositions that go to make up my character—then it is mine and I am responsible for it.[12]

If this is right, then there are two tests of responsibility at work rather than one. One is a test of *volition*: it holds my responsibility for a thing to be bound up with claims about my control and intentions in respect of that thing. The other is a test of *affirmation*: it holds my responsibility for a thing to be bound up with claims about whether I endorse that thing, regardless of whether it was within my control to have or be that thing to begin with.[13] I should say that I offer up these two as tests of responsibility in the knowledge that the gap between them may be narrower than I have suggested. From the fact that my being or having a thing was not within my control *to begin with* it does not follow that my being or having that thing is not within my control now and that it is this fact about my present, rather than some fact about my past, that establishes the relevant degree of responsibility on my part. Indeed, from here it is a short step to the idea that a necessary condition of my endorsing or affirming a thing is precisely that it is within my control to rid myself of it. Even allowing this, however, I want to resist the idea that claims about affirmation simply *collapse* into claims about control and intentionality and to resist also the idea that claims about affirmation are nothing more than a sophisticated rendering of the demands of the volitional test. The fact of my endorsing a thing does, it seems to me, carry some *independent* weight in assessing my responsibility for that thing, regardless of any claims about my capacity to jettison it.

As it is, neither the volitional nor the affirmational account of the preconditions of responsibility appears to rest upon deep metaphysical premises. It does seem that we can talk about whether something is within my control, or whether I affirm it as my own, without feeling compelled to follow the trail of cause and effect back to a free and self-causing will, stripped of causal antecedents and contingent characteristics, from which all responsibility proceeds. To this extent, the search for a set of specifically political preconditions of responsibility and human agency seems to have succeeded. Or, at least, that is how things appear to me. Let me concede, however, that things may appear that way to me because I do not have much time for *any* view of responsibility—political or otherwise—that holds my responsibility for a thing to require that I have a free and undetermined will. In other words, my belief that we can arrive at a distinctively political conception of responsibility may just be a sign—perhaps *another* sign—of a more general attachment to compatibilism on my part.

All of which allows for the possibility that the quest for a distinctively political conception of responsibility and its preconditions is doomed to failure. After all, there is a perfectly respectable view holding that control and affirmation *matter* in our thinking about responsibility only if or because we make certain assumptions about the metaphysics of the will, most obviously that each of us has a will that is the free and originating source of our actions and intentions. Without such assumptions, the argument runs, there is no reason to regard my affirming or being in control of a thing as *my* doing in the deep sense required in order for me to be held *responsible* for it. Whether or not I affirm a thing may be of explanatory value in understanding why I am contented or why I act one way rather than another but such explanations cannot, of themselves, supply us with grounds for assessing an individual's moral standing. The possibility remains, therefore, that affirmation and control, as I have described them, are illusory and that the human individual is no more than the locus of a set of causes and chance events. This means, in turn, that we cannot insulate claims about responsibility from claims about free will and universal determinism: any attempt to do so will produce an account of responsibility and agency that, however attractive *politically*, is not compelling and may even be misconceived *philosophically*. In short, to take the metaphysics out of responsibility and agency is to risk propounding a philosophical nonsense. It is to relegate claims made in the name of individual responsibility to the status of claims made in the name of conventional practice or (even) etiquette.

I cannot hope to resolve these disputes here (or anywhere else for that matter). The best I can do is recall that I have pointed to three possible accounts of the preconditions of responsibility, the first focusing on *volition*, the second on *affirmation*, and the third on *origination*. I have pointed also to the fact that these three preconditions may well pull in different directions: the argument from origination, for instance, might forbid attributions of responsibility that the arguments from affirmation and volition would permit.

How can we break the deadlock? On the one hand, we could opt for the account that best matches our view of the conditions under which individuals acquire responsibility for a thing—regardless of whether the deliverances of that account match our view of the sorts of things individuals are and are not responsible *for*. On the other hand, we could opt for the account whose deliverances best match our view of the sorts of things individuals are and are not responsible for—regardless of whether the conditions under which that account holds individuals to acquire responsibility for a thing best match our ordinary view. In the first case, we are claiming that the question of whether responsibility should be attributed to X in respect of b can and should be resolved by appealing to a set of preconditions constructed with no particular answer to this question in mind. In the second case, we are opting for the set of preconditions for attributing responsibility to an individual that is most likely to deliver the answer in respect of X's responsibility for b that we favour in advance.

I suspect that much of our ordinary thinking about responsibility—and I include in this the ordinary thinking of egalitarians—follows the second trajectory rather than the first. We start with a conclusion—namely that individuals are not responsible for things of type b—and we construct premises in support of that conclusion. We then test those premises against things of type c. If the premises we have constructed do not yield the conclusion we would otherwise have anticipated in respect of c, then we are faced with a choice. *Either* we modify the premises in order to yield the conclusion we would have anticipated in respect of c *or* we accept the conclusion, even though it is unanticipated, and (thereby) preserve the premises—and so on and so forth. This method of thinking about political and moral questions, or something like it at least, is what Rawls calls 'reflective equilibrium'.[14] According to this method, we arrive at conclusions through testing our intuitions against our theory and our theory against our intuitions, modifying each, where necessary, as we go along.

When it comes to testing claims of individual responsibility, the temptation—methodologically—is to *appear* to adopt the approach(es) I've been describing whilst leaving the premises of the argument both unexamined (initially) and untested (subsequently). If we succumb to this temptation, then we will start moving *from* the claim that individuals are not responsible for b via the claim that there is no relevant difference between b and c *to* the claim that individuals are not (therefore) responsible for c. And we will do this even though at no time will we have spelled out the preconditions of responsibility that supported our initial position in respect of b, nor whether these preconditions would apply to c considered in isolation from b, nor whether we might have reached a different conclusion had we started the argument with c instead of b. Indeed, the danger is that we will start moving between *different* accounts of the preconditions of responsibility and that we will appeal to the argument from volition in respect of some things, the argument from affirmation in respect of others, and, perhaps, the argument from origination in respect of others still.

It so happens that many egalitarians are drawn to Rawls's general approach in the matter of the relation between intuitions and theory and drawn also to what they take to be his specific approach in the matter of determining the scope and preconditions of individual responsibility. I say what they *take* Rawls's position to be because Rawls couches his arguments in the language of moral arbitrariness rather than that of responsibility and, as a matter of exegesis, it would not be faithful to Rawls's intentions to use these two notions interchangeably.[15] Allowing for this, what gives the Rawlsian argument its compelling quality is that it appears to lay bare and dismantle the underlying logic of the principle of equal opportunity and, in so doing, to highlight incongruities in the ordinary interpretation of that principle. Rawls works his way into the argument by mounting, in *A Theory of Justice*, an attack on two conceptions of (distributive) equality. These are what he calls 'the system of natural liberty' and the 'liberal interpretation' of equality. The former advances a doctrine of formal equality of opportunity: it requires no more than that all should have 'the same legal rights of access to all advantaged social positions'.[16] Rawls thinks this unfair because it permits distributive shares 'to be improperly influenced . . . by factors so arbitrary from the moral point of view',[17] the particular factors Rawls has in mind here being differential good fortune and social position. But Rawls has no truck either with the liberal interpretation of equality, which, whilst seeking to mitigate the effects of the natural and social contingencies described above, nonetheless permits distributive shares to vary according to differences in natural talents and abilities. Although the liberal conception is, according to Rawls, 'clearly preferable' to the natural liberty view, it too is defective. This is because it

permits the distribution of wealth and income to be determined by the natural lottery of abilities and talents . . . distributive shares are decided by the outcome of a natural lottery; and this outcome is arbitrary from a moral perspective. There is no more reason to permit the distribution of income and wealth to be settled by the distribution of natural assets than by historical and social fortune.[18]

From this, it seems that Rawls has made a powerful case for expanding the class of things for which individuals cannot be held responsible and he has done so by pushing at the logic of the equal opportunity principle itself. On the interpretation of the equal opportunity principle I am considering here, the force of that principle lies in the idea that there are certain differences between individuals for which they are not responsible and which *for that reason* ought not to prejudice their access to opportunities and resources.

Note that the argument is directed at *differences* between individuals and their responsibility for those differences. The argument asks whether X is responsible for being different from Y in respect of b, where b might or might not be the sort of thing that we can speak of individuals having more or less of than one another. It does not ask—or at least it does *necessarily* ask—whether X is responsible for b according to an absolute or non-relational standard of responsibility. According to the argument I have in mind, if we think that individuals are not responsible for differences in the colour of their skin, then these differences are not something that in and of themselves should restrict their access to opportunities and resources. And if we think that individuals are not responsible for differences in their skin colour, so the argument runs, we will presumably think also that they are not responsible for differences in their gender or in the social class into which they were born. This is because there does not seem to be anything in the underlying structure of these differences to distinguish one from the other. What the Rawlsian argument appears to do is extend this thought into the realm of natural talents such that whatever it is about differences in skin colour, gender, and social background that makes us think they ought not to prejudice access to opportunities and resources applies with equal force to differences in natural talents.

I shall have more to say about natural talents in Chapter 6. Let me concentrate here on the assumptions that seem to support what I have styled as the Rawlsian argument. The argument says that *if* individuals are not responsible for differences between them in respect of b, and if there is no relevant difference between b and c, then they are not responsible for differences between them in respect of c also. We can, of course, sign up to this argument whilst remaining agnostic on the question of whether individuals *are* responsible for differences between them in respect of b. To see this, we need only recall that Rawls says merely that there is no *more* reason to allow free play to differences in natural talents than there is to allow free play to other manifestations of differential luck. This is compatible with believing there to be no reason *not* to allow free play to both. Unless we know *why* individuals are held not to be responsible for differences in skin colour—or gender, or social background, or whatever else is taken as the point of orientation for the rest of the equal opportunity argument—then we shall be deploying an untested premise in the service of an unwarranted conclusion.

In this context, the claim that I am not responsible for my b being different from yours—where b might comprehend skin colour, or gender, or social background—seems to draw its force from the idea that my being (or having) b_1 and your being (or having) b_2 is in some sense outside *my*—and indeed *our*—control. This might mean one of several things. It might mean (1) that it *was* outside my control that I should not have been (or had) other than b_1 to begin with. Or it might mean (2) that it is *at present* outside my control not to be (or have) other than b_1. Or it might mean (3) that it *will be* outside my control not to be (or have) other than b_1 in the future. In considering how these distinctions apply to different facts—or classes of facts—about individuals, we need to think about how we are to characterize the b_1 in question. If, for instance, b_1 is *being male*—as opposed to b_2 *being female*—then (1) applies. But—and allowing here for a certain latitude in our understanding of the effect of surgical procedures upon our definition of an individual's gender— (2) and (3) do not *necessarily* apply. If, however, b_1 is being *born* male, as opposed to b_2 being *born* female, then all of (1), (2), and (3) apply. Indeed, (2) and (3) apply trivially. Clearly it is not, nor will it ever be, within my control to change a fact about my past.

Does the Rawlsian argument target differences between individuals that are *logically* outside their control or does it target differences that are *circumstantially* outside their control? As I have suggested, my being *born* male is logically outside my control—it is an ineradicable feature of my life. My *being* male, in contrast, is circumstantially outside my control—it is an eradicable feature of my life, albeit one that can be eradicated only at great cost to me. If the Rawlsian argument targets differences between individuals that are necessarily ineradicable, such as my having been *born* a man and your having been *born* a woman, then we will soon be drawn into a tight analytical circle within which the presence or absence of control for a thing is established logically rather than circumstantially.

My worry about this argument is not that it fails on its own logical terms. My worry is that it misconstrues the normative force of the equal opportunity principle from which it purportedly derives, a normative force that I am pretty sure stems from circumstantial rather than logical claims about responsibility. It is the fact of my *being* male—not the fact of my being *born* male—that ought not to prejudice my access to opportunities and resources. My being born male may indeed be relevant to the argument but only in so far as it contributes to establishing that my being male is something that it would be peculiarly difficult for me to change. After all, not every difference between individuals that is present at birth is circumstantially ineradicable nor every circumstantially ineradicable difference between individuals present at birth. The relevant normative distinction here is between what is and what is not circumstantially ineradicable, not between what is and is not present at birth.

Perhaps there is another way of thinking about this. In the matter of access to opportunities and resources, the relevance of some being born male and others being born female is only in part that these differences are circumstantially ineradicable. Perhaps it is also that these differences are not self-induced: there is no sense in which they reflect choices made by the individuals concerned. Even if we accept, however, that what marks out differences of this kind is the conjunction of their ineradicable character with the fact of their not being self-induced, still this will not tell us why differences that are present at birth should be of any more concern to us than other sorts of differences that are ineradicable and not self-induced. Moreover, if we allow that it is not only differences between individuals present at birth that should concern us, then we shall have to entertain the possibility that access to resources and opportunities should not be prejudiced also by certain *acquired* differences between agents—at least where these fail the relevant test of control and responsibility. Prominent amongst such differences might be differences between individuals in their values, beliefs, and preferences. If we apply to these the test of control and responsibility I suggested applies in the case of differences in skin colour or gender—namely, that these differences are not self-induced and that they are circumstantially ineradicable—then we must allow that there may be cases where (differences in) values, beliefs, and preferences are, in terms of an individual's responsibility for them, indistinguishable from (differences in) skin colour and gender. In other words, if we are to conduct the argument about responsibility by way of contrast and analogy— if we are to say that if X is assumed not to be responsible for b, and if b is structurally indistinguishable from c, then X is assumed not to be responsible for c also—then we have no reason to call a halt to the argument when we reach variations in natural talents, thereby precluding differences in values, beliefs, and preferences from the reckoning. If, on the other hand, we are to conduct the argument by appealing to certain tightly defined preconditions of responsibility—such as that X is responsible for b where X affirms b, or where X is not coerced in respect of b, regardless of whether b was within X's control to begin with—then we cannot apply that test of responsibility to one class of differences (such as those in values, beliefs, and preferences) but not to others (such as those in natural talent or social position).

In short, we must go where the argument takes us. And it seems to me that it takes us from the idea that we are not responsible for the circumstances of our birth to the idea that then we may not be responsible *in this sense* for the values and preferences we have in adulthood. From there it takes us back to where we started—if we are responsible for the values and preferences we have in adulthood then we may be responsible *in this sense* for the circumstances of our birth. My thought here is not that there is no difference between, on the one hand, having a belief or making an effort in adulthood and, on the other, being born poor or being born talentless. After all, our intuitions tell us that being born one thing rather than another is not so much something we *do* as something that *happens* to us. Granted this, perhaps we should simply fall back on our intuitions. Perhaps we should accept that claiming of someone that he is responsible for something is just another way of saying that he did it and that claiming of someone that he is not responsible for something is just another way of saying that it happened to him.[19] This intuitive distinction does not point to some truth about individual responsibility that lies beyond our intuitions. Indeed, our intuitive distinction between doing and happening is really all we have to go on. There is no theory or fact of the matter lying *out there* beyond that distinction.

Perhaps we could, or even should, leave matters standing there because it is not as if the other routes I have taken in this chapter have yielded convincing results—or indeed any *results* at all. For all this, I cannot shake off the idea that to fall back on the intuitive distinction between doing and happening is to postpone something rather than to resolve it. Leaving aside any concerns there might be about the status of intuitive distinctions of this kind, the fact is that we disagree in our understanding of what we do and of what happens to us. I do not mean that we disagree all the way down. We do not, I think, disagree over whether feeding ourselves is something we do and being struck by lightning is something that happens to us. Beyond these sorts of cases, however, I suspect that our intuitions just differ. Where they differ, we shall have to start offering one another *arguments* accounting for why some things should come under the heading of doing and others of happening. And the deeper we get into the enterprise of advancing arguments about what our intuitions reveal, rather than just describing what those intuitions *are*, the more that enterprise will come to resemble the enterprise with which this chapter has been concerned all along—namely, the enterprise of identifying what makes individuals *responsible* for some things but not for others.

I suspect that, as things stand, we are still struggling to find a basis, other than conventional practice and raw intuition, for saying of individuals that they are responsible for some things but not for others. As such, claims about what individuals are responsible for are often no more than stipulations about what the state should be prepared to do for them and they for themselves. Sometimes these claims rest on an appeal to certain capacities we impute to individuals and other times they do not. But quite what it is about individuals that makes us think it reasonable, given the kind of beings they are, to draw the line in one place rather than another is unclear. This said, I do not believe that all arguments about what individuals are responsible for lead, inexorably, towards the various puzzles that surround the metaphysics of the will. Nor do I believe that arguments about the importance of personal responsibility are, in some sense, on hold pending a breakthrough in our ability to make sense of these puzzles. The temptation, of course, is to think that if only we could achieve such a breakthrough—if only we could get our understanding of the metaphysics of the will nailed down once and for all— then everything else would fall into place. That is, we would know what to do with the notion of responsibility, whether to hold on to it or to abandon it. But just as resolving the metaphysical puzzles would not, of itself, resolve the question of what test of responsibility to apply to the man accused of stealing chickens, so resolving those puzzles would not of itself resolve the question of what test of responsibility to apply to the more general issue of who should get what.

In the end, we have to decide how far we want the writ of justice to extend. The deeper judgements of justice go—the more closely they are tied to claims about our motivations and intentions rather than claims about what needs we happen to have or what property we happen to be entitled to—the more captivating these judgements become. Those, for instance, who baulk at the idea of the selfish securing a benefit whilst the unselfish lose out are, I think, offering a captivating vision of just this kind. But there is nothing shallow or matter of fact about the judgement that someone is selfish or unselfish—as I said before, these are deep judgements about individuals—and what makes such judgements captivating is also what makes them contentious. The question is whether some of what makes the vision captivating should be surrendered in favour of some what makes it less contentious. That question cannot altogether be divorced from the metaphysical puzzles I have been describing, but we do not need to resolve those puzzles in order to answer it.

4

The social division of responsibility

At this point I want to tie up some of the loose ends generated by the discussion so far. Quite which loose ends I have in mind will soon become clear. In order to work my way into them, I begin with the observation that arguments about justice focus on two broad issues. One is the issue of *what* should be apportioned in the name of justice. The other is the issue of *how* these things should be apportioned. For the sake of brevity I shall refer to these two as, respectively, the issues of goods and criteria.[1] When we argue about goods we are arguing about what sorts of things individuals have a claim to, allowing for the possibility that these things might range from tangibles such as food and shelter to intangibles such as rights and opportunities. When we argue about criteria we are arguing about the basis upon which these things, whatever they might be, should be apportioned.

My concern in this chapter is to locate the place of claims about individual responsibility within broader arguments made under these two headings. In order to make headway with this I shall, however, need to retrace my steps to some extent. In particular, I shall need to revisit an idea I have had cause to touch on already, namely, the idea of a *social division of responsibility* between citizen and state. I revisit this idea because it is one that appears to bring together claims about goods and criteria under the banner of claims about individual responsibility and, in so doing, to make responsibility the connecting thread in arguments about who should get what. What is more, getting on to the arguments in this area allows me to honour the undertaking I made in the previous chapter to say something more about how the *interplay* of claims about conditions and claims about capacities makes for a distinctively political conception of individual responsibility. In this latter enterprise I am to some extent following in the footsteps of Scanlon. My aim, however, is to open up new lines of enquiry as the argument unfolds.

By way of a preliminary, let me note that claims made under the heading of criteria are sometimes claims about allocations or distributions *viewed as such*. It is in these terms that we should understand arguments about whether we should favour equal distributions over unequal ones or indeed whether we should in all cases favour the distribution that maximizes the absolute position of the worse off. Arguments of this kind do not just abstract from claims about what particular goods we should address our attention to. Often, they also abstract from claims about the particular *concerns* motivating our account of justice. They do not ask, for example, whether we should apportion things in the name of meeting basic needs or of honouring desert. For the most part, they assume that we already have an answer to that question at our disposal. Of course, not *all* accounts of justice incorporate a view as to the merits of different distributions or allocations viewed as such. Not all think that we should aim for one kind of distribution or allocation rather than another. Indeed, some think that claims about such things have no place in arguments about justice, arguments that they think should eschew claims about the patterns and structures of allocation we should aim for.[2]

Arguments about motivating concerns follow their own distinctive trajectory. Here, the starting point will, typically, be a claim as to what it is about individuals that *matters*—what should be regarded as being of essential interest or fundamental importance—for the purpose of devising rules of justice.[3] Indeed, there is a sense in which the arguments under this heading are arguments about the *point* of our account of justice. They are arguments about the values and interests that that account exists to honour, protect, or promote. I have already highlighted two possibilities falling under this heading, one being that justice requires us to meet basic needs and the other that it requires us to honour desert. To these possibilities might be added others: a narrow view of justice might require us to respect nothing more than certain rights of and to private property, whilst a broad view might direct us towards the promotion of happiness.[4]

I make these points in the knowledge of there being a certain artificiality in separating out the component elements of justice in this way—what I have offered so far is a set of simplifying assumptions whose principal value is illustrative. It would seem obvious enough, for instance, that claims about what should be apportioned in the name of justice will be intimately related to claims about the concerns that our theory of justice embodies. This will be particularly so where the concerns in question are directed towards an end such as the promotion of happiness. In cases of this kind, claims about what sorts of things should be apportioned will to a large extent *fall in behind* claims about the concerns at which those things are to be directed, perhaps to the point where the content of the former is straightforwardly derived from the character of the latter. Certain versions of utilitarianism would, I think, come under this heading. In other cases, however, there will be no great distance between claims about goods and claims about concerns because the former will merely be an *articulation* of the latter. Take the case of an account of justice, such as Nozick's entitlement theory, telling us that we should respect individual property rights. Here, claims about goods and concerns come together: we respect the property rights of individuals not in order to promote some end but because in and through respecting such rights we fulfil the demands of justice. In between, stand cases where what is apportioned is indeed a means of a kind but not a means directed towards securing a particular end or, at least, not directly. It is in these terms that I understand John Rawls's *primary goods* (more of which shortly) and Ronald Dworkin's *resources*.[5]

Often enough, claims about individual responsibility make an appearance not when we are discussing what should be apportioned in the name of justice nor even when we are discussing the motivating concerns of our theory. Instead, they make an appearance when we are discussing, in abstract terms, the merits of different allocations or distributions. Where the discussion is conducted in these terms, egalitarians often *combine* arguments about equality with arguments about individual responsibility. Having committed themselves to the idea that equal distributions are to be preferred, in some way and to some extent, to unequal distributions, they advance the further claim that departures from equality may be permitted or required in certain cases. One such case, which I shall not be discussing here, arises where departures from equality would serve to improve the position of the worse off. Another case arises where a relevant test of responsibility is met by the parties concerned. Where that test is not met—and where inequalities none the less exist—the distribution in question falls foul of the requirements of egalitarian justice. Indeed, it is precisely this thought that underpins, and is captured by, what I have called the egalitarian intuition, namely, the intuition that it is objectionable for some to be worse off than others through no fault of their own. As I am construing it here, the egalitarian intuition—and the more general attempt to combine concerns about equality with concerns about responsibility—is part of a view of what makes one distribution *viewed in the abstract* preferable to others. It follows from this that different egalitarians might endorse this intuition—and incorporate it into their distributive schemes—whilst disagreeing in the matter of what sorts of goods should in principle be distributed and of the ultimate concerns at which that distribution should be directed.

What I have said so far relies, of course, on the diagnosis I offered earlier concerning the place of individual responsibility in arguments about justice, according to which claims about responsibility operate principally in the realm of abstract arguments about allocations or distributions viewed as such and barely at all in arguments about goods and concerns. Imagine now that we operate with an altogether different diagnosis. Imagine we believe that claims about individual responsibility cannot enter our thinking about justice simply at the stage where we are adjudicating between permissible and impermissible distributions. Imagine we think that they have to enter our thinking earlier on, so to speak, at the stage where we are deciding upon what sorts of things should be apportioned in the name of justice and (even) at the stage where we are thinking about ultimate concerns. The thought here may well be that claims about responsibility, being the kind of *fundamental* claims that they are, do not lend themselves to being confined to one area of our thinking about justice and excluded from others. In other words, we are faced with a choice: *either* we make no mention of responsibility in any quarter of our account of justice *or* we make responsibility the connecting thread of that account. What we cannot do is to make mention of responsibility in one quarter but not in others. On this view, it would be incongruous, if not inconsistent, to defer to claims about individual responsibility in deciding how things should be apportioned while at the same time ignoring claims about responsibility in determining what those things should be or indeed in thinking about the ultimate concerns at which they should be directed.[6] In other words, the nature of our commitments in one area seems to have implications, normatively if not logically, for the nature of our commitments in others. Take, for instance, a view which says that the distribution of goods should, on the one hand, be directed towards the relief of suffering but that it should, on the other, be regulated by a principle of individual responsibility. These two judgements seem to emphasize quite different aspects of the human individual, one passively attracting suffering, the other actively choosing and deciding. Is it not odd to have the active and the passive sitting alongside one another within a single distributive ideal?

On the face of it, it *is* odd. Perhaps, then, we should favour a more ambitious role for individual responsibility in arguments about who should get what, according to which individuals are, in the name of justice, owed compensation in respect of those things they can nothing about but not owed compensation in respect of those things they can do something about.[7] Obviously enough, a very broad formulation of this kind will soon lead us into difficult questions of interpretation in the matter of what individuals are responsible *for*. Those difficulties, however, are not of immediate concern to me. For the time being, let me put to one side problems of interpretation and assume that we have at our disposal a stable and reliable account of what—in terms of capacities and control—people are and are not responsible for. Granted this assumption, I want to assess the attraction of pivoting claims of justice around the axis of individual responsibility in the manner I have been describing and thereby bringing claims about goods and criteria together under the banner of what I referred to earlier as a social division of responsibility between citizen and state.

It so happens that this approach *does* seem to have intuitive pull—and not just by virtue of its apparent symmetry and completeness. It has intuitive pull because it appears faithful to the demands of the responsibility principle, according to which it is objectionable for someone to suffer a loss through no fault of their own. On the face of it, there does not seem to be anything in the nature of that principle restricting it to some losses but not to others. It may so happen that the force of the responsibility principle comes into sharpest relief where the losses in question are in some sense *tangible*, such as when I am injured by a reckless driver or bankrupted in circumstances that were wholly unforseeable. From the fact, however, that tangible losses serve to make the principle vivid it certainly does not follow that intangible losses lie outside its compass. If you, constituted as you are, wake up one morning to find yourself in the grip of a deep depression, I do not see that the responsibility principle *per se* tells us that depression is not the sort of loss with which the principle is concerned. Clearly enough, in applying the responsibility principle we have to impose *some* restrictions upon our understanding of what should *count* as a loss, if only the restrictions that arise from the way we use the term in ordinary language. But, however much we push at it, ordinary language will not tell us what sorts of losses are, and are not, the proper concern of principles of this kind.

Two things seem, then, to be true of the responsibility principle. On the one hand, there does not seem to be anything internal to it implying that it is *applicable* to losses of one kind rather than another. On the other, it actually seems to be *applied* to a range of loss circumscribed by the prior demands of justice. The puzzle in all this is obvious. The responsibility principle appears, first, to be a demand of justice; second, to be in direct competition with other demands of justice; and, third, to be itself bounded by those other demands in some way. The attraction of pivoting an account of justice around the responsibility principle, and thereby around a clear-cut division between what individuals are and are not responsible for, is in part that it appears to give the idea of responsibility a much clearer role to play in arguments about who should get what. But the attraction is also that it accords claims about individual responsibility the sort of *fundamental* status they seem to warrant. Claims about responsibility thereby come to set the boundaries of our account of justice, rather than vice versa, and that account is in turn judged by how well it explicates and promotes the demands of responsibility.

I offer up this possibility in the knowledge that concerns about responsibility cannot really constitute the *starting point* in arguments about who should get what. Indeed, I suggested as much in the second chapter when I said that to accord considerations of responsibility independent weight is not thereby to believe that claims about control, intentionality, and the like can tell us what is, and what is not, a concern of justice to begin with. Concerns about control and intentionality commonly enter the picture once we have specified why some kinds of conduct are to be rewarded, others penalized, and others still ignored. From the fact, for instance, that I am unlucky in love—in the sense of suffering what Dworkin would call bad brute luck—it does not *follow* that I am owed compensation by the state. Similarly, from the fact that I am not responsible for the pleasure I take in causing others pain—it just so happens that I am built that way and can do nothing about it—it does not *follow* that there is anything objectionable about the loss I suffer when others shun me. Whether this suggests that frustrated malevolence does not qualify to be regarded as *a loss* or whether it is a loss that is outweighed by other considerations, I am not sure. My claim is that in order to establish what sorts of losses are relevant, or dominant, from the perspective of justice we need a developed view of what individuals owe to and may expect from one another. If claims about capacities and control are to assume importance it will be within the margins of such a view. But claims as to the content of our background rights and duties, and the content of harm and loss, cannot be *derived*, in any straightforward way, from claims about capacities and control.

As I have already made clear, the very least this does is put a dent in the idea that an absence or presence of control on my part for having, being, or doing a thing is sufficient to establish whether I should be compensated or penalized in respect of that thing. On the view I am describing, knowing whether I have control over a thing becomes at most a necessary condition of determining the strength of my claims in respect of it. Indeed, it would be as well also to record that conferring upon an individual the opportunity to avoid a loss does not, in and of itself, render that loss unobjectionable. A loss, to be legitimate, must surely be so on *independent* grounds. In other words, to say to an individual 'you were told' is at most a necessary condition of it being unobjectionable that he suffer a loss. Warnings are not licences: from the fact that someone warned you of their habit of breaking people's hearts it does not follow that they have *carte blanche* to break your heart as well.

But it is not merely these kinds of background duties and rights that impose constraints on the sorts of claims that can legitimately be advanced in the name of justice. Sometimes it is simply not *feasible* to cater for certain kinds of claims, regardless of the capacities of the parties concerned. Return to the example of my being unlucky in love. Is this a matter with which a theory of justice should be concerned? Intuitively, the answer is no. It seems we can grant that it would be *better*—for me or indeed for the world—were I to find love without thereby granting that it would be *unjust* were I not to do so. And it would not be unjust, on this view, because emotional fulfilment is not the sort of thing to which agents have a *claim* and whose allocation and distribution social institutions should, in the name of justice at least, be concerned with. It seems pretty obvious, moreover, that our impulse to exclude emotional fulfilment from the ambit of justice has more to do with our views about the nature of emotional fulfilment than it does with our views about the control individuals enjoy in matters of the heart. Emotional fulfilment, in short, is not the sort of thing that lends itself to being distributed or provided by a third party. This is because it is in the nature of emotional *fulfilment* that it arises and persists spontaneously—it cannot be conjured up by a third party. The same might be said also of friendship. Even if we could arrive at a satisfactory measure of what it was for one individual to have or not to have this thing, or to have more or less of it than another, it is not clear how a third party might go about supplying friendship to those who had hitherto been deprived of its satisfactions. (Of course, it may be that this establishes less than I suggest. From the fact that it is outside the competence of a third party to supply me directly with emotional fulfilment it does not follow that I am ineligible for compensation of some kind in respect of any lack of emotional fulfilment that I might suffer through no fault of my own. Nor does it follow that a third party might not promote emotional fulfilment indirectly through putting in place the relevant enabling conditions.)

I have suggested, then, that considerations both of desirability and of feasibility impose constraints upon the sorts of claims that can be advanced in the name of justice, constraints that operate quite independently of claims about individual responsibility. These two considerations are not, however, the only ones that condition our thinking about who should get what. That thinking is conditioned also by how we characterize the *circumstances* of justice—by which I have in mind the background social conditions under which claims to goods arise. What are the background social facts and what bearing do these facts have on the principles governing the exercise of public power and the tests of legitimacy that should be applied to social institutions? Clearly enough, claims about circumstances of this kind take us into contentious territory because what is at issue is nothing less than the question of how we should approach the task of thinking about and constructing a theory of justice itself. Perhaps it is enough for a theory of justice to be regarded as such that it consists in an informal alliance of commitments each of which has intuitive plausibility in its own right. In other words, it is legitimate to *compartmentalize* questions of justice on the basis that each engages a circumscribed range of concerns and applies to needs and interests of a particular kind. On this view, our pronouncements on what should be apportioned in the name of justice neither require nor presuppose a particular stance on the issue of whether the state may legitimately advance one view of human flourishing over others nor on the issue of the tests of public justifiability that the relevant goods must satisfy if they are to provide a stable basis for servicing citizens' claims. The approach to constructing a theory of justice that I am describing here is not primitive. It does not deny that different values and concerns stand in competition with one another any more than it denies that theories of justice must strive for some measure of consistency. It simply assumes it possible to distil those concerns that are purely distributive—as these apply to distributive goods, for instance—from those concerns that are essentially non-distributive in character.

In contrast to this stands what might be called the *integrated* approach to thinking about and constructing a theory of justice. This approach denies that theories of justice comprise distinct and more or less free-standing elements, elements that can with propriety be considered in isolation from one another. In the work of Rawls, for instance, the distributive elements of the theory are, as we shall see, informed and conditioned by considerations imported from the non-distributive elements. Each element is constructed, so to speak, with an eye to the others. This being so, the issue is not so much that of identifying the pure distributive component of the theory but of determining whether it makes sense to speak of there being one to begin with. Certainly, the goods with whose distribution Rawls thinks we should be concerned—what he calls primary goods—are restricted in scope. But they are restricted in deference not only to arguments of substantive moral principle. They are restricted in deference to what Rawls takes to be the peculiar constraints that attach to a theory of *justice*—as opposed to a substantive moral theory—in terms of its public justifiability and enforceability.[8] It is with this in mind that we might say that primary goods follow from the underlying assumptions of Rawls's theory of justice as does prescription from diagnosis.

Let me say more about Rawls's theory here. His primary goods comprise rights, liberties, opportunities, and resources of various kinds. Rawls believes that the case for primary goods can be deduced from two conceptions that lie at the core of his theory. One is his *political* conception of the person as free and equal. The other is his conception of society as a fair system of cooperation. Rawls denies that the argument for primary goods can be made in terms of the contribution these make to the well-being or utility of those who have them. Instead, he specifies primary goods as all-purpose means to the pursuit of a variety of different ends. Rawls's argument for primary goods rests on the claim that they can serve as 'the focus of a reasonable overlapping consensus' amongst those who otherwise disagree on what is of fundamental value in human life. These are his *political* arguments for primary goods, arguments that are in turn buttressed by what Rawls calls 'the limits of the practicable'.[9] Rawls does not, seemingly, conceive of these two sets of concerns as mutually exclusive, for there is a clear sense in which they intertwine: a public basis of interpersonal comparison that was not practicable in the required (Rawlsian) sense would be unstable as a political conception of justice intended to serve as the focus of an overlapping consensus. It is precisely because primary goods offer a basis of interpersonal comparison deriving from 'objective features of citizens' social circumstances open to view'[10] that Rawls believes them to be fitting for a society characterized by what he terms 'reasonable pluralism'.[11] To tie claims about what should be apportioned to claims about how far these things contribute to the satisfaction of preferences would, Rawls believes, be to violate 'the constraints of simplicity and availability of information'[12] as well as to leave open the way to 'socially divisive and irreconcilable conflicts'.[13]

Rawls does not deny that the case for primary goods over rival possibilities is underpinned by certain 'restrictive assumptions'.[14] Nor does he claim that primary goods are of ultimate moral value. What Rawls claims instead is that a specifically *political* conception of justice, as opposed to a comprehensive moral doctrine, must provide a basis of interpersonal comparison that meets certain tests of *public* acceptability and justification. Thus, for Rawls, the attraction of primary goods is that they constitute a common political currency. They are open to public view and scrutiny in a way that goods tied to the promotion of intangibles such as happiness or welfare satisfaction cannot be.

I mention the arguments of Rawls in particular not to suggest that his primary goods are the last word in distributive currencies but because I join Norman Daniels and others in thinking that Rawls's claims concerning the *public* character of justice—and his claims about the constraints he believes this public character imposes on the sorts of things whose allocation and distribution should be of concern to us—are particularly telling against any attempt to determine the scope of justice in terms of an appeal to a bare notion of (capacity) responsibility.[15] The reason why we should reject such an approach is only in part that people *disagree* over what people can and what they cannot do anything about. Even to the extent that there is consensus on this issue, applying that consensus might be too open-ended an enterprise for allegiance to the principles of justice in question to be sustained. Imagine, for instance, there is agreement that, generally speaking, individuals do not have it within their power to satisfy their preferences to the full and that it is *therefore* with the levels and distribution of preference satisfaction that a theory of justice should be concerned. When it comes to enforcing and applying this requirement, problems will arise in measuring the extent to which an individual's preferences have been satisfied and, still more so, in venturing comparisons of preference satisfaction between individuals. If each is to be the judge of how far their preferences have been satisfied, then I have only your word for it that you have not taken more resources and opportunities than you need in order to satisfy your preferences to the same extent as I satisfy mine.[16] This being so, the prudent strategy for me might be to anticipate your possible dishonesty in this matter by being dishonest myself. Nor will these problems necessarily go away if we remit decisions about preference satisfaction to a third party—so long as there remains *something* that is not publicly accessible about the basis upon which interpersonal judgements are made, the potential for fractiousness and dispute in the matter of such judgements will remain.

Where does all this leave the idea I started with, namely, the idea of a social division of responsibility? At the very least, we must abandon that idea in its most ambitious form, one that tries to set the boundaries of justice wholly by way of an appeal to claims about control, intentionality, and affirmation. This said, perhaps we can reject the most ambitious version of the social division of responsibility argument but substitute a modified version in its place. This modified version might defer to some, if not all, of the constraints I have been describing but none the less retain the idea that claims about goods and criteria do *in some sense* form two sides of a broader argument that is *in some sense* held together by concerns about individual responsibility. Obviously enough, the senses in which these connections obtain would need to be robust enough for the social division of responsibility argument to be recognizably one about *responsibility*. This means, I think, that the argument must steer a middle course between diluting the role of responsibility beyond recognition and emphasizing that role beyond plausibility. To see what such an argument might *look like*—and the difficulties it faces—I want now to examine what I think remains the most sophisticated attempt on offer to bring the idea of a social division of responsibility to life. This is the attempt made by Rawls, in particular as part of his defence of primary goods.[17] Rawls provides several statements of his position of which one of the most recent is as follows:

The . . . account of primary goods includes what we may call 'a social division of responsibility': society, citizens as a collective body, accepts responsibility for maintaining the equal basic liberties and fair equality of opportunity, and for providing a fair share of the primary goods for all within this framework; while citizens as individuals and associations accept responsibility for revising and adjusting their ends and aspirations in view of the all-purpose means they can expect, given their present and forseeable situation. This division of responsibility relies on the capacity of persons to assume responsibility for their ends and to moderate the claims they make on their social institutions accordingly.[18]

What are we to make of this statement? Perhaps Rawls's idea is this. In deciding upon what sorts of things should be apportioned in the name of justice we need to ask ourselves what sorts of things are, and what sorts of things are not, within the control of individuals. Our access to resources and opportunities—which taken together constitute the all-purpose means with which we pursue our ends in life—is not something that would be fully within our control under, for instance, a *laissez-faire* economy. Under such an economy, our access to these all-purpose means would be shaped by the differing circumstances of our birth and upbringing, amongst other things. This being so, we must reject *laissez-faire* if we are to take seriously the idea that the means at the disposal of individuals should be determined by factors within their control. In place of *laissez-faire* we must favour an arrangement in which responsibility for providing individuals with these means rests with social institutions. This is one half of the social division of responsibility argument.

Whilst, however, our access to resources and opportunities is outside our control, or at least would be under *laissez-faire*, the same cannot be said about our ends in life. Our wants and aspirations are not outside our control in the same way as is our access to resources and opportunities—in so far as such access is tied to the circumstances of our birth and upbringing at least. It is for this reason that social institutions may legitimately distinguish between the provision of means and the satisfaction of ends. And indeed this is the other half of the social division of responsibility argument—as I have chosen to construe it here at least.

Viewed in this light, the social division of responsibility argument appears to enjoy precisely the symmetry I alluded to earlier: social institutions assume responsibility for that which is outside individual control and individuals assume responsibility for that which is within their control. If this is the gist of Rawls's argument, however, then the symmetry in question has been purchased at the cost of something approaching incoherence. Recall that I was able to make sense of the claim that we should fix the boundaries of our distributive good according to an account of what is, and what is not, within the control of agents only by placing claims about the presence or absence of control in the context of a particular social arrangement, namely *laissez-faire*. Having done so, I pointed to the fact that under *laissez-faire*, the extent of our access to the relevant means—by which I mean here resources and opportunities—is determined by, amongst other things, the circumstances of our birth and upbringing. If, for the purposes of the argument, we allow that these circumstances are outside our control, then it follows that the extent of our access to resources and opportunities, in so far as it is shaped by these circumstances, is likewise outside our control. But that claim only follows in the context of *laissez-faire*. It does not follow in all contexts—it does not follow regardless of the bases upon which our access to resources and opportunities are determined. All of which suggests that we cannot claim it to be true of means *considered in the abstract* that they are outside the control of individuals—unless that is we take the circumstances of our birth and upbringing to be, in and of themselves, means of the relevant kind. In this context, however, it seems to make more sense to think of these circumstances as bases upon which claims to resources and opportunities might, or might not, be determined. That being so, the argument is really one about whether access to resources and opportunities should be tied to bases that are within the control of agents, not one about whether access to resources and opportunities *per se* is within the control of agents. In short, the boundaries of a distributive good, Rawls's or otherwise, cannot be fixed in advance by claims about the presence or absence of control for one kind of means rather than another.

And even if the argument is not incoherent, it is at the very least question-begging. It would seem obvious enough that whether something is a means or an end is an altogether separate matter from whether that thing is within or outside our control—there appears to be nothing about the inner logic of means and ends which holds it to be in the *nature* of means that they are outside our control and in the *nature* of ends that they are within our control. At different points Rawls does appear to meet such doubts. Thus he writes

that the responsibility of free persons is implicit in the use of primary goods can be seen in the following way. We are assuming that people are able to control and to revise their wants and desires in the light of circumstances and that they are to have responsibility for doing so, provided that the principles of justice are fulfilled, as they are in a well-ordered society. Persons do not take their wants and desires as determined by happenings beyond their control. We are not, so to speak, assailed by them, as we are perhaps by diseases and illness so that wants and desires fail to support claims to the means of satisfaction in the way that disease and illness support claims to medicine and treatment.[19]

Taken at face value, however, this argument seems unlikely to satisfy those already disposed to doubt the force of Rawls's distinctions. The claim here seems to be that wants and desires are in some sense within our control in a way that disease and illness are not. But that is precisely what Rawls has to demonstrate, not what he is entitled to assume.

In defence of Rawls it will be recalled that earlier on I provided an account of why he opts for primary goods over rival possibilities that made no mention of concerns about individual responsibility. I pointed to Rawls's belief that the case for favouring primary goods can be made by way of an appeal to the limits of the political and the practicable. It is these arguments—arguments deriving their force from, amongst other things, the demands of public justi-fiability—that tell us why the jurisdiction of the state does not extend to a concern with the satisfaction or promotion of ends. As a jurisdictional matter, responsibility for the satisfaction of ends falls, *by default*, upon citizens. On this reading, the case for setting the jurisdictional boundaries of citizen and state in one place rather than another can be made without invoking claims about the degree of control individuals have over their ends.

Clearly enough, however, this defence of Rawls's position does not tell the whole story. After all, it was not I who introduced into the social division of responsibility argument a claim about the relevance of control. It was Rawls himself. That being so, what is the standing of claims about control in his argument? Two possibilities suggest themselves. On the one hand, Rawls might be advancing a weak claim about the relevance of control to the social division of responsibility argument. He might believe that in order to deny my claim on the state in respect of b it is *sufficient* to show that my having or not having b is within my control. On the other hand, Rawls might be advancing a strong claim about control and its relevance. He might believe that in order to deny my claim on the state in respect of b it is *necessary* to show that my having or not having b is within my control. In support of the latter view we need only recall that Rawls claims of the social division of responsibility argument that it 'relies' on certain capacities we have in respect of our ends. This would suggest that he believes the injunction that citizens *ought* to take responsibility for their ends implies that they *can* do so.

For all this, Rawls does not claim that the *can* in question presupposes that we choose our ends and aspirations as we might choose soap powder in a supermarket.[20] Nor does he claim that our ends and aspirations are somehow created *out of nothing*. Instead, his claims are more modest. Rawls speaks of people 'adjusting' or 'revising' or 'moderating' their aims such that these fall into line with the share of primary goods they can reasonably expect. From the Rawlsian perspective, we may be regarded as being capable of adapting our ends to the circumstances in which we find ourselves, taking our upbringing to be a circumstance of the relevant kind. Indeed, Rawls's argument might be read as resting, in part at least, upon a quasi-empirical claim about adaptive preference formation. On this view, our preferences are formed within, and they are endowed with content by, our *social* world: their content is context-dependent. Change that social world and it is to be expected that our preferences will change with it. The same is not true of our biological needs for these are not socially conditioned in the same way. The content of illness or pain is context-independent. That being so, it would be unreasonable, if only as an empirical matter, to expect individuals to adapt their biological needs to the social arrangements in force.

And, indeed, it is at this point that arguments about the social division of responsibility shade into arguments about the interplay of conditions and capacities. Rawls, like Mill, *does* think that the causal history of our tastes and preferences is relevant to whether we bear responsibility for them. But like Mill also, Rawls thinks this causal history is relevant not because causal laws *per se* are relevant but because the historical conditions under which we come to have those tastes and preferences are relevant. On Rawls's view it is neither sensible nor attractive to think of preferences as being formed *in vacuo*, in a world stripped of social forms and the expectations that attach to those forms. What we should do instead is recognize that the content of our preferences is shaped by these social forms and expectations. What we should recognize also is that certain background conditions have more to commend them, *as* background conditions, than others. Indeed, Rawls wants to reject the idea that we should take people's preferences as the starting point in devising rules of justice and from there ask how those rules might fall into line with the (equal) satisfaction of those preferences. In fact, Rawls thinks that we should do something very different. We should take our theory of justice as the starting point in the argument and then ask how our preferences might fall into line with it. The question that the social division of responsibility argument addresses itself to is: 'Is it reasonable to expect people's preferences to fall in behind the demands of justice?'. It is *not*: 'How best can a theory of justice fall in behind people's preference satisfaction?'.

Moreover, it is clear that Rawls does not believe that this process of adaptation to society's basic structure is one that can or should be undertaken overnight. Instead, it is one that takes place over time.[21] To the argument that this still leaves open the possibility that some will be *unable* to adapt or moderate their ends in the required way, Rawls's reply is that this will be true only of those who lack 'at least to the essential minimum degree, the moral, intellectual, and physical capacities that enable them to be fully cooperating members of a society over a complete life'.[22] In other words, the objection has force, on Rawls's reckoning at least, only in the case of those who suffer from a physiological or psychological disorder—and Rawls wants to relegate to the margins of his theory those who find themselves in this predicament.[23] Viewed in this way, Rawls is claiming no more than that individuals have—or may be regarded as having—a capacity to adapt their aims and ambitions to the social arrangements in place and that it is reasonable to expect them to do so where those arrangements meet the requirements of justice.[24]

By way of illustrating Rawls's argument here, imagine we have a society that, through its institutions, systematically discriminates against a particular minority group in terms of the distribution of socio-economic goods and favourable positions. No doubt, over time, the members of the minority group will form and adapt their ambitions in the light of the unfavourable treatment they can expect from those institutions: as a group they might, for instance, gravitate towards some occupations and away from others. That it is within the mental and physical capacities of all but a handful of those concerned to adjust their expectations in this way seems an indisputable empirical truth—indeed, it matches the experience of certain minority groups within Britain and other liberal states. But this empirical truth does not make them *responsible* for the ambitions and expectations so adapted in the (Rawlsian) sense that they have no reasonable claim in justice beyond the satisfaction of those expectations and ambitions, for it is clear that these have been formed against the background of unjust conditions. Where, however, the relevant background conditions are just—and provided those concerned possess the minimum capacities Rawls speaks of—then the individuals in question *are* responsible for the satisfaction of their ambitions. And they are responsible for those ambitions not because they have it in their power to satisfy them to the full, whatever they may be, but because they will have formed those ambitions according to an understanding of the demands they can legitimately make upon others.

So, Rawls does not appear to be advancing a deep claim about the genealogy of want or desire formation. Indeed, recall that he claims no more than that individuals may be held responsible for their 'wants and desires . . . *provided that the principles of justice are fulfilled*'.[25] The attribution of responsibility for such 'wants and desires' is contingent upon a background set of just rules and institutions: individuals may be regarded as having the capacity to assume responsibility for these things where these conditions hold good. Where they do not, such attributions of responsibility no longer apply—it is the fact of the social arrangements in question being just that both demands and legitimates the process of adaptive preference formation to which Rawls alludes. Moreover, from the fact that Rawls thinks it reasonable that we should tailor our demands to prevailing social conditions it certainly does not follow that he is out to homogenize our tastes and preferences, still less to penalize us for having some kinds of preferences rather than others.[26]

But even if we accept Rawls's specifications in the matter of what constitute favourable background conditions, it strikes me that important doubts remain when it comes to the capacities he attributes to individuals and to the interplay between capacities and conditions. As I suggested earlier, the thought seems to be that the content of preferences, wants, and aspirations is conditioned by the social context in which these things are formed, something that is not true of our biological needs. It is for this reason Rawls believes that persons are not 'assailed' by their 'wants and desires' in the way that they are by 'disease and illness'. In advancing this argument, Rawls seems to be trading on the intuitive distinction I mentioned in the previous chapter, namely, the distinction between what we do and what happens to us. Forming preferences, wants, and aspirations is something we *do* and indeed something we do against the backdrop of the expectations our social world instils in us. Acquiring diseases and illnesses is something that happens to us, regardless seemingly of our social expectations.

Perhaps there is some force in this argument—the content of preferences and aspirations does indeed vary between communities and, over time, within communities. It is not a universal fact of human life that individuals aspire to, and indeed expect, the creature comforts of the bourgeoisie. Similarly, there are many diseases and illnesses to which human beings, wherever in the world they might live, are vulnerable. But this does not establish that one *happens* to us and the other does not. Perhaps *both* happen to us, one by virtue of conditions that are local and the other by virtue of conditions that are universal.

That we tend to *look upon* preferences and illness as being importantly different—in terms not only of how we come to have them but in terms also of our capacity to do something about them once we have them—does not tell us anything about the basis, beyond raw intuition, upon which we distinguish between the two, still less about whether these distinctions can withstand close scrutiny. As I suggested in Chapter 3, we cannot keep on appealing to our intuitions in order to resolve the puzzles that our intuitions throw up—our intuitions are not infallible. This comes into sharper relief when we are faced with hard cases—such as whether homosexuality should be regarded as a preference formed in a particular context against the backdrop of certain social expectations or whether it is a biological characteristic that might, in principle, arise and develop under pretty much any social arrangements we can imagine.[27]

In the end, my suspicion is that Rawls moves between two views of the capacity to assume responsibility for our ends. One view characterizes this capacity, be it an underlying capacity or a capacity that is exercised, in terms that invite us to think of it in causal or empirical terms. As such—and allowing for the florid terms in which I expressed the thought—the capacity in question is akin to a power that issues from within and that affords agents a degree of control in respect of their preferences that they lack in respect of disease and illness. The other view characterizes this capacity as a *moral* capacity, which I assume means a capacity that, on the one hand, might be neither causal nor empirical or, on the other, might be causal or empirical in some sort of distinctive way. Either way, that capacity is not such as to afford agents greater control over their preferences than they have in respect of disease and illness.

Let me allow that the capacity in question is of the first kind rather than the second. Let me allow also that Rawls is advancing what I termed earlier a strong claim about the relevance of control to the social division of responsibility, namely, that to deny my claim on the state in respect of b it is *necessary* to show that having or not having b is within my control. Even if Rawls has failed to show that individuals' satisfaction of their own ends is within their control in the relevant way, that undermines the case for focusing on primary goods rather than outcomes only *in so far* as that case rests upon the social division of responsibility so construed. But if the case for primary goods does no more than *include* an appeal to a social division of responsibility, and include it not as a necessary feature, then that case may be able to withstand any shortcomings there might be in such an appeal. It is the constraints of politics and practice that directed us away from preference satisfaction and towards primary goods in the first place. In thinking about what sorts of goods should be apportioned in the name of justice we can, and indeed should, recognize the importance of these constraints and recognize also that arguments about control and responsibility must fit in behind these constraints, not seek to challenge them.

I do not want to deny that there are attractions, philosophically and politically, in appealing to a social division of responsibility between citizen and state. Philosophically, it appears to bring clarity to arguments about who should get what through pivoting such arguments around a single and simple principle—namely, the principle that we are owed compensation for those things we can do little or nothing about, but that we are not owed compensation for those things we can do something or everything about. Politically, talk of a *division* of responsibility sends out the signal that the arrangement in question is a happy balance between two extremes: it is neither a minimalist arrangement (under which the state is responsible for nothing and the individual for everything) nor a totalitarian one (where the state is responsible for everything and the individual for nothing). The temptation is to exaggerate the work that claims about individual responsibility can do for us in putting together a fully worked out account of who should get what. But claims about what people can and what they cannot do something about do not *resolve* the question of what sorts of goods they have a claim to any more than they *resolve* the question of what ultimate concerns our theory should be directed towards. Where such claims do come into their own is in judging what makes some distributions better, *qua* distributions, than others. The egalitarian intuition embodies a judgement of just this kind and it is to that intuition I turn in the chapter that follows.

5

The egalitarian intuition

Some people believe justice to be served where individuals are responsible for the holdings to their name. Others believe justice to be served where holdings are equal. Others still believe justice to be served by neither of these demands. Egalitarians, as we have seen, believe justice to be served by both. I have already said something about the points of intersection between arguments about equality and arguments about individual responsibility—but not yet enough. My aim in this chapter is to draw the contours of these intersections more sharply than I have done so far in order to address a doubt that hangs over the egalitarian enterprise as a whole. This doubt has it that the attempt to combine concerns about equality with those about individual responsibility is flawed. It is flawed not just because there exists no natural affinity between the two sets of concerns. It is flawed because the two sometimes pull in quite different directions. As such, any moves towards combining them will be at best *ad hoc* and at worst unstable. By way of addressing these charges I begin by saying something about the *level* at which the two sets of concerns are supposed to be combined—whether, that is, they make an appearance together in the foreground or in the background of schemes of distributive justice or, indeed, whether they are not really combined at all. From there I move on to test the claim that concerns about equality and responsibility may, on occasion, be in competition with one another. Where they are in competition, my aim is to find out which commitment egalitarians see as dominant.

Two thoughts in particular will preoccupy me as the discussion proceeds. One is that schemes of justice lend themselves to being characterized in terms of a background and a foreground. The other is that how much equality there exists in the background bears upon the legitimacy of inequalities in the foreground. Of course, it is not just in the context of claims about equality and responsibility that these two thoughts make an appearance. They make an appearance also in analogous claims about opportunities and outcomes. The two sets of claims are analogous because, on my construal at least, opportunities *belong* in the realm of background conditions just as outcomes *belong* in the realm of the foreground.

Whichever pair of distinctions we favour, it is a familiar enough idea that unequal outcomes (represented as they are in the foreground of justice) are legitimate only if they issue from equal opportunities (represented in the background). Indeed, it is a familiar enough idea that unequal outcomes trigger our interest in questions of justice to begin with, questions that we try to answer by examining whether the relevant enabling conditions *cum* opportunities were in place when the unequal outcomes arose. The dividing line between what should *count* as an opportunity and what should *count* as an outcome has, however, always been somewhat blurred. Just as there is a sense in which background is *prior* to foreground so there is a sense in which opportunities are *prior* to outcomes. In fact, there might be several senses—temporal, logical, normative—in which the latter is true. Opportunities might be prior to outcomes in the sense in which causes are prior to effects, or in which means are prior to ends, or in which the right is prior to the good. Precisely *how* we should characterize the relation between background and foreground—and between opportunities and outcomes—is not something I can hope to resolve here and now. For my purposes, the point of more immediate concern is this: from the bare fact of your being worse off than me, judged in terms of our respective *foreground* positions, it does not follow for egalitarians that the inequality between us is objectionable. This is because (many) egalitarians believe that a just distribution of foreground goods need not be an equal distribution. They believe that inequalities in social goods may be acceptable provided that certain things are true of those inequalities. One such thing is that a relevant test of responsibility is met—or, at least, not violated—by the parties in question. This view, as I have suggested, is articulated, for some at least, in the form of the egalitarian intuition, which holds it to be objectionable for some to be worse off than others through no fault of their own.

So, the egalitarian intuition brings together concerns about equality and responsibility and applies those concerns to inequalities in the foreground of justice. But it is not only within the margins of the egalitarian intuition itself that claims about responsibility might be tied to claims about equality. Foreground inequalities may usher the egalitarian intuition on the scene—they may, as I said before, trigger our interest in questions of justice to begin with. If, however, we want to know *what would have to be true* in order for you and I to be responsible for our foreground holdings, then we shall need to address our attention to the background or enabling conditions against which we came to have the holdings that we do. Inspection of these background conditions will not *of itself* tell us whether we two are responsible for our holdings: in order to make *that* judgement something would need also to be said in the matter of whether we possessed or exhibited the relevant degree of agency. None the less, our responsibility for our holdings requires that the background conditions against which we acquired them be suitably favourable. I am not *responsible* for my holdings if, for instance, the background social conditions against which I acquired them were such that others were able to impose their will upon me or to frustrate me in the pursuit of my purposes. Quite what it is that makes one set of background conditions favourable and another otherwise is, as I have said already, a matter on which egalitarians disagree with their opponents. But I think it must be right that my decisions, preferences, and actions can properly be regarded as *mine*—in the sense necessary for me to be held responsible for them—only where various opportunities, resources, and liberties are made available to me.

Of course, from the fact that my being responsible for a thing requires that opportunities and the like be *available* to me it does not follow that my responsibility requires that these things be *equally* available. Provided that I have available to me *adequate* opportunities and resources there seems no reason to hold my responsibility to be undermined merely through having fewer of these things than you nor indeed to hold your responsibility to be enhanced merely through having more of these things than I do. In order to establish a link between responsibility, as it appears in the foreground of claims about justice, and *equality*, as it appears in the background, more work needs to be done.

In fact, I think that there may well *be* such a link. Indeed, my instinct is that concerns about equality and concerns about responsibility are joined together by way of a deeper ideal of *independence*, in the foreground of which the egalitarian intuition itself make its appearance. To see what this ideal of independence might involve, return to the distinction I drew in Chapter 1 between interpersonal and intrapersonal advantages. In my discussion of the former I said that on occasion it did indeed make sense to speak of one person suffering disadvantage merely by virtue of having less of something than another. The bare fact, for instance, of my having less purchasing power *than* you gives you purchasing power *over* me. In other words, my demands must fall in behind, and be fitted around, yours: it is as if you are ahead of me in the queue and I am to be left with whatever you choose not to take for yourself. From here it is, I think, a short and not implausible step to the idea that through your superior purchasing power you are able to impose your will upon me and to frame the options that are available to me.

I do not want to exaggerate a point that may already be suffering from exaggeration. All I want to suggest is that it is quite in order to think of certain forms of inequality—particularly *entrenched* inequalities of inherited wealth and social position—as both cause and effect of the systematic imposition of the will of some upon that of others. In caste societies, for instance, it is not an open question whether the demands of those of a lower caste should fall in behind the demands of those of a higher caste. This is because part of what it *means* for a caste society to be such is precisely that the purposes of some are subordinated to those of others. Similarly, in certain market economies it is not an open question whether the demands of the poor should fall in behind those of the rich—to say of such societies that they are run for the convenience of the rich is no idle piece of political rhetoric. So, whether our concern is with certain market or caste societies there seems to be nothing coincidental or accidental about the fact that the will of some prevails systematically over the will of others. In short, relations of domination and subservience are part of the inner logic of such systems—they are not an unfortunate, benign, or otherwise neutral by product of them.

If we allow that certain kinds of inequalities are inseparable from relations of domination and subservience—and if we allow also that my decisions, preferences, and actions cannot properly be regarded as *mine* if they are formed and transacted within the margins of such relations—then the features of the ideal of independence I sketched earlier start to become clearer. According to that ideal, I cannot be responsible for a thing unless I come to do, be, or have it against the background of conditions that protect or promote my independence. If the relevant relations undermine my independence—if they are coercive and suffocating rather than uncoercive and stimulating—then my responsibility for the thing in question is also undermined. In short, my being responsible for a thing requires that there exist background *equalities* of various kinds. With equality comes independence and with independence comes responsibility.

It should, however, be clear from what I have said so far that the link between independence and *equality* relies on the assumption that inequalities go hand in hand with relations of domination and subservience. Of some inequalities—inequalities in status, title, and inherited wealth—this seems to me obviously true. But it is not true of *all* inequalities. The bare fact, for instance, that you are healthier and happier than I am does not mean that you dominate me or that I am subservient to you. Relations of domination and subservience are precisely that—*relations* between individuals rather than bare facts about how they stand relative to one another along a certain dimension. From the fact that my will is subservient to yours by virtue of being your slave it does not follow that my will is subservient to yours whenever I have less of something than you do. Relations of domination and subservience are, it is true, a species of inequality. But not all inequalities involve relations between individuals, still less conflictual relations in which the will of one is pitted against that of another. You do not impose your *will* upon me merely by virtue of having an easier life than I do.

Of course, it might still be said that our concern in the cases I have described is not really with *inequality* but with something objectionable that lies beyond the inequality itself, namely, domination and subservience. As such, I am wrong to think that independence is compromised by inequality *per se* even if I am right to think that it is compromised by relations of domination and subservience. Nowhere have I claimed, however, that inequality *per se* compromises independence. My claim instead is that it is in the nature of the kinds of relations that *do* compromise independence that they are unequal. Indeed, they cannot be other than unequal: there is no such thing as a relation between two parties that is both equal *and* characterized by domination and subservience. Clearly enough, this may just be another way of describing the relevant relations *as* relations of domination and subservience, in which case I am merely trading in tautologies. I remain pretty sure, however, that to accept that the objectionable thing in question does not consist in the inequality itself, but in what inequality means for the way we relate to each other, is not thereby to deny that there exists a logical relation between the two. Nor, indeed, is it to deny that there is a sense in which objecting to one is indistinguishable from objecting to the other.

The significance of all this is as follows. At the very least, my being responsible for a thing requires that others not impose their will upon me or subordinate my purposes to theirs. It requires, that is, the elimination of certain kinds of inequalities from the background conditions against which claims to social goods arise. It is by this route that the link between responsibility and equality—mediated by an ideal of independence—appears to be established. But just as the link between independence and equality is bound up with certain assumptions we make about the underlying character of equal distributions, so the link between responsibility and equality is also bound up with those assumptions. As I have made clear already, the link applies not between responsibility and equality *per se* but between responsibility and equality if, where, or because certain things are held to be true of such equality. That is, it applies to equality on the assumption that equal distributions, and equal distributions only, are uncontaminated by relations of domination and subservience of the kind I have been describing. Where our concern is with interpersonal advantages of certain kinds—advantages that are valuable not in themselves but by virtue of the social power they confer upon those who possess them—then there *is* a correspondence between inequality and domination. Indeed, it is surely uncontentious to claim that my responsibility for my position in life would be undermined were I to find myself in a society, such as apartheid South Africa, that withheld from me, and others like me, various rights of citizenship that it conferred upon a privileged few. I have emphasized all along, however, that not all advantages are of this interpersonal kind. The intrapersonal advantages of health, nourishment, and so on are advantageous to me regardless of how other people are doing in the same respects. My independence—and thus my responsibility—may indeed demand that I be adequately provided for in terms of these things. The language of adequate provision is, however, the language of a principle of *sufficiency* rather than one of equality. It may be true that my decisions, preferences, and actions can be regarded as *mine* only if I have been provided with the basic wherewithal necessary to make my way in the world. From this, however, it does not follow that those decisions, preferences, and actions would be any *more* mine were I to have had available to me the same stock of intrapersonal advantages as those who are better off than me.

I have said, then, that there may well be a link of some sort between arguments about responsibility and those about equality, one that connects up claims about responsibility as they feature in the foreground of arguments about justice with claims about equality as these feature in the background. What I have denied is that this link is such as to require background equality *in all things* as a precondition of holding people responsible for their foreground holdings. Whether my being responsible for a thing requires no more than that I be unimpeded by others, or whether it requires also that certain goods be made available to me, the fact is that the demand for background *equality* appears at its strongest in the realm of interpersonal advantages and at its weakest in the realm of intrapersonal ones.

Indeed, in the realm of intrapersonal advantages, given a choice between background conditions that are equal but sufficient and those that are sufficient but unequal it seems that the cause of responsibility encourages us to favour the latter over the former. I can be responsible for a decision, choice, or action—to the extent of its being mine in a sufficiently deep sense to render me liable to pay the costs or secure the benefits of it—even if the background conditions confronting me were *less* favourable than those confronting others. This is what we might call the *non-relational* view of responsibility.

The non-relational view is not, however, the only one on offer. Some believe that my being responsible for something—for being well off, for instance—requires not so much that the background opportunities and resources available to me be adequate or sufficient. It requires that these opportunities and resources be the same as, or equal to, those available to others. Only where background conditions are *equal* in this way are we permitted to say of the parties to a given distribution that they are responsible for their position in life. This is the *relational* view of responsibility. This relational view seems, in turn, to be a close cousin of the view that fairness in distribution requires that each of us starts from the same position in life or that each of us has the same chance of doing well or badly in life as everyone else. According to the conception of fairness I have in mind—the equal opportunity conception—how much equality there exists in background conditions bears upon the legitimacy of inequalities in foreground holdings.

The doubt I have in all this is whether the relational view of responsibility is not something *more* than a close cousin of the equal opportunity conception of fairness. Indeed, it seems to me that the former view very often *is* the latter expressed in the idiom of responsibility rather than opportunity. If I am right about this, then those who advance the relational view of responsibility are often doing no more than announcing their allegiance to the equal opportunity conception of fairness. I venture this thought in part because I doubt whether the relational view really does represent a sensible interpretation of the demands of individual responsibility. That is, I doubt whether it is not in the *nature* of claims about responsibility that they cannot rest wholly upon relational preconditions. I am not suggesting that it is foolish or misguided to think of an attachment to equal opportunity as being in some sense related to claims about responsibility. Indeed, in the third chapter I examined an interpretation of the equal opportunity principle that made precisely this connection. What I *am* suggesting is that claims about responsibility do not necessarily carry the force in the equal opportunity argument that they appear to. Clearly enough, there is a sense on the equal opportunity view in which outcome inequalities are objectionable where and because individuals are not *responsible* for them. But often this is just another way of saying that these inequalities are objectionable where and because the relevant equal opportunities are not in place. In other words, there no *distinctive* work being done here by the notion of responsibility over and above that of capturing the idea that individuals are or are not liable to certain kinds of treatment according to the rules of justice in question. The appeal to responsibility in this context makes no essential reference to the capacities and dispositions whose existence and exercise is part of what gives claims about responsibility their peculiar force. The presence of equal opportunity is not at all the same thing as the presence of agency and it is the presence of agency that gets claims about individual responsibility up and running. Nor, by the same token, is the presence of identical *luck* the same as the presence of agency. From the fact that luck may undermine agency it does not follow that agency is present wherever luck, differential or otherwise, is absent. We can, after all, quite easily imagine a world purged of capriciousness—one that in all its operations observes certain regularities—that is nonetheless inert and in which no one *does* anything.

I make these points because it strikes me that, in devising their distributive schemes, egalitarians are often confused as to whether their mission is to reward individual responsibility, to promote equal opportunity, or to eliminate differential luck. These, however, are quite different and sometimes competing demands. To see this, we need only turn our attention to the work of a representative sample of egalitarians. Thomas Nagel, for his part, launches his argument with the following statement:

To embody egalitarian values in a political ideal would be an involved task. An essential part of that task would be to introduce an appropriate condition of non-responsibility into the specification of those goods and evils whose equal possession is desirable. What seems bad is not that people should be unequal in advantages or disadvantages generally, but that they should be unequal in the advantages or disadvantages for which they are not responsible. Only then must priority be given to the interests of the worse off. Two people born into a situation which gave them equal life chances can end up leading lives of very different quality as a result of their own free choices, and that should not be objectionable to an egalitarian.[1]

Nagel's principle appears to take claims of responsibility seriously. It appears that my being responsible for something constitutes an important— if not necessarily a decisive—reason for insulating my claims in respect of that thing from the claims of others and indeed for protecting others from claims of mine. But now we must ask whether Nagel's principle only *appears* to do this—we must ask how much my being responsible for my holdings *matters* in determining the strength of my claim to them. One answer to this is that my being responsible for my holdings matters to Nagel in ways analogous to those in which my deserving my holdings matters to a desert theorist and analogous also to the ways in which my being entitled to my holdings matters to an entitlement theorist. Of course, these analogies might not be altogether sustainable. They might break down on the grounds of its being in the nature of claims involving desert and entitlement—unlike Nagel's claims involving responsibility—that they outweigh other sorts of concerns that apply to questions of distribution. I am pretty sure, however, that few desert theorists, at least, think that claims of desert are the only sorts of claims relevant to the issue of who should get what. Indeed, my intuition—and it may be no more than that—is that it is not the *force* of claims of desert and entitlement that marks them out from the claims Nagel advances in the name of responsibility. What marks them out is the terms in which the commitment to desert and to entitlement is conceived and expressed. Judgements in the matter of whether I deserve or whether I am entitled to a thing turn on whether I have or have not done enough to establish a claim to the relevant good. If *I* have done enough, then I have a claim to that good. If *I* have not done enough, I have no such claim. The emphasis is on the requital of something, be it desert or entitlement, rather than on the elimination of its negative, be this what we might think of as non-desert or non-entitlement.

In this, the commitments to desert and to entitlement operate in a quite different way from Nagel's apparent commitment to distributing goods on the basis of the responsible agency of each. To see this, note what Nagel has to say in another passage:

If A gains a benefit for which he is responsible, becoming better off than B, who is not responsible for the change, the resulting inequality is still acceptable, since the [egalitarian] principle does not object to *inequalities* for which the parties are not responsible, but only to the parties' being unequal in goods or evils for the *possession of which* they are not responsible—where merely having less than someone else is not in itself counted as an evil. So if A and B are each responsible for how much of a particular good he has, the non-responsibility condition fails and inequality is unobjectionable. It is perfectly all right if A has more of the good, even though B is not responsible for the inequality, since he is not responsible for how much A has.[2]

Imagine now that we have before us a distribution in which Anne has 100 units and Bill's holdings are unknown. If we want to know whether this distribution is permissible according to Nagel's principle the starting point will be to ask whether Anne and Bill are responsible for the holdings to their name. If Anne *is* responsible for her 100 units this confers upon her a (prima facie) claim to those 100 units. But Bill would have a claim to some part of Anne's holdings were (1) Bill not to be responsible for having holdings of less than 100 units. He would have no such claim were (2) his own holdings also to be 100 units, or were (3) he to be responsible for the fact that his holdings were less than 100 units.

The upshot of this is that Anne's responsibility for her holdings is of only limited significance in determining the strength of her claims to them. After all, her responsibility is irrelevant in cases (1) and (2). Bill would, seemingly, have the same claim on Anne in (1) whether or not she was responsible for her holdings. It is Bill's non-responsibility for having less than 100, rather than Anne's responsibility, that is at issue. Similarly, Bill would have the same claim (or non-claim) on Anne's holdings in (2) regardless of her responsibility for her holdings since, where the two parties have equal holdings, the principle does not apply. Only in respect of (3) does Anne's responsibility for her holdings appear to be of independent relevance. But even this is deceptive, because it is relevant only because Bill is responsible for having less than she. That is, Anne's responsibility for her holdings is relevant only to the extent that Bill's responsibility for his holdings is taken as a given.

So, Anne being responsible for her holdings establishes no more than a neutral claim on her part to those holdings—*neutral* in the sense of being lexically inferior to, or otherwise trumpable by, other claims. As such, Anne's is a claim that can resist the predations of others who, by virtue of their responsibility for their own holdings, have similarly neutral claims. But neutral claims of this kind are defeated by the positive claims of those who are not responsible for the fact of their holdings being less than others. Moreover, the relevant conflict here is not between concerns about responsibility and concerns unrelated to it—as we might expect, on occasion, there to be a conflict between the demands of desert theory or entitlement theory and the demands of some form of consequentialism. Instead, the conflict is *internal* to the commitment to responsibility itself. Nor is this surprising. As Nagel says, his is really a *non*-responsibility rather than a responsibility principle. Its focus is not so much on what individuals are responsible for having as on what they are not responsible for not having. What is more, judgements about what they are not responsible for not having are made having regard to how much those who have more than they have, be those others responsible for what they have or not.

My earlier suggestion that Nagel's principle takes seriously the claims of individual responsibility may, then, need to be modified. That principle does not embody a *positive* commitment to the requital of individual responsibility in the manner of the positive commitment to desert embodied in desert theory and to entitlement in entitlement theory. Indeed, as we have seen, the concern with responsibility drops out of the picture altogether where individuals have equal holdings. In fairness to Nagel, he recognizes the tensions that this creates. He recognizes that a concern with the absence of responsibility on the part of the disadvantaged agent must be reconciled with a concern for the presence of responsibility on the part of the advantaged agent if the commitment to responsibility as a determinant of distributive reward is to have any credibility at all. Thus we find Nagel offering the following example:

suppose A gains a benefit for which he *is* responsible, but that in addition to benefiting A, A's gain positively harms B in a way for which B is *not* responsible (by taking away all his customers or simply making him poor). If the evil for which B is not responsible is always allowed to dominate the good for which A is responsible, rendering the inequality unacceptable, very little will be left.[3]

Some philosophical egalitarians are not as alive to this problem as they might be. G. A. Cohen, for instance, seems to attach less weight to choice and responsibility than he imagines. At various points Cohen claims that 'the primary egalitarian impulse is to extinguish the influence on distribution of . . . brute luck';[4] that the 'purpose [of egalitarianism] is to eliminate involuntary disadvantage, by which I (stipulatively) mean disadvantage for which the sufferer cannot be held responsible';[5] and that '[b]rute luck is an enemy of just equality, and, since the effects of genuine choice contrast with brute luck, genuine choice excuses otherwise unacceptable inequalities'.[6] Note that, in the first two quotations, Cohen's principal concern is with eliminating the (differential) effects of chance rather than distributing advantages on the basis of the responsible agency of each. But the more interesting quotation is the third one in which Cohen claims that 'genuine choice excuses otherwise unacceptable inequalities'. On whose part must there be genuine choice(s) in order to excuse what would otherwise be unacceptable inequalities? If my holdings are greater than yours, and if they are the product of factors for which I am responsible, this might be thought to establish a claim on my part to those holdings. Cohen, seemingly, wants to deny this. Like Nagel, he wants to say that I have a claim to my holdings in this case if and only if you are also responsible for the holdings that you have. If we two are not *both* responsible for our holdings in this way, then the inequality between us does not reflect the 'effects of genuine choice', as Cohen's principle demands. For an inequality to be acceptable it is not enough that it should reflect the (effects of the) genuine choice(s) of one party. It must reflect the (effects of the) genuine choice(s) of both.

And this, in turn, means that the fact of *my* holdings being a matter of genuine choice on *my* part is irrelevant to the question of who should have what unless *your* holdings are also a matter of genuine choice on *your* part. In and of itself, the fact that I am responsible for my holdings establishes nothing: it gives me no claim to those holdings independently of your responsibility for your holdings. Thus, ideas of choice and responsibility seem to function in Cohen's scheme in an essentially negative way. Where the claims of responsibility and non-responsibility come into conflict, it is the latter that must prevail, for there exists no positive commitment to confer advantages upon individuals on the basis of their responsible actions and choices. In this sense, Nagel's claim that very little will be left of the commitment to having distributive holdings vary according to choice and responsibility seems vindicated.

Nor do the ambiguities end there. Both Cohen and Nagel trade on the idea that the presence of background equal opportunity—coupled with the absence of background unequal luck—is bound up in some way with the question of whether individuals can be held *responsible* for the foreground holdings to their name. Recall here that Nagel, for instance, thinks that the question of whether each of us is responsible for his position in life is related to the question of whether we enjoyed equal life chances. But it is not always clear to me how Cohen and Nagel conceive of the connection between background and foreground legitimacy. On some occasions the thought seems to be that background equality is a necessary condition of holding individuals responsible for their foreground holdings. On other occasions the thought seems to be that it is sufficient. I have already indicated, however, why we should be suspicious of such views. From the fact that my being responsible for a thing requires that background conditions be suitably favourable it certainly does not follow that what makes them favourable is that they are equal. Indeed, equalizing those conditions may serve to diminish the responsibility of the parties concerned rather than to promote it. If I suffer the same bad luck as you—or if I am cursed by the same paltry array of options—it seems that I bear as little responsibility for my life as you bear for yours rather than that you now bear as much responsibility for your life as I once did for mine. From the thought that neither of us is responsible for his holdings I suppose it might follow that each of us is responsible for his holdings to the same extent. But the latter formulation hardly makes the case, on the grounds of the requital of individual responsibility, for distributing goods in one way rather than another. Moreover, it is not just in terms of background conditions that attributions of responsibility seem to rest upon non-relational premises. Part of what makes me responsible for a thing is that I affirm it as my own or that I exhibit the relevant intentions in respect of it. It is, however, in the nature of such judgements that they are non-relational in character. My intentions do not become more or less *my intentions* according to how far your intentions are yours and we would simply be misunderstanding the individualized nature of claims about agency were we to absorb into them a relational standard.

So, the question of whether there is *equal* background opportunity or luck (or both) is quite separate from the question of whether individuals are responsible for their foreground holdings. In this regard, I think that there exists an important tension in the argument that Cohen in particular develops. This tension centres around the difference between Cohen's claim that the 'effects of genuine choice contrast with brute luck' and the claim that 'a large part of the fundamental egalitarian aim is to extinguish the influence of brute luck on distribution'. By the latter, Cohen might mean that distributive inequalities are impermissible if they spring from *inequalities* in brute luck. If so, it would seem that distributive inequalities are not impermissible if they do not spring from unequal brute luck, even if they spring from *equal* brute luck. If, however, the effects of genuine choice 'contrast' with brute luck, and if a choice is 'genuine' in so far as it is purged of brute luck, then it would seem that distributive inequalities are impermissible even where the brute luck of the distributees is equal. And they are impermissible because it is only 'genuine choice' that 'excuses otherwise unacceptable inequalities': all inequalities that are not the product of 'genuine choice', so construed, are inexcusable.

All of which suggests to me that Cohen, like Nagel, offers a brand of egalitarianism whose commitment to the values of responsibility and choice is more fragile than first impressions would suggest. If my responsibility for my holdings is judged wholly in relational terms—by considering whether the life chances or opportunities of all relevant parties were equal—then the positive commitment to distributing according to the responsible choices of each is really a negative commitment to eliminating unequal opportunities and the unequal effects of luck. If, instead, my responsibility for my holdings is judged according to a non-relational standard, then it still remains the case that, for the egalitarians I have been examining, the claims of the disadvantaged agent who is *not* responsible for his holdings trump the claims of the advantaged agent who *is* responsible for his holdings.

Ronald Dworkin too is moved to specify the conditions under which it is, and it is not, permissible for foreground inequalities to arise between individuals. This he does by way of a distinction between what he calls option luck and brute luck—a distinction I have already had cause to touch upon obliquely. On Dworkin's view, it isn't objectionable for A to be better off than B if B could, in principle, have been as well off as A. Applying this to the case of Nagel's shopkeepers, it is not objectionable for A to put B out of business provided there is a sense in which A and B were competing against one another on equal terms or that each had before them the same set of options. If either party chooses to take a risk or gamble, then they are opening themselves up to the effects of option luck. If the risk pays off they enjoy good option luck. If it does not they experience bad option luck. Either way, each is responsible for the outcome because each is responsible for the decision to take the risk in the first place. The fact that the actions of shopkeeper A have been such as to reduce B's stock of goods does not necessarily render B's loss a loss for which he is not responsible even though, strictly speaking, he is not responsible for the fact that A took the action that he did. Dworkinian justice is offended against in this case only to the extent we assume that (the effects of) A's action were not part and parcel of B's option luck. Were it to be the case that A's intervention was, from B's perspective, a matter not of option luck but of brute luck then the case would be different: the resulting inequality *would* offend against the egalitarian intuition.

More specifically, Dworkin describes the two kinds of luck in the following terms:

Option luck is a matter of how deliberate and calculated gambles turn out—whether someone gains or loses through accepting an isolated risk he or she should have anticipated and might have declined. Brute luck is a matter of how risks fall out that are not in that sense deliberate gambles. If I buy a stock on the exchange that rises, then my option luck is good. If I am hit by a falling meteorite whose course could not have been predicted, then my bad luck is brute.[7]

Dworkin then asks us to consider whether there is any objection to distributive holdings varying according to differences in option luck and he answers that there is not:

We have no general reason for forbidding gambles altogether in the bare fact that in the event winners will control more resources than losers, any more than in the fact that winners will have more than those who do not gamble at all.[8]

But an important rider is subsequently added to this claim:

the argument in favour of allowing differences in option luck to affect income and wealth assumes that everyone has in principle the same gambles available to him. Someone who never had the opportunity to run a similar risk, and would have taken the opportunity had it been available, will still envy some of those who did have it.[9]

Thus, in Dworkin's scheme, two conditions must be met in order for

distributive inequalities to be permissible. One is that the gambles available
to A and B must be equal 'in principle'. The other is that the gambles be
'genuine and calculated'. Only when *both* requirements are met are inequalities legitimate. But we can see again how the commitment to responsibility
and choice is significantly qualified by the commitment to equality. Consider
here Dworkin's example of someone who gambles on the stock market. If my
gamble is indeed 'genuine and calculated', then I will want to say that the
outcome of that gamble is a matter of genuine choice on my part. But this is
not enough for Dworkin's purposes. He wants to claim that a genuine choice
on my part is relevant if and only if the same genuine choice was 'in principle' open to you. If it was not open to you, then any inequality between us is
impermissible. But my genuine choice is no less *genuine* in this case for not
being open to you because, on Dworkin's own account, what makes a choice
a matter of option rather than brute luck is that it involves calculation and
deliberation on the part of the choosing agent. That is, in his description of
what makes something a matter of option luck, Dworkin makes no reference
to the nature of the choices facing others. The element of comparison enters
the picture only *after* Dworkin has set up the option versus brute luck distinction and its effect is to constrain the very inequalities that that distinction
appears to license. Once the concern with relativities is introduced, it seems
that cases will arise where what is a matter of option luck from one perspective is a matter of brute luck from another. And this, in turn, seems to be
because judgements about what counts as option and brute luck are at their
most compelling when made from within a single perspective rather from an
overarching perspective that seeks to apply these notions to relations between
individuals.

There is a second peculiarity in Dworkin's scheme. He says that the case for
letting differences in option luck affect people's levels of income and wealth
requires that the same option luck be open to all because '[s]omeone who
never had the opportunity to run a similar risk, and *would have taken the
opportunity had it been available*, will still envy those who did have it'. For the
purposes of the argument, let us agree with Dworkin that you would have a
legitimate complaint against me if you would have taken the same gambles as
me had those gambles been open to you. The corollary of this seems to be
that you can have no such complaint against me if you would *not* have taken
the same gambles as me. If this is right, then it is unclear what conclusions we
should draw from the bare fact that we two did not enjoy *equal* opportunities
to gamble. We know that Dworkin would refuse to license an inequality
between us where we were equally disposed to gamble but had unequal opportunities to do so. We know that he would be happy to license an inequality
between us were we unequally disposed to gamble but had equal opportunities to do so. But what of the case where we are unequally disposed to gamble

and have unequal opportunities before us? The question is apt because Dworkin's argument works primarily if we assume that there exists an inequality of treatment if some have before them more choices than others. But Dworkin seems to recognize that this is not always so, thereby raising the question of why formal equality of choice should be taken to be the test of a just distribution to begin with.

Let me recap. Up until now, I have been examining the thought that arguments about equality and those about responsibility may intersect by way of an underlying ideal of independence that draws the two naturally and necessarily together. According to that ideal, my being responsible for my holdings requires that I come to have those holdings against the background of conditions that are, in some respects, equal. (I say *in some respects* equal because I have already denied that background equality in all respects is a precondition of independence and responsibility). It is not in these terms, however, that we can understand the intersection between equality and responsibility within the egalitarian intuition itself—the intuition that, in respect of *foreground* holdings, it is objectionable for some to be worse off than others through no fault of their own. Indeed, my suspicion is that the intuition seeks to combine what are, in this context, two quite independent tests of fairness in distribution. One test has it that fairness demands equality. The other has it that fairness demands each receive what he is responsible for. The temptation is to assume that these two tests belong naturally together. In what remains of this chapter I want to examine whether that assumption is warranted and indeed whether the egalitarian intuition itself combines concerns about equality and those about responsibility in a manner that is stable and sustainable.

That claims about equality and responsibility should be *thought* to belong together is understandable. After all, egalitarians have long felt themselves vulnerable to the charge that an unbridled commitment to equality—a commitment to equality in holdings come what may—is counter-intuitive. It is counter-intuitive precisely because the demand to preserve equality in distribution appears to require that resources be systematically diverted from the prudent to the profligate. This is the counter-intuition that the expensive tastes argument identifies. The way to head off worries about expensive tastes seems, in turn, to qualify the commitment to equality by holding departures from equality to be permissible in certain cases, namely, when a relevant test of responsibility is met by the party with the expensive taste. This ensures that the spendthrift has no claim to have his resources continually topped up by the prudent.

From the fact that unbridled egalitarianism becomes more attractive when it incorporates claims about responsibility it would be wrong to infer, however, that *whatever it is* that draws us to equality as the benchmark of a just distribution draws us also to individual responsibility. On the face of it, there is nothing discernibly *egalitarian* in the idea that individuals should benefit or suffer according to what they are responsible for. Indeed, the impulse to qualify the commitment to equality by incorporating claims about responsibility seems designed not so much to explicate the true nature of underlying egalitarian concerns as to help egalitarians get out of a philosophical and political fix. In this, the role played in egalitarian thinking by principles of individual responsibility, in the matter of meeting the expensive tastes objection, seems to me quite different from the role played in egalitarian thinking by principles of priority, in the matter of meeting the levelling down objection. Whereas priority principles serve to explicate the concerns underlying the putative attachment to equality, principles of responsibility appear to operate quite independently of that attachment. In short, it is easy enough to make sense of the idea that egalitarians sometimes *think* they are arguing for equality when *in fact* they are arguing for some notion of priority or sufficiency. The same cannot be said of the idea that egalitarians sometimes *think* they are arguing for equality when *in fact* they are arguing for individual responsibility. Indeed, it is not obvious what it is that concerns about equality *add* to concerns about responsibility if all the time the thought driving the argument along is that it is objectionable for the profligate to free-ride on the prudent. Why is that thought not strong enough *in itself* to do the work required of it by those who are impressed by the expensive tastes objection? From the fact that we might find it objectionable for some to displace the cost of their lifestyles on to others it does not follow that *what* we see as objectionable in such cases is connected in any way to claims about the *patterns* of distribution that precede such free-riding or result from it. Of course, judgements about what constitutes prudence and profligacy cannot be made *in vacuo*: they are intelligible only if we have in mind a norm of what should count as prudence and profligacy. It is obvious enough, however, that the norm in question need not be one of *equal* distribution. We can repudiate free-riding without committing ourselves to the idea that equality should enjoy some sort of privileged status when it comes to assessing the acceptability, or otherwise, of different distributions. I imagine that, for most people, whatever it is about free-riding that is objectionable—such as that it involves one person being unwillingly called upon to benefit another—is objectionable for reasons that are independent of the patterns of distribution it results in. It is just not clear to me why we should worry more about free-riding that produces a move from an equal distribution to an unequal one than we should about free-riding that produces a move from an unequal distribution to an equal one. Even if the thought is that the mischief of free-riding is *compounded by* the alleged mischief of inequality, this does not bear out the idea that the two mischiefs are joined by way of an underlying ideal so much as that they constitute separate and independent tests of rightness in distribution.

Either way, I do not want to exaggerate how much headway these arguments have enabled me to make. From the observation that a commitment to equality does not entail a commitment to responsibility, and vice versa, it does not follow that the attempt to bring the two together is somehow improper. Still less can we assume that incorporating both within a single distributive ideal leads inevitably to instability and confusion. To this end, I want now to move away from the thought that the egalitarian intuition explicates concerns about expensive tastes and free-riding and to address head on an altogether different sort of appeal it makes. That appeal rests on two thoughts. One is that it is objectionable for someone to suffer a disadvantage through no fault of their own—what I described earlier as the responsibility principle. The other is that there exists an intimate relation between someone's suffering a disadvantage and their being worse off than someone else. Those who sign up to the latter view are not committed to the idea that disadvantages are *necessarily* relational. Only a myopic egalitarian—and there are one or two about—would believe that individuals are disadvantaged *only* where they are worse off than others. Instead, the thought is that inequalities are a species of disadvantage: they are *analogous* if not identical to punishment, pain, and malnourishment. Just as we find something objectionable in the idea of someone incurring punishment or pain through no fault of their own, so, on this view, do we find something objectionable in the idea of someone being worse off than others through no fault of their own.

What are we to make of this line of argument? On the one hand, the analogies in question seem to break down as soon as we move from the idea that there is something *inherently* disadvantageous about being punished or about being in pain to the idea that there is nothing *inherently* disadvantageous about being worse off than someone else. And if there is nothing inherently disadvantageous about being worse off than someone else then there is no reason to single out *inequality* as the sort of thing that engages our concerns about responsibility. On the other hand, there is nothing mysterious in the thought that certain kinds of inequalities are linked inextricably to certain kinds of disadvantage or indeed in the thought that part of what it means to be worse off than someone else is that of being in a position of disadvantage relative to them.

The temptation at this point is to insist that whilst relational disadvantage is *one* kind of disadvantage it is not *the* kind of disadvantage to which the responsibility principle might legitimately be applied. But that is the view the egalitarian intuition challenges, not one that its proponents are obliged, by definitional fiat, to accept. I should confess that I am not sure how to resolve disputes of this kind—disputes about what kind of thing should *count* as an advantage or disadvantage to begin with and indeed disputes about whether it is in the nature of some kinds of disadvantage that they engage our concerns about responsibility but of others that they do not. At the very least, it seems clear that the egalitarian intuition is at its most compelling where inequalities are associated—perhaps *logically* associated—with disadvantages and losses whose standing *as* disadvantages and losses is recognized by egalitarians and non-egalitarians alike. If you believe, for instance, that unchosen inequalities are necessarily exploitative, then you will sign up to the egalitarian intuition as part of a more general objection to exploitation. Similarly, if you believe that inequalities serve to demoralize the worse off, then you will sign up to the egalitarian intuition on the grounds that people ought not to be demoralized through no fault of their own. The worry, of course, is that adopting either tack does not so much rescue the egalitarian intuition from implausibility as subvert it altogether. To hold, for instance, our commitment to that intuition is contingent upon a prior and non-relational conception of advantage and disadvantage is to abandon the idea that the bare fact of some being worse off than others is something that ought to engage our concern to begin with. In the example in question, we can replace all talk of equality and inequality with the claim that it is objectionable for someone to be demoralized through no fault of their own no matter the distributive route by which it comes about.

In assessing the egalitarian intuition we need then to be clear whether its target is all inequalities or only some. We need also to be clear whether the intuition targets inequalities on the basis of their being advantageous or disadvantageous in themselves, or on the basis of there being a logical relation between inequality and something disadvantageous that lies beyond the inequality itself, or indeed of there being no more than a contingent relation of the latter kind. These doubts about the target of the egalitarian intuition only strengthen once we recognize the ambiguous terms in which that intuition is couched. The claim that it is objectionable for me to be worse off than you through no fault of my own might apply where *either* (1) it is not my fault that our holdings are unequal; *or* (2) it is not my fault that my holdings happen to be what they are (and what they are is less than yours). These, of course, are two quite different ideas. Imagine, for instance, that you and I are born with equal life chances: we have the same range of options before us. I choose to produce rather than to consume and you to consume rather than to produce. Clearly enough, there is a sense in which it is not your fault if you end up with less than me since it is not your fault that I choose the sort of life that I do. My lifestyle, and its attendant rewards, are not something over which you have any direct control. Since you had no direct control over my choosing to acquire a greater stock of goods than you, there is an obvious sense in which it was not your fault that there came to exist an inequality between us.[10] (1) is therefore violated.

Perhaps there are some for whom (1) captures the concerns underlying the egalitarian intuition. But if that *is* so, then we shall soon find that (1) is capable of licensing few, if any, departures from an equal distribution. What (1) claims is that *any* inequality that comes to pass as a result of decisions and actions other than those of the individual in question is thereby an inequality that is not *his fault* in the required sense. From the perspective of that individual, a cause of inequality is impermissible if it is one over which he has no direct control. And this, of course, is to rule out of court almost any inequality that we can imagine since an inequality that in no way depends on the acts or omissions of others is difficult to picture. If we want to confer a more prominent role upon concerns about responsibility than (1) appears to allow, then we shall have to reject (1) in favour of (2). According to (2), what is at issue is not whether you and I are responsible for any *inequality* between us. Instead, what is at issue is whether each of us is responsible for his holdings being what they are. If each of us is responsible for his holdings, then there can, according to (2), be no objection to any inequality between us. This indeed is Nagel's position, as I cited it earlier.

But now we must return to a question I raised in Chapter 1. Imagine that you *are* responsible for your holdings. Why is it that, if I am *not* responsible for mine, the level of your holdings (and the extent of the inequality between us) is of all-consuming importance, whereas if I *am* responsible for my holdings the level of your holdings (and the extent of the inequality between us) is a matter of indifference? If it was a matter of indifference in one context why should it not be a matter of indifference in the other? Nagel, for one, acknowledges that 'merely having less than someone is not in itself counted as an evil'. But if it is true that an inequality is 'not in itself counted as an evil' in cases where each of us is responsible for the holdings to his name, then it is unclear why it is not also true in those cases where one or other of us is *not* responsible for our holdings. The argument is meant to show that there are independent reasons for thinking that my having less than you in such cases is objectionable. But these reasons are obscure: it is unclear why they operate in one context but not in another.

To illustrate these points, consider the following case. You and I start with 100 units to our name. Through choices and decisions of mine I come to have 200 units. Through sheer bad luck your holdings dip to 50 units. To claim it to be no fault of yours that your holdings are 50 units implies that it is no fault of yours that your holdings are not *more than* 50. So you are not responsible for the fact that you do not have 50 + *a*. What, however, should *a* be taken to be? If we take our cue from (2), then it would seem that *a* is the amount that needs to be taken from me and given to you such that our holdings would be equal. But this was supposed to be an argument about your not being responsible for having less than *you* should have had—according to some view about what constitutes an equitable baseline or starting point. If we follow

(2), it becomes an argument about your having less than me. On Nagel's account, however, the latter fact, taken by itself, is unexceptionable. That is, the fact that you are not responsible for my having more than you—such that there is an inequality between us—is not, strictly speaking, relevant. Thus to claim that you should have 50 + *a* is not to establish that we should be equal in our holdings. After all, the supposed concern of the argument is with the fact that you were not responsible for not having 50 + *a*. It is not with the fact that your holdings fall short of mine. To be sure, in a two-person world you can have 50 + *a* units only by drawing upon some of my 200 units. But if the concern is with you and your absence of responsibility, then it does not follow that our holdings should be equal.

Nagel, for his part, seems to acknowledge this. He claims that where this principle is violated we should respond by giving 'priority . . . to the interests of the worse off'.[11] This enables him to avoid the levelling down objection and thereby to rescue (his version of) the egalitarian intuition from one of its more obvious deficiencies. The corollary of this manoeuvre, however, is to shift the focus of the egalitarian intuition away from concerns about equality *per se* and towards concerns about compensating individuals for shortfalls in the absolute level of their holdings that are not their fault. In the example under discussion, no longer is the focus of the objection upon your *having less than me* through no fault of your own—objectionable though that might be in its own right. What is now the focus of the objection is that you have less than you should have had according to some suitably constructed counterfactual or, at least, to some absolute baseline. It is in order to *compensate* you for the bad luck you have suffered that we should increase the absolute level of your holdings.

Recasting the egalitarian intuition in these terms allows us to compensate those who suffer from bad luck. But it does not give us grounds for taking away from those who enjoy good luck. We can believe there to be something objectionable about *your* holdings being diminished in absolute terms through bad luck without believing there to be anything objectionable about *my* holdings being increased in absolute terms through good luck. I say this in the knowledge that it might still be open to egalitarians to couch the argument in terms that might meet this doubt. They might claim that we should eliminate the unequal effects on distribution of all forms of luck, be it good or bad, because it is as objectionable for me to be better off than you through good luck as it is for you to be worse off than me through bad luck. But this begs the question, for we shall have to ask what intuitions support this view. Certainly not those underscoring a principle of compensation of the kind that I described before: such a principle is addressed only to those whose holdings are depleted as a consequence of bad luck. This being so, we shall be forced back into appealing to the egalitarian intuition in its original form—and it is precisely the appeal of that intuition that I am doubtful about.

In interpreting the egalitarian intuition, egalitarians must decide whether the target of their concern is equality or whether it is compensation. Exclusive reliance on concerns about equality leaves the egalitarian case vulnerable to the levelling down objection. But exclusive reliance on concerns about compensation undermines the claim that A being *worse off* than B through no fault of his own is objectionable at all still less on the grounds of its being an *inequality*.

Perhaps egalitarians do not have to choose between concerns about equality and concerns about compensation. Perhaps they can balance the two concerns against one another according to the circumstances of the case. In this way, they might be able to avoid the counter-intuitive consequences that would spring from an exclusive reliance on one or other concern.[12] But there will remain a dilemma none the less, for there is an obvious sense in which the appeal to concerns about compensation challenges the basis of the egalitarian intuition itself. To appeal to a principle of compensation is not merely to claim that, in cases where A is worse off than B through no fault of his own, our concern is not *primarily* with equality. Instead, it is to claim that our concern is not with equality *at all*. Redistributions undertaken in the name of compensation are egalitarian in effect rather than in intent: they are undertaken for the purpose of increasing the holdings of those whose luck has been bad rather than for the purpose of reducing the gap between them and those whose luck has been good.[13]

Thus it is concerns about compensation rather than equality that appear to lend the egalitarian intuition such intuitive appeal as it possesses. And as if to bear this out, recall that the egalitarian intuition concerns itself with those who cannot be faulted for being *worse off* than others, not with those who cannot take credit for being better off than others. That is, the phrasing of the egalitarian intuition is suggestive of an asymmetry in its concerns. The intuition does, then, embody an *egalitarian* commitment of a kind. But it is not, seemingly, a commitment to equality in distribution. Instead, it is a commitment to the view that an improvement in the absolute position of the least fortunate carries greater moral weight than an improvement in the position of those further up the scale—what Parfit calls the Priority View.[14]

Recall now that I began this chapter by asking how concerns about equality and those about individual responsibility might fit together, in the egalitarian intuition and elsewhere. In particular, I wanted to know whether the view that we should prefer equal distributions over unequal ones sat happily alongside the view what people receive by way of advantages and disadvantages should depend on what they are responsible for. Having allowed that certain kinds of background equalities might indeed be required in the name of holding individuals responsible for their foreground holdings, I then sought to separate claims about responsibility in particular from those about equal opportunity in general. From there I moved on to test, and to cast doubt upon, the thought that there exists some sort of natural affinity between a commitment to distributing goods equally and a commitment to distributing goods on the basis of individual responsibility. Indeed, I highlighted several examples where the two commitments seem to pull in opposite directions. Nor should we be surprised by this: the impulse to reward and to penalize on the basis of responsibility is bound up with a view of *the individual* as the locus of moral assessment. On this view, how I am treated should depend upon facts about *me*—facts about what *I* do and what *I* am. It should not depend on facts about others—facts about what *they* do, what *they* are, and what *they* have.

Armed with the thought that the egalitarian intuition is driven by concerns about how individuals fare relative to one another, I proceeded to suggest that the object of comparison—and therefore the basis of the intuition itself—was unclear. The intuition might be motivated by an objection to some being *worse off than others* through no fault of their own or it might be motivated by an objection to some being *badly off* through no fault of their own regardless of the position of others. Although the point at issue here may appear to be one between principles that are comparative and those that are non-comparative, I suppose that there is a sense in which this is not so. The real dispute is about the *sort* of comparative judgement that is being made and the relevance of different kinds of counterfactual to that judgement. Nor is the issue one of how best to combine two mutually compatible concerns, for the claim that we should compensate those who are badly off appears to undercut altogether the claim that we should aim for a position of equality between the parties concerned.

In addition to its negative demands, the egalitarian intuition leaves open the possibility that inequalities might be justified where they spring from choices, decisions, and actions for which the parties to the distribution are responsible. But what *appears* to be a commitment to distributing the good and bad things in life according to factors for which you and I are responsible often turns out, upon closer inspection, to be something rather different. On the egalitarian account, what legitimates my having more than you is not that my holdings are attributable to choices of mine that are genuine according to some non-relational standard. In and of itself, that often decides nothing. Instead, what makes such inequalities legitimate is that my greater holdings are the result of no choice available to me that was not *also* available to you. The choices in question must, in principle, be equally open to us and equally open to us in one or both of two puzzling ways—namely, in the sense of being identical in kind or equal in quantity. Only these choices, seemingly, are relevant from the standpoint of egalitarian theory. There is no commitment to distributing according to choices that are not, or cannot be made, equally open to all, even though those choices themselves might be genuine in the sense of being rationally reflected upon against the background of relevant information and favourable conditions. It is the concern with relativities that defines what makes a choice *genuine* to begin with.

If I believe that ideas of choice and responsibility should play a positive role in our distributive theory I will think that my being responsible for my holdings ought to carry some independent moral weight, regardless of whether you are likewise responsible for your holdings. But this is not, seemingly, what philosophical egalitarians believe. They believe that we should impose a relational concern—a concern with equality—upon what is in essence a non-relational principle—the principle that how people fare in life should be determined by that for which they are responsible. It is not just that arguments about responsibility enter the picture only against the background of a fair initial distribution of resources and advantages. It is also that part of what makes an initial distribution fair is that choices themselves, as well as resources and advantages, are equal, namely that they are, in principle, equally open to all. Thus the comparative judgement egalitarians take to be decisive is one focused on whether the choices facing different individuals are equal. It is not one focused on the question of my responsibility for my holdings taken by itself.

6

Natural talents, luck, and the market

The egalitarian intuition stands as one of the hallmarks of philosophical egalitarianism and it is an intuition to which political egalitarians have shown themselves sympathetic. Another hallmark of philosophical egalitarianism is the claim that the distribution of natural talents is arbitrary from a moral point of view and that, as such, natural talents stand as an illegitimate cause, source, or basis of unequal social reward. On the face of it, this claim is nothing more than an innocent development of now familiar ideas in the matter of what constitutes fairness in distribution. After all, the objection to natural inequalities as a basis of unequal social reward fits nicely with the thought that whether inequalities in outcome are legitimate is bound up in some way with whether opportunities are equal. Indeed, the egalitarian stance on natural talents seems, in essence, to be an extension of the logic of principles of equal opportunity. If I think it objectionable that some should end up with fewer goods than others as a result of their place in the *social* hierarchy, then presumably I will find it no less objectionable that some should end up with fewer goods than others as a result of their place in the *natural* hierarchy. The mischief in the two cases seems to be the same, namely that some end up being worse off than others through no fault of their own. Hanging over these arguments, of course, are the general doubts I have talked about already, namely, doubts about why inequalities *per se* should be thought to require justification of any kind and doubts also about why background equality should be thought to be a condition of legitimate foreground inequality. But these are, as I say, *general* doubts about the shape of the argument as a whole rather than specific doubts about egalitarian claims concerning the status of natural talents—claims whose logic, *within* the terms of the overall argument, appears unimpeachable. And yet the position adopted by philosophical egalitarians on the question of natural talents has shown itself to have less political appeal than the egalitarian intuition itself because, unlike that intuition, it appears to be at best counterintuitive and at worst pernicious. And it appears to be these things despite its apparently close *logical* connection to the egalitarian intuition.

It so happens that I think there *is* something troubling about the claims made by certain (philosophical) egalitarians when discussing natural talents, and in what follows I try to identify what that something is. Having tested the egalitarian argument under this heading, I then take that argument forward into an analysis of the egalitarian stance towards markets and market outcomes.

Let me begin here by saying something about what I understand by the idea of there being an arbitrary distribution of natural talents. In ordinary usage, to have a talent is to have a faculty or aptitude for something, be that something of a kind that promotes our well-being or diminishes it or for which there exists some demand on the part of others or none at all. Thus, according to the ordinary view, my talent for stepping over the lines between paving stones is no less *a talent* than is the talent that I would like to have, but regrettably lack, for picking winners on the stock market. Talents, as I am construing them here, are *all-purpose* aptitudes or faculties. There is nothing in the *idea* of a talent that allows us to say of one aptitude that it is a talent and of another that it is not, just as there is nothing in the idea of a talent that requires it to be something that benefits those who possess it, or indeed benefits anyone.

I make these points in the knowledge that when philosophical egalitarians claim there to be a distribution of (natural) talents, they often have in mind a narrower account of talents that I have offered so far. The talents they have in mind are of a kind that it is in some sense advantageous to possess. Indeed, it may even be that the talents in question are thought to be such that, given the choice, any rational agent would prefer to possess more rather than fewer. It is not by accident, however, that I have said that possessing the relevant talents is regarded as being in *some* sense advantageous (and not possessing them is regarded as being in *some* sense disadvantageous). I have couched the claims of egalitarians in these terms precisely because there exist deep ambiguities as to *what* sense of advantage and disadvantage is being appealed to. To see this, return to the example I used earlier of my talent in the matter of stepping over the lines between paving stones. There is *some* sense in which possessing this talent is advantageous to me—I enjoy the particular thrill I get from putting that talent to the test, a thrill that is denied to those who lack my talent in this respect. But the inner satisfaction I derive from my talent is not matched by an external demand for it. I cannot make a living out of my aptitude for dodging the lines in the pavement because it is not an aptitude that attracts tangible reward. In terms of its contribution to the stock of tangible goods I have to my name, my talent as a pavement walker is not advantageous to me. But this is not all that follows the argument. What follows also is that, in terms of its contribution to the stock of tangible goods I have to my name, my lack of talent as a pavement walker is not *disadvantageous* to me.

In thinking about what makes some aptitudes *talents* and others not, we need then to resolve not one question but two. We need to resolve the question of whether talents are such only where they are advantageous to those who possess them. From there we need to resolve the question of what qualifies something to be regarded *as* advantageous. Imagine, for instance, we do hold that the more talents we have the more advantageous it is to us. Imagine also we think that something is advantageous where and because it gives rise to some sort of inner satisfaction. If that is our view, then we are already in deeply contentious territory. This is because my understanding of what inner satisfaction consists in may not be the same as yours. Even if it is the same— even if we can agree on the characteristics and properties of inner satisfaction—then we shall still encounter difficulties when it comes to determining whether you, constituted as you are, have a more developed aptitude for inner satisfaction than do I, constituted as I am. And if we cannot resolve *that* question, then we will be unable to resolve the question of whether you have the same talents at your disposal as do I at mine.

Perhaps the way round this is to claim that what makes something a talent is not the contribution it makes to our inner satisfaction, nebulous idea that that is, but the fact that it attracts or commands tangible reward. On this view, I may have an *aptitude* for avoiding the lines between paving stones but this aptitude is not a talent properly so called. Whilst all talents are aptitudes, only those aptitudes that attract tangible reward (such as the aptitude I would like to have in the matter of playing the stock market) are talents. And indeed, construing talents in this way seems to navigate us past worries about the impenetrability of claims concerning inner satisfaction. Having done so, however, fresh worries begin to appear. If what makes a talent *a talent* is that it attracts tangible reward, then it would seem that what is a talent in one context may not be a talent in another. Imagine, for instance, I live in a society that bestows tangible rewards upon those who step over the lines between paving stones but not upon those who pick winners on the stock market. In *that* context it is the former that counts as a talent and the latter as a mere aptitude. In other words, talents are neither universal nor self-evident: nature cannot direct us towards them. If we are to define talents as aptitudes that it so happens attract tangible reward, then we shall need to make clear what context we have in mind and indeed whether our concern is with the link between aptitude and reward under the status quo or under some actual or possible alternative to it. And even if it *is* the status quo, we will still have to make further efforts in the direction of marking off the boundaries of our enquiry. If we do not, then we may find ourselves wondering whether talents should encompass all the aptitudes from which individuals can derive material gain in a market economy, including the aptitude some have for dealing in crack cocaine, or for demeaning themselves on national television, or for engaging in other such potentially lucrative pursuits.

I made clear at the outset, however, that the philosophical claim with which I am concerned focuses not on the general idea that people have talents but on the specific idea that there exists a *distribution* of *natural* talents. This idea is a puzzling one. If part of what it means for a talent to be a talent is that it attracts some sort of social value, then it cannot be in terms of the bare fact of having or not having social value that a natural talent differs from a non-natural one. Instead, I think that what makes talents distinctively *natural* is the thought that they are somehow crafted by nature and nature alone, or that they are acquired from nature rather than cultivated by human hand or, perhaps, that they are crafted by nature to a greater extent than they are cultivated by human hand. Admittedly, these thoughts are suffused with vagueness and it may just be that the distinction between doing and happening will once again go some way towards helping us understand the intuitions at work. Natural talents are talents that happen to us rather than talents that have come to be as a result of something we have done. Thus, being tall or fleet of foot are natural talents because they happen to us in much the same way as getting wet in the rain or being subject to gravity happen to us.[1] Non-natural talents are talents that have come to be because of something we have done or that others have done for us, for instance, through bringing us up or educating us. They are talents that have in some way been worked upon or cultivated: examples would include the talent some have for writing poetry, or for assembling pieces of machinery, or for understanding a balance sheet.

A number of things follow from the distinction between the natural and the non-natural, as I have drawn it. The first is that there is likely to be no such thing, empirically if not conceptually, as a pure case of a natural talent and a pure case of a non-natural talent. The second is that natural talents need not be innate: we can be endowed by nature with a talent at any point in our life. The third is that natural talents need not be permanent: just as we can acquire new natural talents so can we lose existing ones. And the fourth is that non-natural talents are not *un*natural: there is nothing unnatural about human beings cultivating their talents in and through doing things. These are not the most important points about natural talents, however. The most important point is one I have made already, namely, that whether something is a talent at all, natural or non-natural, depends on whether it has social value in a given context. Thus, whilst it might be nature that *causes* you to have a given natural talent, nature does not determine whether that kind of aptitude counts as a *talent*, in any given context, in the first place. I may have a natural talent one day that, as a result of a shift in social valuation, is no longer a talent the next: my natural strength, for instance, may no longer command a premium in the market because a new piece of machinery can do the work of ten men at half of what it formerly cost to pay one. In other words, natural talents can and do cease to be talents for reasons that have nothing to do with the workings of nature and everything to do with social decisions. I am not disputing here that natural talents have some sort of independent existence as facts about the world. What I am claiming that we cannot make the move from identifying something as an independent fact about the world to classifying as a talent without interposing the notion of social value.

So much for the idea of *natural* talents. What of the thought that there exists a distribution of these things and that this distribution is morally arbitrary? To claim of natural talents that they are *distributed* is to invite three broad objections. The first holds that we cannot claim of something that it is distributed without at the same time believing there to be a distributor, namely an agent or agency *doing* the distributing.[2] In the case of welfare benefits or university places it is clear enough that there does indeed exist a distributor of the required kind. In the case of the supposed distribution of natural talents, however, the question arises as to whom or what the distributor should be taken to be—and indeed of whether it makes sense to speak of there being such a thing.[3]

For the record, I do not see that it *is* an analytical truth about distributions that they can only be such where there exists a clearly identifiable distributor. And even if it were so, it might still be open to philosophical egalitarians to preserve the content of the claim that some enjoy greater natural talents than others but to recast it in a form that saw off objections to that claim—for instance, by holding there to be a *spread* of natural talents rather than a distribution of them *per se*. I say that this possibility *might* still be open to egalitarians because there is a second doubt about talk of a natural distribution, one that has nothing to do with analytical claims about distributions and distributors. This doubt says that it is simply misleading to imagine that distributions of things somehow inhere in nature. Of course, there is a trivial sense in which this doubt has force, namely, that distributions are categories that we impose upon the material world so as to order and make sense of it. From the crude thought that mountains and oceans have to them some sort of tangible reality and independent existence it is clearly a long way to the further thought that these things lie naturally together along a scale that allows us to compare them and to speak of a *distribution* of mountain heights and ocean depths. Nature, after all, does not distribute anything: distributions are intangibles that we project into the world according to our categories of more and less, similar and different, height and weight. Distributions are constructed out of these categories, categories that tell us which cluster of facts to group together and what common scale to apply to them.

The doubt hanging over claims about the distribution of natural talents is not, however, the trivial one I have just been describing. It is not a doubt over whether the idea of such a distribution can be defended only through assuming it to be part of the furniture of the universe. Instead, the doubt centres over whether talk of such a distribution is so infected with imprecision as to be distracting. Often enough, appeal is made to the idea of a distribution of natural talents in order to capture the idea of natural human diversity—the idea, that is, that some are beautiful and others ugly, some fat and others thin, some tall and others short, and so on. But being beautiful or being tall is not, in and of itself, *a talent*, any more than is the inequality in height between the tall and the short an inequality *in talent*, any more than is the difference between the beautiful and the ugly in *inequality* of any kind. I do not mean that, in these examples, the relevant descriptions and comparisons are being applied to things other than independent facts nor that we lack a common scale in comparing these facts. Indeed, I have already said that natural talents *are* independent facts about individuals. They are, however, facts conceptualized in a quite specific way: natural talents are facts about individuals whose status as natural *talents* is a function of their having social value. From this it not only follows, as I suggested earlier, that something cannot be a natural talent unless it commands social value. It seems also to follow that there are degrees of natural talent, properly so called, only to the extent that there are degrees of corresponding social value. Indeed, it is not at all clear how we can completely separate claims about the distribution of natural talent from claims about the distribution of its associated social value.[4] Again, let me emphasize that I am not out to deny that there are natural *differences* between people. What I do want to cast doubt over is whether such differences can, except by presupposing some facts about which aptitudes are valued and to what extent, be redescribed in the language of inequalities and distributions. If they cannot, then it is not simply that what *counts* as a natural talent one day may not, as a result of changes in social valuation, count as a natural talent the next. It is also that the distribution of natural talents can vary from one day to the next, again according to shifts in the relevant social valuations. This suggests, in turn, that we should stop thinking of talents and their distribution as something fixed in nature in the way of mountains and oceans and start thinking of them as incorporating the capriciousness and fluidity of the process by which social value is ascribed to some things but not to others.

This brings me to the third objection in the matter of the claimed distribution of natural talents. Distributions standardly, if not analytically, involve a distributor, a distributed, and a distributee. If we take as an example the distribution of welfare benefits in Britain, it is clear enough who or what attracts these descriptions. The distributor is the Department of Social Security, the distributed is the department's annual budget, and the distributees are the claimants. The example of welfare benefits might be extended into other areas of social distribution, relating for instance to the distribution of educational opportunities. The question I want now to consider is whether the natural distribution is possessed of the same formal properties as the social distributions I have been describing. Putting to one side the issue of who or what the distributor should be taken to be—an issue I have dealt with already—it seems clear that there exists a further disanalogy between the natural distribution and these social distributions. This disanalogy arises from the fact that, in the case of the natural distribution, the distributed and the distributee are indistinguishable—or, at least, indistinguishable unless we make some ambitious metaphysical claims about the person. On the ordinary view of the person, the distributee—the person—is part constituted by what is being distributed—namely, talents and aptitudes. This is plainly not something that can be said of the distribution of social advantages such as opportunities and money.

The significance of this disanalogy comes into sharper relief when we recall that those who speak of a natural distribution are commonly given to describe that distribution as *arbitrary* or a *lottery*. Quite what is meant in applying the charge of arbitrariness to the natural distribution is something I examine below. In the meantime, let me point to some of the oddities to which the image of a natural lottery gives rise. That image seems to encourage us to think of our physical and mental constitution as analogous to the outcome of a game of chance. According to this view, it is a matter of chance that my physical and mental constitution should be of one kind and yours of another. Had the workings of chance been other than they were—and, it being chance, they might have been—then I might have had your constitution and you might have had mine. But does not this just imply that, had chance worked other than in the way that it did, I might have been you and you might have been me? We might, I suppose, be able to make sense of this idea were we to join Plato in believing that a pre-existent human soul enters the body at birth and leaves it at death, a view that fits nicely with the image of our entering a lottery before birth and of our finding out at birth whether or not we have hit the jackpot in the matter of our mental and physical constitution. If, however, that is not our view of what it is that makes me *me* and you *you*, then we may have to contemplate abandoning the image of a natural lottery altogether.[5] Presumably, there *does* come a point where we have to demarcate the subject matter of our enquiry and to indicate where the person ends and where his social world begins: claims about who should get what certainly seem to presuppose that the *what* of the enquiry should occupy a conceptual space distinct from that of the *who*.

Let me concede here that I may be wrong in thinking that claims about the natural lottery are *necessarily* bound up with the sort of exotic metaphysics I have been describing—and indeed with any kind of psychological thesis about the constitutive materials of the human personality. Perhaps when Rawls and others recoil from the thought of benefits and burdens being distributed on the basis of natural differences between people they do so out of a more everyday belief that the workings of nature are random and primitive. On this view, the fact that some are born beautiful and others ugly is simply a matter of how the genetic chips happen to fall. There is no good reason for their having fallen one way rather than another and no good reason (therefore) why we should make appeal to these natural facts in deciding who should get what. This intuition—and it is one that I opt to associate with Rawls—seems to be a powerful one. Indeed, it is reflected in everyday language such as when it is said, in criticism, that the distribution of a particular good—such as employment or educational opportunities—is 'simply a lottery'.

Having said this, I think that there is an altogether different way we might respond to the idea of goods being distributed on the basis of a lottery or its equivalent, one which also accords with our everyday beliefs and indeed which is appealed to by Rawls himself. Rawls cites gambling—which we may count as a lottery equivalent—as an example of what he calls 'pure procedural justice'.[6] Here it is precisely because the process in question *is* random that its outcome qualifies to be regarded as, in Rawls's words, 'not unjust'—provided that all the participants in the lottery have an equal chance of winning under it. Similarly, there are numerous examples in everyday life where we think that the right way to decide who should get what is to draw lots or pick a card at random. It is precisely the randomness of the process that renders it immune to the charge of bias. Chance is impartial—we each of us stand equal before it. So, we seem to hold lotteries and their equivalents to be subversive of distributive rectitude in some cases and definitive of distributive rectitude in others—and it is claims about the propriety of deferring to randomness that support these diametrically opposed positions.

Thus, critics of Rawls, such as David Gauthier, can claim it to be at the very least an open question whether deferring to the natural lottery does indeed offend against ordinary principles of justice. After all, since nature does not single out in advance who is to be talented or untalented—since, that is, nature is blind—it would seem to be no more objectionable to defer to the natural lottery than it is to defer to a lottery of any other kind. As determinants of who should get what, either we should repudiate both or we should repudiate neither. What we cannot do, on this view, is repudiate one but not the other.[7]

This argument does seem to me vulnerable to counter-objections, but it also seems to highlight an ambiguity in the egalitarian position. The counter-objections are threefold. First, we often resort to chance where we have no alternative but to distribute a particular good to some but not to others: we have, that is, to decide how a good that is scarce or indivisible (or both) is to be unequally distributed and lotteries provide one means of doing so. In respect of the distribution of the social product, however, there is no such necessity. The issue is not one of *how* the social product is to be unequally distributed but *whether* it is. Second, there exists an important difference between a lottery one (voluntarily) enters in to and a lottery one is (involuntarily) entered in for. What legitimates the outcome of the lottery in the first case is, in part, the element of voluntariness absent from the second. This suggests to me that the intuition at work is to some extent an intuition about the legitimating role of voluntariness rather than merely one about the moral acceptability of random distribution. Voluntary participation, in short, is a necessary condition of regarding the outcome of a lottery as binding—and it is precisely the element of voluntariness that is absent from the *natural* lottery. Third, it seems obvious that we find it intuitively appealing to defer to chance only in those cases where there exists no other criterion for assessing the claims of different individuals or where the claims of such individuals are, in all relevant respects, identical. But this is precisely what Rawls and others would claim does *not* hold true in respect of issues of distributive justice. On their view, there exists a powerful case against translating natural differences into inequalities in social goods.

Perhaps, however, the image of a natural lottery is intended and recognized to be precisely that—an *image* or metaphor. As if to bear this out, I note that Rawls for one is more disposed to describe the natural distribution as *morally arbitrary* than he is to describe it as a lottery. The invocation of arbitrariness in this context may, however, be more distracting than revealing. It may be distracting because it leads us towards the thought there is something about the distribution of natural talents, as a basis of unequal reward, that marks it out from other sorts of distribution to which we might take exception. It makes us think, that is, that natural differences are not just one objectionable baseline, or set of initial circumstances, from which claims to unequal reward might be launched. It makes us think that there is something *peculiarly* objectionable, not to say reprehensible, in allowing free play to natural differences, something that is not present where free play is allowed to social differences between individuals. I do not say that this is Rawls's intention, merely that the appeal to arbitrariness tempts us down this path. As it is, we owe to both Robert Nozick and Thomas Nagel the thought that claiming of the distribution of natural talents that it is *morally arbitrary* might mean one of two things.[8] It might mean, non-pejoratively, that the natural distribution is possessed of no intrinsic moral weight or force. Or it might mean, pejoratively, that there is something morally pernicious about the natural distribution.[9]

Let me begin with the first, non-pejorative, view. If we adopt this view, we will believe that in determining who should get what, we have no reason, morally speaking, to defer to the distribution of natural talents just as we have no reason, morally speaking, to defer to the pattern of clouds in the sky. The more talented cannot hold themselves to have a stronger moral claim upon the social product that the less talented simply by virtue of being more talented. Certainly they cannot claim to *deserve* a greater share of the social product by virtue of their superior talents, for that would be to endow the natural distribution with precisely the intrinsic moral force that the first view refuses to confer upon it. As such, claims of desert grounded in differences in natural talents are morally impermissible.

On the view I am describing, there are no moral reasons, such as reasons of desert, for conferring greater social rewards upon the more talented by virtue of their being the more talented. Strictly speaking, the distribution of natural talents is *irrelevant* to the issue of who should get what in terms of social benefits and burdens. But note that this argument does not altogether extract us from the ambiguity I have just been describing. To claim that we have no moral reason to defer to the distribution of natural talents is not thereby to claim that we have some moral reason *not* to defer to that distribution. We can grant that there are no moral reasons for distributing social goods unequally on the basis of differences in natural talents without thereby granting that there are moral reasons for *not* distributing them on that basis. What the non-pejorative view does is to render inadmissible certain kinds of claim to unequal distributive reward, paradigmatically claims that hold differences in natural talent to be in some sense deserved. What the non-pejorative view does not do is establish that any and all social inequalities arising from the natural distribution are *ipso facto* pernicious.

On the second view I am concerned with, the distribution of natural talents is not morally irrelevant, as it is on the first view, to the question of who should get what. In distributing social goods we should not be blind to the natural distribution. This is because there is a clear sense in which the social distribution should track the natural one: there should be some measure of fit between the two. However, the tracking in question is not of the kind that we would associate with the sort of desert theory I identified earlier, according to which the more talented deserve greater social benefits than the less talented. Indeed, the tracking works the other way: those with fewer natural talents have a stronger claim to social benefits than those with greater natural talents. This is so for precisely the reason that the spread of natural talents is pernicious. In claiming of the natural distribution that it is arbitrary we are not therefore claiming that it should, for distributive purposes, be ignored. Instead, we are claiming that it should be corrected for: we have positive moral reasons to undo nature's work rather than simply to ignore it.

Although this second view of the moral status of the natural distribution is often deployed by those hostile to the desert account—or, at least, a certain conception of it—it is also true that it overlaps with the desert account in a way that the first view does not. Proponents of the second view agree with desert theorists that individuals are owed certain forms of treatment by virtue of their place within the natural hierarchy. In this sense, and to this extent, they go along with desert theorists in holding the natural distribution to be possessed of intrinsic moral weight. Indeed, their aim is not so much to *subvert* the claims of desert theory as to *invert* them. Whereas certain desert theorists might think that the more talented are owed greater social reward than the less talented by virtue of being more talented, those who view the natural distribution in a pejorative light claim that the less talented are owed greater social reward than the more talented by virtue of being less talented.

Which of these two views best captures the egalitarian's intuitions as to the moral arbitrariness of the distribution of natural talents? The drawback of the first view is that it stops short of providing egalitarians with what they seemingly want, namely, out and out condemnation of an allocation of social goods that in some way tracks natural differences between individuals. By this I do not mean that this first view cannot be marshalled in the service of such condemnation. Indeed, there is a sense in which the non-pejorative view depends for its prescriptive force on being conjoined to other commitments to which egalitarians such as Rawls subscribe: the non-pejorative view receives something of a unfair press in being isolated from those commitments. Once we make those commitments explicit, we can begin to see that to claim of the natural distribution that it is not pernicious, in and of itself, is not thereby to deny that it would be pernicious to allow, unquestioningly, the allocation of social benefits and burdens to be affected by our place within the natural hierarchy. The first view, in short, does not exclude talk of perniciousness in the matter of the natural distribution. What it does do is direct—or, more precisely perhaps, displace—the charge of perniciousness away from the working of nature and towards the workings of *social institutions*. According to the first view, there is nothing pernicious about the natural distribution *per se*. Indeed, as Rawls makes clear, the natural distribution is neither just nor unjust—it is simply a fact of nature.[10] Questions of justice and injustice—and of perniciousness—arise in respect of the way that social institutions *respond* to these natural facts, not in respect of the facts themselves. Were social institutions to defer, unquestioningly, to the natural distribution, then that would indeed be pernicious on their part, for it would mean that those institutions were failing in their task of applying the relevant test of justice to social distributions. And they would be failing in this task because it is a requirement of justice, on this account, that such institutions distinguish in their treatment of individuals only where there exist relevant reasons for doing so. As I suggested in Chapter 1, for a reason to be a relevant reason in this context it is not enough that it should not be irrelevant. Inequalities, being the kinds of things that they are, require *justification* and it is precisely this justification that egalitarians who adopt the first interpretation of the moral arbitrariness argument might want to withhold from natural talents. They might want to claim that there are *no* justifying moral reasons—and certainly no justifying moral reasons grounded in considerations of desert—to confer greater social rewards upon the more talented over the less talented merely because they *are* the more talented.

If the first, non-pejorative, view of the natural distribution can be, and stan-dardly is, deployed by egalitarians in order to call into question the accept-ability of distributing social burdens and benefits on the basis of differential talents, why should this not be enough to satisfy proponents of the second, pejorative, view of the natural distribution? Is the point of dispute between the two views essentially *rhetorical* in character? The answer to the second question is, I think, no. It is not that proponents of the two views agree on a conclusion but disagree on its premises, for it is not simply that proponents of the second view are bolder in their characterization of the natural distri-bution than proponents of the first view. Those who hold the natural distri-bution to be arbitrary in a pejorative sense think that it is not enough to ignore natural differences in deciding who should get what. Instead, they think that we are required in the name of justice to do something to put those differ-ences right. We are required, that is, to rectify or mitigate natural differences, for instance through offering compensation of some kind to those with fewer natural talents than others.

In other words, there exists amongst philosophical egalitarians an impor-tant division concerning the extent to which justice requires us to eliminate the unequal effects of natural differences between individuals. For Rawls and Nagel, the demands of justice do not extend *all the way down*. Nagel takes the claim that the distribution of natural talents is morally arbitrary to be syn-onymous with—or an entailment of—the claim that natural differences are differences for which individuals are not responsible. From there, he argues that

[a]ny advantage to the better off at no cost to the worse off is all to the good, even if it is due to causes for which the recipients are not responsible. This seems to me the only correct view to take of inequalities that arise naturally. For example, there can be no possible objection to some people's naturally enjoying immunity to certain dis-eases or perfect health or sunny dispositions, even though this makes them much better off than those who are constitutionally sick or depressed.[11]

This statement seems difficult, however, to square with others that Nagel offers. Elsewhere, for instance, he writes that

[a] society that permits significant inequalities among its members, in advantages and disadvantages for which they are not responsible, will be perceived as failing to treat them equally: it distinguishes in its treatment of them along morally arbitrary lines.[12]

Having acknowledged that superior natural health and the like are indeed 'advantages'—and that inequalities in advantages of this kind are 'due to causes for which the recipients are not responsible' and (therefore) morally arbitrary bases of unequal distribution on that count—Nagel has to explain why some morally arbitrary facts about individuals may legitimately in-fluence how well off they are relative to others and others not. If my sunny disposition is as arbitrary a fact about me as my talent as a singer, what possible objection to the latter making me better off than others would not also apply to the former? Nagel's answer to this is to say that the moral conception with which he is concerned is one which relates

to equality of treatment rather than impartial concern for well-being. It applies to inequalities generated by the social system rather than inequality in general.[13]

So it is, in respect of those possessed of sunny dispositions or rude good health

[b]etter is simply better in such cases because no inequality of treatment is implied. But once social mechanisms enter into the causation of a benefit its unequal distribution becomes a form of unequal treatment by the society of its members, and the sense of unfairness makes its appearance.[14]

Thus, on Nagel's account, social mechanisms do not cause or generate the natural benefits that come a person's way by virtue of his particular internal constitution. This is true not simply of health and happiness but of the internal benefits deriving from natural talents since (differences in) talents, according to Nagel, are not 'socially created'. Such natural blessings, and their attendant satisfactions, lie outside the scope of social mechanisms in the sense that they have not been brought about through their operation. These mechanisms do, however, cause or generate—or can be regarded as causing or generating—the external or social benefits that come a person's way in the form of advantages and disadvantages. These advantages and disadvantages include more than income or wealth, but they none the less share with income something of their external character.

For Nagel, then, egalitarians must concern themselves with the external dimension and see to it that *social* goods are not distributed unequally on the basis of factors that are arbitrary from the moral point of view. The congenitally talented or healthy may legitimately derive what internal satisfaction they can from their natural attributes, even though the distribution of those attributes is morally arbitrary. They have, that is, a claim to the internal product of their natural attributes. But they have no such claim to the (external) social product by virtue of these attributes.

Once we recognize that the concern of egalitarians, such as Nagel and Rawls, is not to *eliminate* natural differences between individuals but, instead, to deny that such differences constitute a proper basis of unequal distributive reward, we can see that John Gray is quite wrong to claim that '[i]t has never been explained satisfactorily by egalitarians why [the abilities and talents we receive via the genetic lottery] should not be subject to redistribution' just as he is quite wrong to claim that '[t]here is nothing in egalitarian morality that can in principle rule out'[15] the forcible transfer of body parts. It should be obvious from what I have said already that egalitarians do not need to invoke the value of bodily integrity in order to meet Gray's objection, for there is nothing in the egalitarian case *demanding* a biological adjustment of the population, whether in pursuit of the unspecified notion of equality of well-being Gray attributes to egalitarians or not. As we have seen, there may be a sense in which egalitarians are concerned to undo nature's work, but it is not the sense that Gray identifies. Indeed, it is difficult to see against which brand of egalitarianism, if any, Gray's argument is telling.[16]

Having said this, Nagel's line of argument is vulnerable to two broad objections. The first concerns its emphasis on the favourably endowed. Nagel thinks it unobjectionable that those blessed by nature should enjoy greater well-being than others: recall here his claim that 'better is simply better in such cases because no inequality of treatment is implied'. But now let us imagine that we are addressing those who fare badly in the natural distribution. Would we want to say *to them* that 'worse is simply worse in such cases'? The point here is that the appeal of Nagel's argument may be asymmetrical. To say that we should not begrudge the better-endowed the (internal) benefits of their superior talents does not commit us to the view that we should be indifferent to the (internal) disbenefits suffered by those of inferior talent.

Nagel makes great play of the role played by social mechanisms in the causation of benefits. But this leads to the second objection to his position, for the fact that social mechanisms do not cause benefits would not, on Nagel's own principles of negative responsibility, seem to entail that we should be indifferent to these (internal) benefits in the distribution of the social product.[17] If Bill derives significantly greater well-being from his bundle of social goods than does Anne from her bundle of the same size, then there seems to be at least a prima-facie case for considering the satisfactoriness or otherwise of the nominal equality that obtains between the two. Clearly, such comparisons are fraught with difficulties, not least those associated with how we measure people's well-being or capacity. But if external resources are not to be regarded merely as an end in themselves, then comparisons of what it is that people can get out of, or are able to do with, their resources seems unavoidable. To say that the extra *internal* benefits that come the way of the fortunately endowed can be excluded from the calculation, on the basis that they are not socially caused, seems too weak a position for Nagel to adopt.

This is especially so if we consider a third objection to this sort of approach, namely, that it appears to violate the non-responsibility condition that Nagel takes as a centrepiece of his egalitarian scheme. Imagine it so happens that I am more efficient than you at converting resources into inner satisfaction. Given that neither of us is, in this case, *responsible* for the efficiency with which we convert our resources, it seems curious that the egalitarian principle should be indifferent to the inequalities in inner satisfaction that arise between us as a result. Of course, there may be practical reasons why inequalities of this kind will prove difficult to address. But Nagel's is an argument from principle. True enough, he believes that the greater inner satisfaction enjoyed by the fortunately endowed is acceptable (only) to the extent that it involves 'no cost to the worse off'. But the notion of *cost* being appealed to here is obscure. Is it always the case that my greater efficiency at converting external resources into inner satisfaction *costs* you nothing or is it only sometimes so? Presumably, whether a given inequality is seen as costing someone something will turn on a view about what sorts of inequalities are and are not the proper concern of justice in the first place. What Nagel seems to be doing is assuming such a view rather than defending it.

In support, however, of the position advanced by Rawls and Nagel, it seems clear that their distributive schemes do not stand or fall on the basis of whether they permit inequalities between people to arise along *some* dimension. Their concern is to devise a distributive scheme that treats citizens as equals in the sense that it does not dispense *social* advantages and disadvantages along morally arbitrary lines. It is no part of their concern to render individuals equal in each and every respect we can think of—logical impossibility that that may be. On the view I am describing, inequalities in the inner satisfaction with which our natural endowments furnish us with are not *social* inequalities at all: they are inequalities that obtain between persons *qua* individuals rather than *qua* citizens.[18] This means that the charge against Rawls and Nagel that they illegitimately permit inequalities in inner satisfaction to arise from differences in natural endowments is telling only if one supposes that the purpose of their distributive schemes is to promote some sort of welfarism. But I said before that this is precisely what Rawls in particular denies. Indeed, his appeal to the limits of the political and the practicable is intended to show why we should eschew an account of justice that judges individual well-being in terms of claims about inner satisfaction. As I have suggested already, Rawls is not out to correct for the unequal effects of nature in the sense of redressing those effects whatever they might be. He believes instead that natural differences should be *ignored*, rather than corrected for, when it comes to deciding how social advantages and disadvantages are to be distributed.[19]

I have said, then, that philosophical egalitarians are committed to the idea that inequalities in social goods should not replicate natural differences—at least not without some sort of further defence of the kind that Rawls's Difference Principle supplies. Given this commitment, and given that *laissez-faire* seems to allow free play to natural differences, it seems to follow that egalitarians must reject *laissez-faire*. But this does no more than prepare the way for thinking about the sort of distributive mechanism that egalitarians believe ought to take the place of *laissez-faire*. The temptation here is to assume that egalitarians should favour some sort of market mechanism, albeit one modified to filter out natural differences of the kind I have been discussing. But the assumption is unwarranted, for it is not clear why egalitarians should want to privilege the market mechanism at all, at least on the grounds of justice rather than efficiency. Indeed, any presumption in favour of the market mechanism would imply that in devising distributive rules our task is that of adjusting the market in order to render it more equitable rather than of questioning its underlying operation. But if the market system has a propensity to produce outcomes that egalitarians find objectionable by the lights of their more general commitments, then perhaps mere adjustment is not enough or, at least, the scale of adjustment required in the name of justice will be such as to render the chosen distributive mechanism unrecognizable as a *market* mechanism at all.

Are there reasons why egalitarians should be approving or suspicious of market outcomes *per se*? Some egalitarians are what we might call contingently suspicious of market outcomes: they are suspicious of market outcomes *given* the world as it is now. And they are suspicious of market outcomes given the *world as it is now* because they believe natural talents to be unevenly spread across the population. Given this uneven spread, given the connection between productive capacity and natural talent, and given that markets dispense rewards according to productive capacity, we have good reason to suppose that inequalities in market rewards will in some way track inequalities in natural endowment. Since natural inequalities are, on the egalitarian account, arbitrary, we will then have good reason to worry that inequalities in market rewards are also contaminated by this arbitrariness.

Nagel is, seemingly, an egalitarian of this stripe. He wants to rule out productive contribution as the primary basis of distributive reward. On his account:

The defence of equality requires that rewards not depend on productive contribution, and in particular that some people receive much more of the social product than they contribute.[20]

Now, it may seem obvious why Nagel should want to sever the link between productive contribution and reward. On his account, how well or badly we do in life ought not to depend on the natural differences between us. From this commitment it seems to follow that how well or badly we do in life ought not to depend on derivative differences in the productive contributions we are able to make within the margins of a competitive economy. Two passages in particular lend credence to this interpretation of Negel's position. At one point he says:

maintenance of a system which allows rewards to be proportional to productivity would have to be regarded as a social choice to permit rewards to depend substantially on differences in natural talent, education and background.[21]

Since these three factors are, for Nagel, arbitrary causes of socio-economic inequality it follows that any distribution grounded upon them would likewise fall to be regarded as arbitrary. Elsewhere, Nagel makes this point more explicitly still, when he says:

[if] the distribution of rewards is too strongly proportional to the natural or social accidents of birth, then the society must be regarded as having chosen to permit the distribution of benefits on morally irrelevant grounds.[22]

I have claimed, then, that Nagel is contingently suspicious of market outcomes. He is suspicious of market outcomes because he has assumed that natural talents are spread unevenly across the population. He has further assumed that market outcomes—and, in particular, market-induced inequalities in social goods—tend to track these differences. This thought is a powerful one. We know, for instance, that the healthy and the beautiful and the clever tend to do better under market systems than the sickly and the ugly and the stupid—and there does seem to be something troubling about any *system* of allocation that allows these sorts of brute facts about individuals to have such a profound impact on the quality of their lives. But imagine now that things evolve in such a way that the sorts of natural differences I have been describing more or less disappear from the scene. No longer are some much more healthy or beautiful or clever than others. Imagine further that many of the deep social differences we see around us disappear also. No longer are individuals confronted by very different levels of opportunities or resources. In these circumstances, should our suspicions about the moral status of market outcomes disappear? Can we now be satisfied that market inequalities are unobjectionable?

Nagel, for one, equivocates in his answer to these questions. In a revealing argument, he claims that

[t]he advantages due to talent are not handed out as a reward for high scores on tests: they come as a result of demand for scarce resources in a competitive economy.[23]

This analogy engages a rather different set of intuitions from those canvassed earlier. Here, the worry is not that individuals bring to the market place a set of brute facts over which, in principle, they have no control and that the market dispenses rewards according to those brute facts. Instead, the worry seems to be about the desirability of the rewarding mechanism itself. Leaving aside any doubts about the uneven spread of natural talents, market rewards cannot be regarded as *rewarding* those talents in the way that academic prizes reward the successful student. The stamp of approval present in the latter is nowhere present in the former because market rewards do not match individual talents in the sense in which academic prizes match intellectual excellence.

All of which seems to return us to the difficulty I identified earlier, namely, the difficulty of separating claims about natural talents and their distribution from claims about social value and its distribution. The temptation is to conceive of *nature* as a lottery or a casino, and as imprisoning human individuals within circumstances over which they have no control—such as the circumstances of being ugly in a society that worships only beauty, or of being sickly in a society that employs only those who enjoy good health. As I have suggested already, however, the natural distribution is not a brute fact about the world but a social fact. Indeed, were there to be no variations in social value—were we all to have claims to identical bundles of social goods regardless of our aptitudes and circumstances—it would seem that we would have to dispense with all talk of there *being* an unequal distribution of natural talents. Human difference and diversity would, of course, remain—but the presence of natural diversity is compatible with the absence of (unequal) natural talent.

Having suggested, then, that Nagel is contingently suspicious of market outcomes—namely, he is suspicious of such outcomes because of certain assumptions he makes concerning the current spread of natural differences—I must now propose that his attitude to markets may be more hostile than I had originally thought. Nagel, that is, my be *intrinsically* suspicious of market outcomes. He may think that markets, in and of themselves, disrupt the demands of fairness in distribution. Perhaps, moreover, he is not alone in adopting this view. Consider, for instance, the following passage from Rawls's *A Theory of Justice*:

in determining wages a competitive economy gives weight to the precept of contribution. But as we have seen, the extent of one's contribution (estimated by one's marginal productivity) depends upon supply and demand. Surely a person's moral worth does not vary according to how many offer similar skills, or happen to want what he can produce. No one supposes that when someone's abilities are less in demand or have deteriorated (as in the case of singers) his moral deservingness undergoes a similar shift. All of this is perfectly obvious and has long been agreed to. It simply *reflects the fact* . . . that it is one of the fixed points of our moral judgements that no one deserves his place in the distribution of natural assets any more than he deserves his starting place in society.[24]

Let us focus here on what it is that Rawls takes to be morally objectionable about the facts under description and why it is he should characterize the distribution of natural talents as morally arbitrary. Most obviously, Rawls is out to undermine the idea that we *deserve* rewards by virtue of our natural endowments or that some deserve to be blessed by nature whilst others do not. On this point, he is on strong ground because it really would be odd to speak of individuals *deserving* to be naturally gifted. But, on Rawls's view, it is not just that we do not deserve to have whatever good or bad fortune nature throws our way. It is that we do not deserve another kind of good or bad fortune, namely, the good or bad fortune that comes our way through (sudden) shifts in the market price attaching to our skills. It is quite consistent, however, to think that fluctuations in the market rate for any given set of skills—and (relatedly) fluctuations in the number of other individuals who have similar skills to sell—are matters for which individuals cannot be credited or faulted *without* thereby subscribing to the view that the fact that some have these skills and others do not is a matter for which those concerned cannot be credited or faulted. The question of whether it is a matter of luck that I have the skills I do is separate from the question of whether it is a matter of luck that those skills happen to command a high or low price at any given time.

Return to Rawls's example of singers. Even if we were to allow that singing abilities are *equally* distributed across the population—or, at least, to allow that it is no more difficult for one person to be a singer than it is for any other—we might still want to say that variations in the *rewards* attached to singing under *laissez-faire* are not a matter for which those concerned can be credited or faulted. To say that the operation of supply and demand is such that, on some occasions, my being a singer brings me a higher than average wage and on others a lower than average one is not at all to say that it is down to luck that I came to be a singer in the first place and that I remain such. It is the *rewards* for my skills that are subject to what is, from my perspective, variable luck rather than my *possession* of those skills—the issue of whether I am lucky to have the talents I do is quite separate from the issue of whether I am lucky that they happen to be marketable. Thus to claim that I cannot be credited or faulted for variations in the preferences and tastes of others, as they bear upon the value that is attached to my particular skills, is not the same as claiming that I cannot be credited or faulted for having those skills in the first place. It may be objectionable that my life chances should be tied so closely to the preferences and tastes of others, over which I have no control. But what is objectionable here consists, partly at least, in factors external to me—namely, the talents and preferences of others, rather than in factors internal to me—namely, my own talents and preferences.

Perhaps it could be countered at this stage that the distinction between the internal and external dimensions of talent is irrelevant, or false, or true but only trivially so. After all, I have already said on several occasions that a talent is only a talent to the extent that it is a productive capacity that is externally valued—valued, that is, by others. The arbitrariness of the external dimension is built into the definition of why it is that the distribution of talents is deemed to be arbitrary from the internal point of view. But even if the two dimensions are not easily separable they are none the less separate. To say that supply is ignorant of demand—such that there exists a strong element of chance in determining what level of demand will attach to a particular supply at any given time—is not therefore to say that the content of supply is a matter of chance. This being so, Rawls seems to be alerting us to two different kinds of arbitrariness as they pertain to questions of distribution. One is the arbitrariness present in the market pricing mechanism. The other is the arbitrariness present in the spread of natural differences. The important thing is not to move between these two views of the source of arbitrariness and to attribute to nature the capriciousness and unpredictability that we find in market systems. One can believe that the market pricing mechanism gives rise to objectionable outcomes without making any assumptions about the spread and moral standing of natural differences. The two issues are distinct and the assumptions that Rawls makes about the one do not necessarily generate his conclusions about the other.

Ronald Dworkin, for his part, appears (perhaps inadvertently) to hint at precisely this distinction in his own discussion of the market:

a liberal cannot . . . accept the market results as defining equal shares. His theory of economic justice must be complex, because he accepts two principles which are difficult to hold in the administration of a dynamic economy. The first requires that people have, at any point in their lives, different amounts of wealth in so far as the genuine choices they have been made have been more or less expensive or beneficial to the community, measured by what other people want for their lives. The second requires that people not have different amounts of wealth just because they have different inherent capacities *to produce what others want*, or are differently favoured by chance.[25]

Note here that the force of the second proposition—that people's shares ought not to be unequal by virtue of their different inherent capacities 'to produce what others want'—is little diminished if one reworks it into the balder claim that it is objectionable that *what others want* should play such a important part in determining what I in fact have. And it is objectionable because what others want is often a matter over which I can have no direct or long-standing control.

Dworkin does not, however, share Nagel's suspicions about the market or, at least, he does not fear that market outcomes may be intrinsically objectionable. Quite the opposite. Dworkin believes that markets are *indispensable* to the realization of egalitarian justice:

the idea of an economic market, as a device for setting prices for a vast variety of goods and services, must be at the center of any attractive theoretical development of equality of resources.[26]

A market, on Dworkin's account, is structurally analogous to an auction: it is the most effective means available for registering and transmitting, to those participating in it, information about the demand for different goods and services. That is, it is a means of registering the opportunity costs of different goods and services and it is the notion of opportunity costs that lies at the heart of Dworkinian ideal equality:

ideal distribution is achieved only when the resources different people control are equal in the *opportunity costs* of those resources, that is, the value they would have in the hands of other people.[27]

Were natural talents, as well as more occasional forms of luck, to be evenly spread across the population as a whole, then we would have no cause to question the moral status of market outcomes. Indeed, we would have good reason to believe that those outcomes not merely conformed to, but in fact expressed, the requirements of egalitarian justice.

So, Dworkin believes that, in the name of equality, the stock of goods at any given individual's disposal should reflect the opportunity cost(s) of those goods to others: it should be contingent upon the extent to which those (particular) goods are in demand by others. On this view, each must pay the price of his lifestyle, as measured by the price that others would be prepared to pay for that same lifestyle, against the background of an (initially) equal division of resources. Not to do this would be to double count the claims of some—namely, those with a taste for goods that are in high demand—at the expense of others—namely, those with a taste for goods that are correspondingly less attractive to others. It would be to violate the dictum that each should be treated with equal concern and respect by the relevant distributive agencies.

This commitment seems difficult to square, however, with Dworkin's objection to welfare-oriented theories of distributive justice. Dworkin is attracted to an egalitarianism focused on *resources* precisely because he believes it to represent a conception of justice that can secure for individuals a distributive share that is immune to incursions arising from the shifting and expanding preferences and tastes of others. Welfare egalitarianism, claims Dworkin, is unable to yield the distributive security that a firmly anchored account of fair shares demands. On Dworkin's reading of the welfarist account, the stock of goods made available to each will *necessarily* be tied to the tastes and preferences of others and to the level of goods required to satisfy their needs. In other words, the defect of welfarist accounts is precisely that they make the stock of goods available to each contingent upon the tastes and preferences of others. That is why Dworkin emphasizes that, under his own scheme, the (equal) stock of goods available to each is 'properly theirs' and '*morally*, mine'.[28]

But these two commitments—the commitment to a market scheme in which the resource holdings of each *are* contingent upon the tastes and preferences of others and the commitment to an anti-welfarist scheme in which the resource holdings of each are *not* so contingent—seem to pull in different directions. This point is well made by David Miller, who argues that changes in (aggregate) preferences and tastes will tend to enhance or diminish the value of any given individual's resource bundle even though the tastes and preferences of the individual(s) in question have remained constant.[29] Indeed, it seems that Dworkin permits the *market* to undertake precisely the taste or preference-led (re)distributions that he would otherwise want to prohibit the *state* from undertaking.

So, as with Nagel and Rawls, we are left with doubts about the moral status of market outcomes and, more pertinently, doubts about whether an egalitarian who is otherwise committed to the sanctity of individual responsibility can condone market outcomes even in cases where there is no suggestion that differences in natural endowments are at work. The thought that how individuals fare in life should be tied to their choices and decisions is not easy to square with the idea of their living in a world that does not so much insulate them from the capriciousness of nature as replicate that capriciousness in social form. It cannot, for instance, plausibly be argued that the demands of choice and control are well served by the violent upheavals and fluctuations we have witnessed in Britain over recent years in terms of salaries and the price of housing. I am not suggesting this is enough to show that the market is unjustified *all things considered*, merely that it seems to come at a price that egalitarians sympathetic to the claims of individual responsibility should find troubling. It is no answer to these doubts to claim, as Dworkin sometimes appears to, that any outcome that is itself the result of innumerable innocent choices qualifies to be regarded as a *chosen* outcome, and therefore unobjectionable on that account: that is merely to repeat the dubious reasoning present in the thought that if an outcome comes about through just steps then that is enough to make it a *just* outcome.[30]

Recall that my concern in this chapter has been to examine the stance adopted by philosophical egalitarians towards natural differences between people. To this end, I have said that egalitarians trade on two intuitively powerful ideas. One is that there exists a distribution of natural talents. The other is that this distribution ought not to dictate how we fare in life. I have suggested, however, that there are deep ambiguities in claiming of something that it is *a talent* and indeed in holding such talents to be *distributed*. I have suggested also that we might be neutral towards the natural distribution or we might be hostile towards it and that which of these positions we adopt will have an important bearing on the scope of the distributive theory we advance. From there, I tested the thought that egalitarians are in the business of correcting for the deficiencies of market systems. I concluded, however, that a more thoroughgoing scrutiny of the underlying operation of the market is needed before egalitarians can commit themselves to deferring to its results, even where those results are ameliorated by redistributive measures.

7

Why work?

In the preceding chapters I have been concentrating on the role that concerns about equality and responsibility should play in our thinking about who should get what. These concerns are not, however, the only ones that egalitarians have been called upon to recognize and defer to. Indeed, Stuart White has recently entered a plea for considerations of *reciprocity* to be given their due by egalitarian thinkers. White's plea has been advanced in several contexts, not least in the context of his rejection of the case for an unconditional basic income.[1] In essence, White believes that an unconditional basic income would be exploitative and it would be so because it would result in those who do make a productive contribution begin exploited by those who do not. The charge of exploitation is, according to White, underpinned and motivated by what he terms the 'reciprocity principle'. This reciprocity principle is clearly seen by him as a, perhaps *the*, core element of any plausible account of distributive justice.

My interest in these arguments is not one that centres on the particular issue of a basic income, unconditional or otherwise. Instead, it is one that centres on how far philosophical egalitarians—amongst whose number White would, I think, count himself—should want to associate themselves with principles of reciprocity of the kind he advances. This is not, however, simply a matter of philosophical interest. As it happens, the Labour Party in Britain—so-called *New Labour*—has for some time been making reciprocity-like noises in its pronouncements upon unemployment and the unemployed, single mothers, and other examples of what it regards as Britain's social flotsam and jetsam. Central to *New Labour*'s concerns is the issue of whether the link between work, on the one hand, and the receipt of benefits, on the other, is one that requires strengthening or weakening. The stance one adopts on this issue will turn, in part, upon how one views work and working as institutions considered in their own right. My suspicion, to be elaborated as the argument develops, is that *New Labour* and Stuart White alike attribute to work *per se* a moral significance that is more in keeping with ideas traditionally associated with desert theory than with the egalitarianism to which one might otherwise think both subscribe. Tony Blair's government has, however, still to provide a compelling *theoretical* defence of its stance in this area. To date, that task has fallen to leftish thinkers such as White. In examining his views, I am, therefore, trying to test what I think is the most well-developed leftish account of the reciprocity principle and its significance for jobs and benefits.

The chapter is in three broad sections. In the first I look at the role and status of claims about reciprocity in general and I examine the extent to which the claims of reciprocity should carry independent weight in arguments about justice. I claim that reciprocity cannot do the independent work that its supporters want it to do. In the second section I scrutinize the use to which claims about reciprocity are put in the context of the issue of jobs and benefits. In this connection, I advance two claims. The first is that what appears to motivate the reciprocity argument is the idea that a just distribution is one in which there obtains a hypothetical balance of benefits and burdens between and among the members of a community. The second is that this argument is to a large extent prosecuted by trading on the thought that, other things being equal, to engage in contributive activity is to incur a burden and not to engage in such activity is to secure a benefit. But what makes an activity *contributive*, still less what makes contributive activity burdensome, are matters that are commonly left unresolved. As such, I believe that further work needs to be done on the principle of reciprocity to render it compelling and, in particular, to render it compelling to those of leftish persuasions. In the third section of the chapter, I consider the relation between egalitarianism and the approach that says that we ought to distribute advantages and disadvantages according to individual desert.

Let me begin by examining the status of the reciprocity principle itself. I take as my starting point the thought that reciprocal relations obtain where there exists between individuals some mutual concession and some mutual benefit. A relation in which all the concessions attached to one party and all the benefits to the other would not qualify to be regarded as a reciprocal relation as we ordinarily understand it. By the same token, there is nothing in the *idea* of reciprocity appearing to require that the advantages or privileges conceded, and the benefits secured, by the parties to the relation need be equal or identical. A relation may properly be termed *reciprocal* even where the relevant concessions and benefits are unequally distributed between the parties in question. It does, however, appear to be an essential feature of the notion of a reciprocal relation that the parties to the relation act, in some sense, in good faith and concede such advantages and privileges as it is appropriate for them, given their individual circumstances, to concede. That is, the relevant concessions must conform to the requirements of proportionality and equity in order for the relation to be reciprocal in character. Thus we find Stuart White claiming of his *egalitarian* conception of reciprocity that 'there is no presumption that one's contribution must be equal or directly proportional

in value to the value of the benefits one recieves'.[2] Indeed, he goes on to assert
that 'reciprocity is now conceived not as a matter of 'putting in as much as
one takes out', but of 'doing one's bit'.[3]

That doing one's bit forms part of our understanding of what makes a
reciprocal relation a *reciprocal* relation, rather than a relation of domination
or one of love, tells us something about the formal properties of relations of
this kind. It tells us something about what would have to be true of a relation
in order for it to be regarded as authentically reciprocal to begin with. But it
does not tell us what it is about reciprocal relations in particular that makes
compliance with the terms of such relations mandatory. It does not tells us,
that is, what makes reciprocal relations *binding* by virtue of their specifically
reciprocal properties. Some reciprocal relations we can think of are indeed
binding. But they seem to be binding for reasons that do not rest upon or
require an appeal to considerations of reciprocity. Contractual relations, for
instance, are often reciprocal relations of the kind I have been describing. Likewise relations of promise-keeping. But if we want to know why we should
comply with the terms of a contract into which we have entered, or why we
should keep our promises, it will surely be introducing into the argument a
needless circuit to claim that we are bound to comply because the relations
are reciprocal in character. Clearly, there is a more straightforward answer at
our disposal. This answer would claim, very simply, that what binds us to stick
to our contracts or to keep our promises is precisely that we have voluntarily
undertaken to do so.[4]

Are reciprocal relations and their concomitant demands necessarily voluntary in character? On this I detect an ambivalence in the literature. Certainly
there exists a tendency to roll together the two notions and thereby to confuse
the terms of the argument. In advancing his own duty of fair play argument,
John Rawls, for instance, hesitated on the question of whether the benefits of
social cooperation to which *his* (reciprocal) duties of fair play applied need
be willingly accepted by those concerned and it is commonly thought to be a
weakness in Rawls's position that his own reciprocal duties lacked the relevant
voluntary component.[5] White, for his part, explicitly incorporates the notion
of *willing* enjoyment into his reciprocity principle.[6] But the more emphasis
one places upon the voluntary character of reciprocal relations the more it
comes to appear that much of what is said in the language of reciprocity could
better be said in the language of voluntariness. Indeed, one wonders whether,
in White's formulation of his own reciprocity principle, it is not the voluntariness implicit in the notion of willing enjoyment, rather than any claims of
reciprocity, that accounts for the requirement to comply with the social practice in question. Like White, I believe that willing participation in a practice
may indeed bind one to comply with its terms and conditions. Like White
also, I believe that the generation of benefits raises important questions about

the moral relations between providers and recipients. But these are distinct issues, each engaging their own set of moral intuitions. My worry is that by rolling them together under the banner of reciprocity the issues at stake are blurred rather than clarified.

It is, then, always open to us to account for the binding force of *voluntary* reciprocal relations by pointing to the fact that the commitment to relations of this kind is voluntarily assumed and by appealing to a principle of fidelity in respect of undertakings we have voluntarily entered into. Perhaps, however, there is another way in which we can test the binding character of the reciprocity principle, namely by removing from the scene its voluntary elements and imagining that the (reciprocal) relations in which we are involved are *involuntary* in character. It might then be shown that involuntary reciprocal relations are binding upon us by virtue of their reciprocal character. Thus it might be said that where I find myself in a relation that might reasonably be characterized as reciprocal, I am bound to comply with the terms of that relation by virtue not of its voluntary character, for it is involuntary, but by virtue of its reciprocal character and its reciprocal character alone.

I am not, however, persuaded that an appeal to the bare notion of reciprocity, considered in isolation from other commitments, is any more revealing in accounting for the binding character of (certain kinds of) involuntary relations than it is in accounting for the binding character of (certain kinds of) voluntary ones. To see this, return to the account of reciprocal relations that I sketched above. Recall my suggestion that implicit in the idea of reciprocity was a principle of proportionate or equitable concession, analogous to the principle of doing one's bit. It cannot, however, be *sufficient* for me to be subject to a requirement to do my bit that others have done theirs. To see why, imagine that we find ourselves living in a society not unlike that of apartheid South Africa in which one group, the Reds, persecutes another, the Greens. Each member of the Reds is required by law to give up one Sunday a month to engage in such persecution. Is it plausible to claim that this Sunday I ought, as a Red, to do my share of persecution because last Sunday my Red neighbour did his? If I believe that claims of reciprocity are binding regardless of *what* is to be reciprocated, then I will answer in the affirmative. And I will answer in the affirmative because I will believe that there are reasons to do one's bit—in the form of conforming to the requirements of a scheme to which others have conformed—regardless of the substantive content of the scheme's rules and principles.[7]

This example points to one of two things: *either* that reciprocity has no independent value *or* that reciprocity does have independent value but that value is outweighed in this particular case. Whichever it is, the bare injunction to do one's bit in return would surely relinquish plausibility were it to justify an individual's acting wickedly or unjustly in cases where he had benefited from someone else's acting wickedly or unjustly. It cannot, then, be convincing in itself as an account of the moral requirements attaching to individuals without the assumption that there exists a prior standard for assessing the moral acceptability of individual conduct and, further, that conduct judged unacceptable by the lights of that standard is conduct in respect of which considerations of reciprocity either do not apply at all or do apply but only weakly. As I indicated earlier, certain minimum standards of equity and proportionality are built into, form part of the make up of, the notion of reciprocity. The demand to reciprocate cannot sensibly be interpreted as being without substantive prerequisites or implications.

This suggests in turn that the (reciprocal) injunction to do one's bit in return will be activated, if it is to be activated at all, only against the background of a set of rules and principles that satisfy the requirements of substantive equity and proportionality or, more generally, of justice.[8] Rawls, for one, was adamant that his own reciprocal duties applied only against the background of distributive rules that were substantively just. Were the background rules in question not to have been just, or to have been unjust, considerations of reciprocal duty would not have applied.[9] Of course, to claim that considerations of reciprocity are not sufficient to establish the existence of a duty to do one's bit leaves open the possibility that they might none the less the *necessary* to do so. If, however, concerns about the content of the background rules of justice assume not merely conceptual but *normative* priority over concerns about reciprocity, then is it not the duty to comply with just rules that motivates the claim that we should do our bit in a just society? In other words, where the background rules are just it may indeed be a matter of injustice if we fail to do our bit. But this is because, in such cases, to do one's bit is to conform to the rules of justice in question. Thus, I do my bit where and if I satisfy the requirements of justice, requirements that will concern themselves with the nature and extent of my duties to others. If doing my bit is taken to be *synonymous* with complying with the requirements of justice, then it will only be trivially or tautologically true that I satisfy the requirements of justice *in and through* doing my bit. A failure to act reciprocally, in the relevant circumstances, may indeed be unjust. But the injustice is parasitic upon claims relating to the content of the background rules in question and one's duty to comply with rules of that character regardless of the extent to which others discharge their own duties. We should indeed *emulate* the just conduct of others, not because we are subject to distinct and independent duties to reciprocate their conduct but because we are subject to the same requirements of justice as they are.

Moreover, if considerations of reciprocity have no independent force in cases where the background rules in question *fail* the test of substantive justice, this raises doubts about whether considerations of reciprocity have independent force in cases where the background rules *pass* the test of substantive justice—in other words whether they have independent force, full stop. If we pursue this line of enquiry, then it seems we are not merely casting doubt on whether any telling conclusions about justice can be *derived* from an appeal to considerations of reciprocity. We are casting doubt on whether considerations of reciprocity themselves occupy a derivative status in moral argument—we are suggesting that much of what is said in the language of reciprocity is said better in the language of substantive principles of justice and their concomitant duties and rights.[10] Stuart White, for his part, appears to me to come close to conceding the derivative view. Having begun by claiming that 'the reciprocity principle *underpins* the [exploitation] objection [to an unconditional basic income]'[11] he then goes on to suggest that violations of reciprocity are objectionable *because* they are unfair[12] or *because* they are exploitative.[13] But if such violations are objectionable because they are unfair or exploitative this suggests that concerns about reciprocity do not occupy the fundamental status he and others appear to want to attribute to the reciprocity principle.

As it happens, White has indicated that he *does* see his reciprocity principle as occupying a derivative status, at least in the sense that it articulates a concern about a certain kind of unfairness.[14] This is the unfairness that I associated in the second chapter with the notion of expensive tastes, namely, the unfairness that is said to arise where people displace the cost of their lifestyle choices upon others. And indeed the appeal to reciprocity appears to capture nicely the thought that fecklessness and wastefulness are the primary political sins. Apart, however, from the doubts that I have expressed already about the substance of this position, I remain to be convinced that it really *is* part of the inner logic of reciprocity that it should be marshalled in the service of one set of values rather than another. My confidence in this is only bolstered by the claim that the demands of reciprocity follow from, articulate, or serve as a shorthand for the demands of a deeper account of the principles that should govern our relations with one another, namely, an account of fairness in distribution.

Let me sum up. In the preceding discussion, I have sought to cast doubt on the claim that an appeal to considerations of reciprocity can succeed in accounting for the binding character of (certain kinds of) involuntary relations. In so doing, I have suggested that a direct appeal to rules of justice and the content of those rules not only can, but generally speaking does, occupy the moral space into which thinkers such as White might otherwise wish to place claims of reciprocity. In short, I have argued that considerations of reciprocity do not constitute a stable basis for determining why one should do one's bit still less what one's bit should be taken to consist in. This mirrors the conclusion I drew in the earlier part of the discussion, namely, that considerations of reciprocity are neither necessary nor sufficient to establish why one should do one's bit in respect of relations one voluntarily enters into.

The temptation to take the notion of reciprocity as the starting point in arguments about justice and to tack on to it certain egalitarian constraints is an obvious one. Indeed, it is a temptation to which thinkers on the left have increasingly succumbed. But this is to launch arguments about justice from the wrong point. If considerations of reciprocity must be modified by background principles of (egalitarian) justice, this suggests that the relevant starting point is or should be the principles of justice themselves. Similarly, if the reciprocity principle applies only to benefits that are willingly accepted by those concerned, this suggests that some of the argument's force rests on an appeal to a principle of voluntarism. In short, the danger is that of trying to smuggle in contentious arguments about distributive justice under the seemingly uncontentious umbrella of an appeal to reciprocity. But a principle of reciprocity is not a theory of justice and we should not appeal to one under the guise of appealing to the other.

Let me now focus on how arguments about reciprocity bear upon the issue of jobs. To this end, I want to begin by noting that the reciprocity principle articulated by Stuart White receives several formulations. In its raw, non-egalitarian form the principle reads as follows:

Those who willingly enjoy the economic benefits of social cooperation have a corresponding obligation to make a productive contribution, if they are so able, to the co-operative community which provides the benefits.[15]

This principle is supplemented and modified by White in order to take account of what he sees as the potentially inegalitarian features of reciprocity principles of this kind. From this process of refinement issues the *egalitarian* reciprocity principle:

Each person is entitled to a share of the economic benefits of social cooperation conferring equal opportunity (or real freedom) in return for the performance of an equal handicap-weighted quantum of contributive activity (hours of socially useful work, let us say, weighted by labour intensity).[16]

In answer to the question of why reciprocity principles of this kind should be taken to be expressive of the demands of justice comes the argument that it is 'unfair' for some to enjoy the (economic) benefits of social cooperation without 'making a relevantly proportionate contribution . . . in return'. But the argument goes beyond the language of fairness for, as I have suggested already, what is being claimed is that it is not merely unfair not to make a productive contribution but that it is *exploitative* not to do so. One who neglects to make a reciprocal contribution of the relevant kind 'claim[s] access to these benefits on what are necessarily advantaged terms, thereby treating [his] fellow citizens . . . as if they were just instruments to [his] own wellbeing'.[17] What we have here, then, is a selection of terms and principles, namely that, under conditions of 'social cooperation', 'economic benefits' are produced as a result of 'contributive activity' undertaken by the members of the cooperative unit in question. Those who 'willingly' claim these benefits, without undertaking reciprocal contributive activity, stand guilty of conduct that is unfair or exploitative, or both.[18]

One might, of course, seek to account for the injunction to engage in contributive activity in terms other than those deployed in the argument I am examining. One might claim that each is under a requirement to offer a social contribution as part of a more general requirement to increase, perhaps even to maximize, the stock of benefits, economic or otherwise, at the disposal of one's community or fellow man. Alternatively, one might claim that contributive activity is virtuous and that each of us is subject to a requirement to do that which is virtuous. In neither case, however, is the injunction to contribute one that draws its force from considerations of reciprocity or mutuality more generally. To understand the reciprocity argument as it bears on the issue of contributive activity, we must focus on the dynamics of mutuality to which it appeals and consider what *sort* of debt arises as a result of my (willingly) accepting a benefit and to whom or what that debt is owed.

Were economic benefits to come into being other than by way of the (contributive) activities of community members—were they to fall upon a community as though manna from heaven—there would be no requirement upon those who claimed such benefits to engage in contributive activity by way of reciprocation, for there would be no human agent or agency to whom such reciprocation was owed. So, what triggers the demand for or requirement of reciprocal activity is not that benefits exist and may be enjoyed, for then the reciprocity in question would be no more than a form of self-denial, a debit in one's own private ledger. What triggers the requirement to *do one's bit in return* is that the particular benefits in question are those that can only come into being and be as a result of human (contributive) activity. They are not the sort of benefits that can arise and persist independent of human activity. What we seem to be reciprocating, then, is human activity directed towards a certain end, namely the provision or generation of economic benefits. Such activity can, seemingly, be reciprocated only in the form of analogous activity on our part, activity that in turn must be reciprocated. And so on and so forth.

But now several puzzles emerge. I suggested that duties of reciprocation are taken to arise in respect only of activity directed towards the provision of economic or what are sometimes called 'socially useful' benefits. That is, the existence of activity and the provision of economic benefits *resulting from that activity* are singly necessary and jointly sufficient to establish that there is placed upon the willing beneficiaries of such activity a duty or requirement of (proportional) reciprocation. This raises the question of whether my reciprocal contribution should be a function of my capacity to contribute, or of the extent of the benefits I claim, or of how much activity on the part of others has gone into producing the benefits that I do claim, or some combination of these.

In respect of the first of these White advances the idea of a 'reasonable work expectation', the thought being that how much time any given individual devotes to productive work should be determined by their ability to contribute and the extent and nature of their non-productive, typically domestic, commitments.[19] But imagine now that we have two individuals, Quick and Slow. Quick produces 10 widgets an hour to Slow's 1 widget an hour. On the assumption that each is claiming access to the same social benefits as the other, what would have to be true for there to be a condition of reciprocal balance between the two, in other words for each to be said to be doing their bit? One answer is that a reciprocal balance obtains between the two where and if each produces the same number of widgets every week or month. This would mean that reciprocity would demand that Slow engage in ten hours of productive activity for every one hour of such activity in which Quick engages. This is not, I am quite certain, the view of reciprocity that its egalitarian proponents are trying to defend. Indeed it would run counter to the egalitarian qualifications embodied in the notion of a 'reasonable work expectation'.

But if reciprocity is not a matter of how much one produces, what *is* it a matter of? The best sense I can make of the argument is that what is to be reciprocated is *time spent engaged in contributive activity* weighted, as I said earlier, for or by labour intensity. That is, it is a matter of how much each puts in to the productive process rather than of how much comes out. Thus, in the example I have been using, a condition of reciprocal balance obtains between Quick and Slow where and if each devotes the same amount of time to contributive endeavour. This would be true even if Quick were now to give way to Very Quick, who produces widgets at the rate of 100 an hour, and Slow were to give way to Very Slow, a producer of 0.1 widgets an hour. In other words, the least able members of the community owe it to everyone else, as a matter of reciprocity, at least to *show willing*. This is so (even) if their productive output, individually or collectively, is (likely to be) dwarfed by that of the most able members of the community. What underpins this view may be the thought, to which I alluded earlier, that the notion of reciprocity appears to carry with it the idea of the parties to the reciprocal relation acting in good faith. Thus it is a matter of good faith that each be prepared to devote as much of their day to contributive activity as everyone else, even where not very much is likely to result from that activity. Indeed, it is in these terms that the requirement that the unemployed make a 'conscientious effort' to find work should, I think, be understood.[20]

But it seems to me that there are two further ideas at work here. The first is that time spend engaged in productive activity, broadly construed, is a form of burden. To see this, return to a passage extracts from which I cited earlier:

To willingly enjoy . . . cooperative benefits without being willing to make . . . a reciprocal contribution is to claim access to these benefits on what are necessarily advantaged terms, thereby treating one's fellow citizens . . . as if they were just instruments to one's own wellbeing.[21]

Note that the claim here is not that those who fail to make a reciprocal contribution are generally or often or likely to be advantaged. It is that they are '*necessarily* advantaged', that is it is stipulatively true in all cases that such a condition of relative advantage obtains. And this is so because what has been assumed is that benefits in the form of economic advantages are in some way *necessarily* offset by way of the burdensomeness of spending time engaged in productive or contributive activity, again broadly construed. This impression is reinforced by the references in White's argument to the idea that engaging in contributive activity is a form of cost to be borne by contributors and to be reciprocated by (willing) beneficiaries.[22]

This connects up with a second idea present in the argument, namely, the (implicit) appeal to a hypothetical balance of benefits and burdens as expressive of the requirements of justice. Such an appeal sits comfortably alongside the notions of balance and proportionality present in principles of reciprocity as indeed does the condemnation of the exploitative character of unforced idleness. On the view of justice being advanced here, economic advantages are taken as beneficial, time spent working as burdensome. In a world of equal needs, talents, domestic commitments, and the rest there would be no call to correct for the effects of *laissez-faire*, for it is assumed, I take it, that some sort of balance of burdens and benefits would naturally arise that was untainted by differences in brute luck. It is in terms of a desire to correct for inequalities in needs, talents, and the like—and thereby to restore the hypothetical balance that would otherwise be upset by such inequalities—that the 'reasonable work expectation' and other putatively egalitarian refinements of the raw reciprocity principle are best understood.

I have suggested, then, that the egalitarian reciprocity principle seems to be underpinned by the thought that productive or contributive work is necessarily burdensome, or disbeneficial, and must be entered as such in the ledger of the reciprocity principle. I am not sure, however, that there really *is* an argument for this position. It seems, rather, to have the status of an unargued premise. Clearly, the claim that contributive activity is burdensome for those who undertake it is empirically contentious.[23] Some activity is costly or burdensome without being especially socially productive just as some is socially productive without being especially costly or burdensome. It cannot plausibly be claimed that a necessary condition of classifying an activity as contributive is that it imposes some burden or cost upon those who engage in it any more than it could plausibly be claimed that a necessary condition of classifying an activity as costly or burdensome is that it is contributive. Even if contributive activity is burdensome for some it is not so for all and may indeed be the most satisfying and fulfilling aspect of life for many. Moreover, there is good reason to think that the burdensomeness of work is asymmetrical, bearing more heavily upon those working at the bottom end of the scale of income and prestige than those at the top. Stuart White is, of course, aware of this asymmetry and to some extent seeks to correct for it. But the adjustments and corrections he makes are somewhat at the margins of his reciprocity principle—they seek to maintain its integrity whilst eradicating its more obvious implausibilities. What I am suggesting, however, is that claims concerning the asymmetry of labour burden affect the argument not merely at the margins but may indeed be subversive of its central thrust. If, for instance, we want to know why the less talented should put in the same number of hours of productive work each day as the more talented it seems neither plausible nor discernibly *egalitarian* to claim this to be so because productive activity of the kind each is qualified to undertake is equally burdensome. This is especially so when we remember that the greater intrinsic satisfaction the talented are likely to accrue from their work will tend to be reinforced by greater extrinsic rewards in terms of income and prestige. If my job is tedious and, from the point of view of its contribution to the common weal, relatively unproductive it seems peculiar to demand that, in the name of reciprocity, I should be putting in the same hours as those whose jobs are neither tedious nor unproductive. Indeed, one cannot help but suspect that the injunction to labour is intended as much as a sop to the more resentful members of the talented as it is a means to inculcating a sense of social responsibility amongst the recipients of social benefits.

Related to this, it remains something of an open question as to what should, and what should not, count as contributive activity.[24] Whilst the focus tends to be on activity directed towards the provision of *economic* benefits, some appeal is also made to the notion of *social usefulness*, thereby allowing for the possibility that socially useful activity takes place outside the 'formal economy'. The latter point is conceded not least in order to bring within the ambit of contributive activity that which relates to the provision of domestic care. But to concede that we can discharge the (reciprocal) duties we owe to our fellow citizens other than by way of holding down a job in the formal economy is surely to put a significant dent in the argument. What activities are, and are not, undertaken in the formal economy is, I take it, a matter that will vary over time according to the contingencies of political tradition, social attitude, and economic circumstance. Certainly it will be insufficiently stable to constitute the foundation of an account of distributive justice that is intended to serve as a critical standard for assessing the justice or otherwise of *existing* social systems. Beyond this, to allow that the realm of the formal economy is not coterminous with that of the socially useful suggests not only that not all socially useful activities are undertaken by way of jobs in the formal economy but also allows for the possibility that not all jobs in the formal economy are socially useful. Indeed, the notion of socially useful activity remains, as is acknowledged, a hazy one. It might be used broadly to refer to any activity that has beneficial effects upon society at large rather than merely the parties directly engaged in it. Or it might be used narrowly to cover activities that, were they not undertaken outside the formal economy, would have to be absorbed within the formal economy and provided for at public expense. The inclusion of domestic labour under the heading of the socially useful fits in with the narrow reading but presupposes that there exists some sort of *social responsibility* to provide domestic care. Were there to exist no such responsibility there would be no duty upon society in general to provide care of this kind, no call (therefore?) to absorb the provision of such care into the formal economy, and no sense (perhaps) in which domestic care was regarded as *socially* useful, that is, useful to society at large rather than merely to the individuals concerned. Thus, in the attempt to offer an account of reciprocal activity that is not simply a creature of the contingencies of existing market arrangements appeal must be made to an account of social responsibilities the content of which can be supplied neither by claims concerning the burdensomeness of work nor the bare principle of reciprocity.

What marks out the position I have been examining from that of conventional egalitarianism is that it combines an appeal to the intrinsic burdensomeness of productive activity with an exhortation to labour and a conception of justice that seeks to maintain a hypothetical balance of burdens and benefits modelled by way of a principle of reciprocity. In these respects at least it strikes me that it has more in common with the desert theory of Wojciech Sadurski[25]—with its emphasis on the intrinsic importance of rewarding people according to their effortful labour—than it does with the liberal egalitarianism of John Rawls.

If there is an intersection between egalitarianism and the desert view, perhaps we should not be surprised by this. After all, desert theorists share with many egalitarians the belief that concerns about individual responsibility have a role to play in our thinking about who should get what. Moreover, there is an obvious sense in which egalitarians pronounce upon what people *deserve* in the way of advantages and disadvantages. But the sense of desert in question is merely the colloquial one, according to which to claim of an individual that he deserves something is to claim in some general sense that he ought to have that thing. The sense of desert to which desert *theorists* appeal is, however, narrower than this. On their view, to claim of an individual that he deserves something is to claim that his qualities or actions are such that they ought to attract certain kinds of treatment. Thus, it is sometimes said of the hard-working and the prudent that they deserve greater reward—just by virtue of *being* hard-working and prudent—than the idle and the feckless. For many people, judgements of this kind are, I imagine, the stuff of justice itself. Indeed, there can be little doubt that the desert view is more entrenched in popular consciousness than any of egalitarianism's philosophical rivals— more so, in fact, than egalitarianism itself.

Desert theorists agree for the most part that the qualities or actions in question must be ones for which individuals are responsible: people cannot be said to be deserving on the basis of brute luck. They disagree, however, in the matter of how to interpret this demand and in particular in the matter of the range of conduct or characteristics that it captures or excludes. Beyond this, desert theorists disagree as to what *grounds* judgements of desert. Whilst David Miller claims that we deserve things on the basis of qualities or actions of ours that are favourably appraised by others,[26] Sadurski claims that desert, as it relates to justice, is a matter of assessing individuals on the basis of conduct of theirs that is burdensome and that 'has socially beneficial effects'.[27] In this, the parallels with the arguments of a nominally egalitarian theory such as Stuart White's are clear.

This is not to say, however, that desert theory is one brand of egalitarianism nor egalitarianism one brand of desert theory. Indeed, philosophical egalitarians and desert theorists alike generally think of themselves as offering distinct and rival conceptions of distributive justice. From the egalitarian perspective, desert theory is thought to suffer from a number of weaknesses and implausibilities. And, indeed, the most trenchant egalitarian repudiation of the desert account comes from Rawls. But whilst it is often supposed that the Rawlsian attack on desert is pivoted around claims about natural talents and the arbitrariness of their distribution, this is only one component of the attack he offers in *A Theory of Justice*. The other components, he believes, are, either singly or taken together, strong enough to defeat the desert account. In what follows, I want to examine the bases upon which egalitarians, such as Rawls, reject desert theory and, in so doing, to assess whether there exists the distance between the two groups of theories that their respective proponents believe there to be. To do this, I am going to examine five charges levelled against desert theory, namely, that (1) it is self-defeating; (2) it rests upon controversial premises concerning the bases of desert; (3) it is derivative; (4) it rests upon implausible pre-institutional assumptions; and (5) it relies on a controversial account of agency and individual responsibility.

As to (1), desert theory is often thought to be self-defeating. To see this, imagine that we have a social rule that is grounded in considerations of desert. This rule rewards certain kinds of conduct or characteristics and penalizes others. Given this constellation of sanction and benefit, acts that are deserving (that is, acts that conform to the rule) will generally be synonymous with, or indistinguishable from, acts that are merely prudential or self-interested, for it will generally be in the agent's prudential or selfish interest to conform to the rule in question. In order to separate out the deserving from the prudential, we will have to ask whether the agent would have performed the action in question even if the relevant sanctions and rewards had not been in place. But this is to ask whether the agent would have conformed to the rule even if there had been no such rule, which seems an impossible test either to set or to pass.

Against this, it seems clear that these arguments are telling principally against a conception of desert that instructs us to distribute the good and bad things in life on the basis of the moral character of the distributees, a conception of desert that appears to require a certain purity of motive on the part of the parties in question. Indeed, a good deal of Rawls's attack on the desert view is made against precisely this principle of moral desert, the notion, as he puts it, that '[j]ustice is happiness according to virtue'.[28] But Rawls himself recognizes that this is not the only kind of desert theory there is. Indeed, he acknowledges that there is 'a familiar although nonmoral' sense of desert.[29] So what appears to be an attack on the concept of desert itself is really an attack on a particular conception of desert, that of moral desert.[30] Desert theory clearly does embody certain value judgements. But not all value judgements are moral judgements *per se*.[31] So, even if the claim that *moral* desert is self-defeating succeeds, it is not a claim that can necessarily be levelled against non-moral accounts of desert.

This brings me to (2). The charge here is that there are irreducible value conflicts concerning what sort of conduct is deserving, whether it is a matter of input (effort), output (contribution), or some combination of the two. This is what Rawls is getting at when he says that '[t]here seems no way of defining the requisite criterion'.[32] Indeed, a good deal of Rawls's case against desert theory rests on the idea that it cannot provide a stable *political* conception of justice. Given, on Rawls's view, its moralizing and moralistic overtones, desert theory cannot help but rest upon or appeal to a substantive conception of the good: its controversial nature renders it incompatible with the 'fact of pluralism' that I discussed before. This objection to desert theory *is* telling in so far as it points to deep-seated disagreements amongst desert theorists themselves as to what should count as a basis or criterion of desert, and why. By the same token, the objection is decisive primarily if we accept Rawls's characterization of desert theory as *moral* desert where the notion of moral desert implies allegiance to a particular view of what gives value to life. The objection is less telling if we view desert theory as a more secular account of distributive justice—an account that applies to the basic structure of society and the basic structure alone—and as intended to command the allegiance of individuals who may otherwise differ markedly in their comprehensive moral commitments.

According to (3), claims of desert are derivative in the sense that they have no independent basis: they are merely an artefact of social institutions and rules. Our judgements about what people deserve are derived from, and would be unintelligible in the absence of, social institutions. To say that X deserves b is to say that X deserves b according to a given social rule R. The statement X deserves b would be unintelligible in the absence of R. From which it seems to follow that claims of desert are really just claims of entitlement by another name: the statement X deserves b according to R is indistinguishable from the statement X is entitled to b according to R. Rawls, for instance, is willing to concede that, under his own scheme, individuals might be said to receive the benefits and burdens that are *due* to them. But he insists that he is using the idea of an individuals's due only to embrace the institutional claims that they have. Members of Rawls's society receive the benefits that are due to them in the sense that they are entitled to those benefits provided they satisfy the relevant established requirements.[33]

The charge that claims of desert are either glorified claims of entitlement, or simply incoherent, is one that has proved appealing to egalitarian thinkers. Indeed, it is a charge that Ronald Dworkin makes considerable play of in his discussion of the pros and cons of affirmative action programmes and, to some extent, his belief in the distance between his own theory and the meritorian one rests upon it. Dworkin wants to deny that affirmative action programmes fail to judge people 'on their merits'. Thus, he writes that:

There is no combination of abilities and skills and traits that constitutes 'merit' in the abstract; if quick hands count as 'merit' in the case of a prospective surgeon, this is because quick hands will enable him to serve the public better and for no other reason. If a black skin will, as a matter of regrettable fact, enable another doctor to do a different medical job better, then that black skin is by the same token 'merit' as well. That argument may strike some as dangerous; but only because they confuse its conclusion—that black skin may be a socially useful trait in particular circumstances—with the very different and despicable idea that one race may be inherently more worthy than another.[34]

This argument against the desert account is less telling than it might appear.[35] To see why, we can distinguish between the content of the claim that individuals should be treated on their merits and its form. Clearly, the *content* of the claim is context-dependent, at least in the sense that what is taken to count as a qualification, or disqualification, for any given position is necessarily conditioned by the nature of that position and the skills it requires of those who occupy, or aspire to occupy, it. We do not fail to treat prospective surgeons on their merits by excluding the clumsy from medical school. This is because, as a general characteristic, the absence or presence of clumsiness is manifestly relevant to the question of whether any given individual is qualified to undertake the duties demanded of a surgeon. But we would fail to treat prospective surgeons on their merits by excluding certain individuals on the basis of factors that were manifestly irrelevant to their ability to exercise the skills in question. That is the formal constraint built into the claim that we should treat people on their merits: we are formally required to exclude extraneous factors from our judgements concerning the allocation of the positions in question.

Once we view the issue in this way we can begin to see that Dworkin's argument rests upon a subtle conflation of two different ideas, namely, the idea of (unobjectionable) exclusion on the one hand and that of (objectionable) discrimination on the other. Dworkin is quite right to suggest that bases of exclusion vary from context to another: my clumsiness may serve as a basis of exclusion in respect of my ambition to be a surgeon but not in respect of my ambition to compose sublime poetry. But medical schools do not discriminate *against* me in excluding me on the basis of my clumsiness because I am not excluded on the basis of a characteristic that ought not to be invoked in determining my treatment. Discrimination, it is true, is a form of exclusion but exclusion is not necessarily a form of discrimination: the two are not synonymous any more than are lying and spitefulness.[36]

So, if a desert theorist were to object that affirmative action programmes fail to treat people on their merits it would be on the basis that the purposes of medical schools and the like do not include the achievement of an ethnic balance in the relevant profession(s). What masquerades as exclusion is in fact discrimination. Dworkin's answer to this is to claim that we could simply redefine the purposes of the institution in question in order to meet the objection. But the objection was never one that ignored the purposes of the institution nor held that there existed a standard of merit wholly abstracted from these purposes. The claim that we should eliminate arbitrariness from the allocation of opportunities, income, and the like is one based upon an appeal to considerations of fairness rather than upon the efficacy of meritocracy. It says that even if there exist instrumental reasons for selecting individuals for jobs and positions on the basis of their social or ethnic background, there is still a rebuttable presumption that it is unfair to do so. We cannot account for this commitment to fairness in terms of a further appeal to the purposes of the institution(s) in question because no appeal to those purposes can account for the value we attach to such fairness. In this sense, the commitment to fairness *is* a non-instrumental or abstract one to begin with. If Dworkin believes in such principles of fairness, as we may reasonably expect he does, then his commitment to them is as abstract as the desert theorist's belief that people should be treated on their merits. Indeed, there is an obvious sense in which the two ideas amount to one and the same thing.[37]

All of which ties in with (4), the charge that desert theory rests upon untenable *pre-institutional* premises. This is the argument Rawls cites when he claims that

> the concept of moral worth does not provide a first principle of distributive justice. This is because it cannot be introduced until after the principles of justice and of natural duty and obligation have been acknowledged . . . Thus the concept of moral worth is secondary to those of right and justice, and it plays no part in the substantive definition of distributive shares.[38]

To illustrate the point, Rawls draws an analogy with the laws relating to property and theft. Just as it makes no sense to speak of there being theft before there are property rules, so too is it nonsensical to speak of their being moral worth before there are moral standards embodied in a conception of justice. 'For a society to organize itself with the aim of rewarding moral desert as a first principle', writes Rawls, 'would be like having an institution of property in order to punish thieves'.[39]

Stated formally, Rawls's attack on the principle of moral worth takes the following form:

(i)   for a person to be deemed worthy he must be worthy according to some principle of justice; **therefore**

(ii) principles of justice are conceptually prior to judgements of worth; **therefore**

(iii) in the absence of antecedently specified principles of justice, judgements of worth are unintelligible; **therefore**

(iv) a theory (such as desert theory) that specifies as a principle of justice that persons ought to be rewarded on the basis of their worth, in the absence of any (further) antecedently specified principles of justice, is unintelligible.

This strand of Rawls's attack on desert theory is subtle and, seemingly, persuasive. But its persuasiveness may rest, to some extent, on the apparent absurdity of (iv). What Rawls claims is that we cannot take as the starting point of our conception of justice the idea that some are morally superior to others in virtue of certain behaviours or dispositions they display or possess since, *ex hypothesi*, no such moral standards exist. But whilst this argument may be telling against the conception of desert I described earlier as *moral* desert, its force against non-moral desert is less obvious. The reason why desert theorists of the latter school believe that burdens and benefits ought to track choice, effort, and the like is not because the effortful are morally superior to the lazy. It is true that this leaves desert theorists in the position of having to account for why effort and the rest constitute a proper basis of distribution.

But it is also true that *any* theory of justice must begin by specifying which properties of individuals are, and are not, to be relevant to claims of justice. To claim that principles of justice, and of natural duty and obligation, must, in some sense, be decided in advance of an account of which kind of conduct or characteristics should determine distributive holdings seems to ignore the fact that it is precisely the relevance of these things to distributive reward that is at issue to begin with. That is, the decision to exclude certain conduct and characteristics as a basis of distributive reward is as much in need in justification as the decision to include them. There is no uncontroversial starting point to the process of constructing a theory of justice.

According to (5), desert theory rests on a controversial account of agency and individual responsibility. Underlying this charge is the thought that arguments about what people deserve are unavoidably bound up with a deep claim about the metaphysics of the will such that to cast doubt on the force of that metaphysical claim is thereby to cast doubt on desert theory itself. In support of this stands the idea that arguments about what an individual deserves do sometimes sound as though they are arguments about what kind of person he is, for instance whether he is evil or whether he is saintly. As I suggested in Chapter 3, these kinds of judgements do seem to address themselves to something sufficiently fundamental about the individual to place a heavy burden of proof upon those making them—there can be nothing trivial or off the cuff about the sorts of things *being* appraised if the relevant judgements are to stick. But from the fact that we *associate* claims of desert with judgements of this kind it is quite wrong to infer that all claims of desert stand or fall on the basis of such judgements. Again, the distinction between moral and non-moral desert comes into play. Indeed, it is not clear to me why claims of desert as they pertain to questions of who should get what—rather than as they pertain to the kind of profound moral judgements I have been describing— are any more bound up with a particular metaphysical view than other accounts of who should get what that appeal to concerns about agency and individual responsibility.

Rawls, for one, does not seek to uproot desert theory on the basis of claims it advances concerning the metaphysics of the will. True enough, he believes that '[n]o one deserves his greater natural capacity nor merits a more favorable starting place in society'[40] and he believes also that it is, therefore, implausible to hold that individuals deserve greater or lesser reward in so far as such reward derives from their starting position in the natural and social hierarchy. But there does not seem to be anything metaphysically contentious in this argument. Who could seriously suggest that individuals *do* deserve to be born into one set of circumstances rather than another? By virtue of what would they have earned their starting place in the world? What *is* contentious in Rawls's argument is his apparent thought that I cannot come to deserve something that I did not deserve to begin with or that in order to deserve an attribute there must be nothing about that attribute that I do not deserve. In the end, Rawls is led to reject desert theory not out of a belief that the bases of desert are contaminated by determinism but that they are contaminated by arbitrariness—coupled with the further thought that justice calls for the elimination of arbitrariness from distribution.

So, unless I am missing something, it strikes me that the conceptions of agency and individual responsibility to which desert theorists appeal need be no more mysterious than the conceptions appealed to by egalitarians, such as Cohen and Nagel. Whether this observation renders egalitarianism more appealing, or desert theory less so, I am not sure. But when it comes to interpreting what individuals are and are not responsible for I am confident that there is not the distance that is commonly supposed to exist between some, at least, of those who think of themselves as egalitarians and some, at least, of those who think of themselves as desert theorists. This comes into sharper relief when we remember that the more egalitarian desert theorists, such as Sadurski, defer to Rawls's views concerning the morally questionable status of natural talents just as the more desert-oriented egalitarians, such as Stuart White, line up alongside desert theorists in wanting to create space within their theories for the operation of choice and responsibility.

All of which suggests to me that desert theory has not wholly disappeared from the theoretical scene. Indeed, the belief that wastefulness and imprudence are the cardinal political sins—when combined with the belief that it is through *labouring* that we express our commitment to and respect for our fellow citizens—indicates that some egalitarians at least remain drawn to the desert view in their attempts to formulate the demands of distributive justice.

Let me sum up the argument of this chapter. I have addressed the arguments concerning reciprocity, jobs, and benefits on two broad fronts. First, I have cast doubt on whether principles of reciprocity in general can occupy the fundamental status in arguments about distributive justice that some appear to think that they can. Second, I have taken issue with the principle of reciprocity as articulated by Stuart White in particular and I have claimed it does not provide a stable basis upon which to maintain the link between working and the receipt of benefits. From there, I have pointed to the theoretical links between claims about reciprocity, equality, and desert.

In terms of its political implications my worry about White's—and, in the British setting, *New Labour's*—prescriptions is that, for all their putatively egalitarian protections, they would be likely to reinforce rather than attenuate existing inequalities in self-respect between those engaged in satisfying work and those unable to find work or to find satisfaction in such work as is available. Only in recent years have western societies begun to face up to the fact that widespread unemployment may be here to stay and many still find it difficult to move beyond the idiom of blame and reproach when discussing the issue of unemployment and welfare benefits. The call for a greater sense of social responsibility is, I know, aimed at *all* members of society and it is part and parcel of the idea of reciprocity that the relevant reciprocal duties work down the income scale from rich to poor just as they work up from it. For all this, those on the left who are attracted by the principle of reciprocity do not, it seems to me, altogether escape from a diagnosis of the underlying nature of contemporary unemployment and underemployment that imports much of the older idiom to which I alluded before. Certainly I find something a little unpalatable in the repeated exhortations to the unemployed to make a conscientious effort to find work, as though the frustrations of unemployment would be ameliorated through being conscientiously pursued. In the United States, for instance, the political impetus to strengthen the link between work and the receipt of benefits is not, for the most part, one rooted in claims of egalitarian justice. In pursuing their work-based principle of social benefits Stuart White and Tony Blair need perhaps to be mindful of the company they are keeping.

CONCLUSION

The temptation when writing a conclusion is either to serve up the Introduction in the past tense or to offer a summary of what has gone before in the order in which it appeared. I want to resist both temptations and to do so by launching my discussion from the chapter that is most recent rather than from the one that is now most remote. Indeed, it seems to me that the argument that we should link the receipt of welfare benefits to a willingness to work—whilst often couched in the language of reciprocity—captures well the *tone* of much recent egalitarian thinking. On the one hand, philosophical and political egalitarians alike have taken to talking as though there is something discernibly *egalitarian* about claiming that people are not responsible for many of the things for which they are ordinarily thought to be responsible. Nowhere is this better illustrated than in the arguments about natural talents that I examined in Chapter 6. On the other hand, egalitarians have also taken to talking as though there is something discernibly *egalitarian* in the thought that people should stand or fall according to factors for which they are responsible and, beyond this, that they should not displace the costs of their chosen lifestyles on to others.

There does not, however, seem to be anything *inconsistent* in thinking that people are indeed responsible for much of what they do and what they are *at the same time* as thinking that we should favour equal distributions over unequal ones. Similarly, there is nothing inconsistent in thinking that people should stand or fall according to whatever they are responsible for *at the same time* as thinking that there is nothing to be said for favouring equal distributions over unequal ones. The temptation is to assume that there exists a natural affinity between these two areas of argument. Indeed, the temptation is to think that whatever it is that is wrong with arguments about equality can be remedied by a good dose of individual responsibility and that whatever it is that is wrong with arguments about individual responsibility can be remedied by a good dose of equality. But if there is no natural affinity between these two areas, it would be curious indeed to hold up either as the salvation of the other. I tried to suggest as much in Chapter 1 when I catalogued some of the deficiencies in the claim that inequalities as such are objectionable and some of the ambiguities surrounding the thought that inequalities are rendered less objectionable when concerns about responsibility are introduced on the scene. If the claim that we should aim for equality is defective for reasons that have nothing to do with responsibility, the danger of fusing concerns about the two will be that that defective ingredients will remain and contaminate. Similarly, if the difficulty with arguments about responsibility is in part that people disagree fundamentally about what renders people responsible for some things but not for others—a point I discussed in Chapter 3—it does not make for a more attractive distributive theory that those disagreements should be combined with disagreements as to whether we should favour equality over inequality.

To some extent I exaggerate in order to illustrate. But what I have tried to illustrate is that equality and responsibility are not always natural bedfellows. Indeed, their union has the air of an arranged marriage rather than a spontaneous elopement. This is nowhere better illustrated than in the egalitarian intuition itself, for it is by way of that intuition that egalitarian concerns about equality are fused with concerns about responsibility. The ideal of independence I described in Chapter 5 lends some support to this fusion—but only some. My being responsible for a thing is not incompatible with my coming to do, be, or have it against the background of unequal conditions, just as my not being responsible for a thing is not incompatible with my coming to do, be, or have it against the background of equal conditions.

Beyond this, I have, at several points, expressed doubts as to the mischief at which the egalitarian intuition is directed. I suggested that the target of that intuition may not so much be the case where individuals are *unequal* in social goods through no fault of their own as where some are badly off, according to some non-relational standard, through no fault of their own. In short, the egalitarian intuition often appears compelling in so far as it concerns itself with compensation rather than equalization *per se*. Moreover, the intuition may pay less heed to the claims of individual responsibility than appearances suggest. On the egalitarian account, it is not enough for my holdings to be mine that these have come to me as a result of my decisions and my conduct. In and of itself, that often establishes nothing. Whether I have a claim on my holdings will depend on the conditions facing others and on their decisions and their conduct. As such, the comparative judgement egalitarians take to be decisive is one focused on whether the choices facing different individuals are, in some sense, equal. It is not one focused on the question of my responsibility for my holdings taken in isolation.

Of course, there is an obvious sense in which egalitarians can claim their schemes to be interpretations of the equal opportunity principle and I have no doubt that there is a certain political capital in their doing so. They can say that the impulse to exclude various natural and social differences as determinants of socio-economic reward merely extends the logic of equal opportunity, rendering the opportunities in question substantive rather than formal along the way. Indeed, it is in these terms that Rawls prosecutes his own case for the prima facie justice of equality of condition and something similar is true of the other egalitarian thinkers I have been examining. Having suggested, however, that there are political attractions for egalitarians in making their case on the basis of an appeal to the equal opportunity principle I must now concede that this strategy runs the risk of exaggerating popular support for some at least of the concerns that I have taken to underlie that principle.

I venture this thought because egalitarians are sometimes given to speak as though principles of equality and responsibility—singly or taken together—pretty much exhaust the stock of principles we have available to us in thinking about who should get what. Certain egalitarians do this, I think, out of a belief that our intuitions in matters of justice are capable of being boiled down to a single or simple set of concerns, concerns that come to define the character of the moral point of view. My suspicion, however, is that most of us prefer not to characterize the moral point of view in terms of one set of concerns, such as concerns about equality and responsibility properly combined, and one set of concerns only. Most of us probably see the moral point of view as embodying a plurality of concerns, with the question of which of these should be decisive being determined according to the circumstances in question. We might, for instance, think the fact that our natural talents form part of what we are is relevant to the question of whether natural talents should attract social reward—even if we do not think that our natural talents are somehow within our control or that they are somehow deserved. Similarly, we might think that effort, being the kind of thing that it is, should attract social reward—even, again, if we do not think that everyone has it in them to be effortful or, at least, to be effortful to the same extent as their neighbour. And we might think these things at the same time as agreeing with egalitarians that claims about control and responsibility are entirely relevant when it comes to countering the arguments of those who would want to see social goods apportioned on the basis of race, gender, or social class.

In other words, resistance to the egalitarian position in respect of talents, effort, and the like arises not from the thought that these are things we choose or have some sort of control over. Instead, such resistance arises from the thought that the moral significance of talent and effort lies elsewhere altogether—in the popular mind, it is the fact they are part of *what we are* that accounts for their significance in deciding upon claims to social goods. In this sense, a major obstacle to the political advancement of egalitarianism is precisely that many would see egalitarians as operating with a picture of the human individual that puts *too much* emphasis on these questions of responsibility rather than not enough or, at least, that puts the emphasis in the wrong place.

Of course, from the fact that we might *think* in these pluralistic terms about distributive justice it certainly does not follow that we are entitled, philosophically, to compartmentalize our thinking about who should get what in the way I have been describing. It may just be that most of us, most of the time, are not thinking clearly. I say this in the knowledge that I do not really have an answer to the question of whether a theory of justice can enjoy philosophical credibility only if it achieves the sort of deep consistency I have said most of us are happy enough to do without in our everyday thinking about justice. I am not saying it is misguided to look for deep principles that might serve to unite our intuitions. Nor am I saying that the account of the moral point of view offered by egalitarians is crazy or unappealing. All I want to say is that how the moral point of view is characterized to begin with is precisely what separates one account of who should get what from another. In the end, I am not sure that it really does make sense to think of there being an overarching account of the moral point of view under the banner of which all accounts of distributive justice operate.

Beyond this, it seems to me an open question whether the force of the intuition that holdings should in some sense track what individuals are responsible for would be diminished were it to be generally accepted that that intuition really *did* have the distributive implications egalitarians attribute to it. Indeed, if egalitarians are to entrust the political advancement of their cause to an appeal to seemingly widespread intuitions concerning the relevance of concerns about responsibility to questions of who should get what, then they must also be alive to the possibility that the intuitions in question may themselves be unstable. That is, a commitment *in the abstract* to the intuitions upon which the egalitarian position rests may wither in the face of *concrete* distributive prescriptions that serve to undermine the force and appeal of the intuitions from which those prescriptions are drawn. It is far from obvious whether principled commitments are generally held in isolation from views about their substantive implications. Seen in this light, the dilemma facing egalitarians is that they must combine an appeal to the status quo with an attempt to subvert it. This is not an insurmountable obstacle nor one peculiar to egalitarianism. Still less is it the case that egalitarians are oblivious to the difficulties involved. The possibility remains, none the less, that the egalitarian conclusion might come to be seen as invalidating its intuitive premises.

Underlying much of this is the worry that it is only egalitarians who see inequalities as unequivocally disadvantageous and only egalitarians who happily move from the claim that individuals should not suffer disadvantages through no fault of their own to the claim that they should not suffer *inequalities* through no fault of their own. Quite how egalitarians go about convincing their opponents that relational disadvantages really are the *kinds* of disadvantages that engage our interest in questions of individual responsibility, I am not sure. Certainly, their cause is not helped by the fact that the worries we think we have about inequalities often turn out to be worries about something that in some sense comes before or lies beyond the inequalities themselves. For all this, my aim in this book has not been to lend support to those who are *anti*-egalitarians. From the thought that some defences of equality do not work it certainly does not follow that all defences of *inequal-*ity do work. Nothing I have said here supports the idea that inequalities are never objectionable. Nor does it support the idea that the supposed benefits of inequalities always outweigh the costs. That there sometimes *are* costs seems to me beyond doubt: there is nothing odd in the thought that luxury and excess are more likely to contaminate human relations than they are to foster a spirit of mutual concern and common purpose. Unfortunately, many thinkers on the political left—in Britain at least—have got it into their heads that a disdain for equality is a mark both of political realism and analytical rigour. But the realism is often no more than cowardice and the rigour no more than dogma. In reviewing its commitments, I for one, hope that the political left will have the courage not to hide behind banalities about markets, globalization, and the internet and to offer instead a clearly thought out view about what it means for a society to do right by its citizens in the distribution of social goods.

ENDNOTES

INTRODUCTION

1. By responsibility I will generally mean *individual* or *personal* responsibility, terms I use more or less interchangeably. Where the context permits, I dispense with these terms and talk simply of *responsibility*.

2. The distinction I draw here between political and philosophical egalitarianism is similar to the distinction drawn by Samuel Scheffler between political and philosophical liberalism: Scheffler, S., 'Responsibility, Reactive Attitudes, and Liberalism in Philosophy and Politics', *Philosophy and Public Affairs*, 21:4 (1992), 299–323, 299–301.

Chapter 1: What is objectionable about inequalities?

1. The distinction between causes and consequences, as it relates to questions of inequality, is one I take from G. A. Cohen, who takes it in turn from Brian Barry. See Cohen, G. A., 'The Pareto Argument for Inequality', *Social Policy and Philosophy*, 12:1 (1995), 160–85, 161–2.

2. Here I follow what Cohen says in 'The Pareto . . .', 162.

3. Derek Parfit makes a similar point in distinguishing between the claim that equality has *instrumental* value and the claim that it has *intrinsic* value: Parfit, D., 'Equality or Priority?', *The Lindley Lecture* (Kansas: University of Kansas, 1995), 5–6.

4. The levelling down objection is discussed at length by Parfit, 'Equality or Priority?', 17–18, 23–8, 31.

5. As it is, Parfit alludes to this distinction in his discussion of Moderate and Strong Egalitarians, 'Equality or Priority?', 30–1.

6. I am endebted to an anonymous referee for pointing this out to me.

7. Again, the source is Parfit, 'Equality or Priority', 28–33.

8. Although quite *why* it is telling may be less obvious than it appears. The objection might point to the fact that equality has no independent value or it might point to the fact that in this case the independent value of equality is outweighed by the independent disvalue of toothache. In short, there may be two kinds of bad at work: one relational, the other non-relational.

9. This said, the possibility remains that what makes us focus on lack of pain rather than equality is not that the former is intrinsically valuable and the latter is not. Both might be intrinsically valuable and we just focus on the lack of pain because it is more tangible—a point I take from an anonymous referee.

10. Here, I concur with Parfit, 'Equality or Priority?', 9.

11. Expressed negatively this principle holds justice to require the removal of unjustified or arbitrary inequality, a position to which Rawls seems sympathetic. See
Rawls, J., *A Theory of Justice* (Cambridge, MA: Harvard University Press, 1971),
5–6. The question of whether egalitarians *do* sign up to presumptive principle is,
of course, separate altogether from that of whether they are *right* to do so and,
more generally, of whether they are right to see there being some sort of necessary relation between justice and equality.

12. Nagel, T., 'Rawls on Justice', *Other Minds: Critical Essays 1969–1994* (New York:
Oxford University Press, 1995), 122.

13. For one of the more recent statements of the Difference Principle, see Rawls, J.,
Political Liberalism (New York: Columbia University Press, 1993), 5–6.

14. A point I pursue further in Chapter 5.

15. Of course, for this argument to work the very least we have to assume is that A
and B operate from an equitable starting point. Quite what constitutes an equitable starting point is, again, something I pursue in Chapter 5.

16. By this I do not mean that we are forbidden to worry about relativities in such
cases, merely that, to the extent they figure in our thinking about the distribution
of intrapersonal disadvantages, concerns about relativities carry little independent
weight.

17. What I say here bears a superficial resemblance to the Marxian view of money as
externalized social power and indeed with the Marxian distinction between *use*
value and *exchange* value, notions I became familiar with largely through G. A.
Cohen's magisterial work in this area. See, especially, Cohen, G. A., *Karl Marx's
Theory of History: A Defence* (Oxford: Clarendon Press, 1978). It goes without
saying, although I shall say it anyway, that what Marx and Cohen have to say on
these matters is of a different order of sophistication from what I say under this
heading.

18. This may *sound* like an objection to inequality on the grounds of its bad consequences, but I do not think that the objection is, straightforwardly, a consequentialist one. It so happens that Richard Norman also claims, although not for quite
the reasons I do, that patterns of distribution *matter* when it comes to certain
rights of citizenship and indeed that the argument in favour of distributing these
things equally is insulated, to some extent, from some of the standard doubts
about the value of equality *per se*: Norman, R., 'The Social Basis of Equality', *Ratio*,
x:3 (1997), 238–52.

19. Raz's views are powerfully expressed in Raz, J., 'Equality', *The Morality of Freedom*
(Oxford: Clarendon Press, 1986), 217–44.

Chapter 2: Responsibility and justice

1. The thought that there are different *senses* in which the statement X is responsible for a can be understood is one I take from Hart, H. L. A., *Punishment and
Responsibility* (Oxford: Clarendon Press, 1968), 211.

2. This characterization of universal determinism is one I take more or less verbatim from Wiggins, D., *Needs, Values, Truth* (3rd edn) (Oxford: Clarendon Press, 1998), 281.

3. Hart, *Punishment and Responsibility*, 212–14.

4. Hart, *Punishment and Responsibility*, 227–30.

5. Hart, *Punishment and Responsibility*, 215–27. Liability responsibility is sometimes referred to as personal responsibility or, in certain contexts, moral responsibility, but it is with Hart's terms that I persevere.

6. Quite what the place of concerns about individual responsibility is in arguments about justice is something I pursue further in Chapter 4.

7. Tom Campbell appears to advance just such a view: Campbell, T. D., *Justice* (London: Macmillan, 1988), 153.

8. In his own analysis of the significance of choice and responsibility, Scanlon distinguishes between consequentialist, or what he calls 'instrumental', arguments of the kind described here and what he calls 'symbolic' and 'demonstrative' arguments of the kind I go on to describe below. See Scanlon, T. M., 'The Significance of Choice', S. McMurrin (ed.), *The Tanner Lectures on Human Values* (Salt Lake City: University of Utah Press, 1988), 149–216, 178–81.

9. Here, I draw heavily on what Roger Scruton has to say in this area: Scruton, R., *An Intelligent Person's Guide to Philosophy* (London: Duckworth, 1996), 97–109.

10. A point I take from Williams, B., *Shame and Necessity* (Berkeley: University of California Press, 1993), 152.

11. Scanlon, 'The Significance of Choice', 174.

12. Waldron, J., 'Theoretical Foundations of Liberalism', *Philosophical Quarterly*, 37:147 (1987), 127–50, 146. In his 'The Significance of Choice', Scanlon seeks to place claims about the significance of choice and responsibility to our thinking about justice within the context of a broader *contractualist* view of the nature of moral and political reasoning. Impressive though Scanlon's achievement is, it is from Waldron I first got the idea that there might exist underlying affinities between the two realms of argument.

13. And indeed there is some overlap between the arguments, consequentialist and otherwise, I cited earlier in attempting to account for the relevance of claims about responsibility to claims about justice and the arguments, instrumental and non-instrumental, cited by Leslie Green in the matter of consent and political authority: Green, L., *The Authority of the State* (New York: Clarendon Press, 1988), 181–7.

14. The expensive tastes argument is one most closely associated with Ronald Dworkin and is mapped out in Dworkin, R., 'What is Equality? Part 1: Equality of Welfare', *Philosophy and Public Affairs*, 10 (1981), 185–246, 228–39.

15. An expression that Rawls has used liberally in his various writings.

16. Jonathan Wolff suggests something further, namely, that pursuing the demands of responsibility may sometimes be incompatible with showing individuals the respect they are owed under the terms of what Wolff calls the 'egalitarian ethos': Wolff, J., 'Fairness, Respect, and the Egalitarian Ethos', *Philosophy and Public Affairs*, 27:2 (1998), 97–122.

Chapter 3: What we are responsible for

1. Whilst the view I describe here has certain parallels with that of Strawson, I do not intend it to be read *as* an interpretation of Strawson's view—although, for what it's worth, I interpret Strawson's position in more anti-philosophical terms than might some. See Strawson, P. F., 'Freedom and Resentment', *Freedom and Resentment and Other Essays* (London: Methuen, 1974), 1–25.

2. See, for instance, Rawls, J., 'Justice as Fairness: Political not Metaphysical', *Philosophy and Public Affairs*, 14 (1985), 223–51.

3. Scanlon, 'The Significance of Choice', 195–6.

4. Scanlon, 'The Significance of Choice', 196.

5. I do not mean by this that, when it comes to arranging our social affairs, *nothing follows* from the truth or falsity of universal determinism. Incompatibilists might favour a social arrangement that seeks not to ameliorate determinism but to acknowledge its impact, for instance, through dropping all pretence that the punishment of individuals is or should be tied to the quality of their will.

6. Williams, *Shame and Necessity*, 154.

7. The commentator in question is Smith, G. W., 'Social Liberty and Free Agency: Some ambiguities in Mill's conception of freedom', John Gray and G. W. Smith (eds.), *J. S. Mill: On Liberty in Focus* (Routledge: London, 1991), 239–59, 246–7. Bernard Williams also acknowledges a debt to Mill, in *Shame and Necessity*, 152.

8. A point I take again from Smith, 'Social Liberty and Free Agency . . .', 246–7.

9. Scanlon, 'The Significance of Choice', 185–90.

10. Frankfurt, H., 'Equality as a Moral Idea', *Ethics*, 98 (1987), 21–43.

11. Points I again take from Scruton, *An Intelligent Person's Guide to Philosophy*, 97–109.

12. Brian Barry advances a similar test of responsibility in Barry, B., 'Chance, Choice, and Justice', *Liberty and Justice: Essays in Political Theory 2* (Oxford: Clarendon Press, 1991), 142–58, 156–8.

13. Barry also thinks that there are two tests of responsibility at work in cases like these but his two tests are not quite the same as mine: Barry, 'Chance, Choice, and Justice', 151.

14. The notion of reflective equilibrium is dealt with by Rawls at various points in sections 4 and 9, chapter 1 of *A Theory of Justice*.

15. I should say that my own understanding of what Rawls might be up to in this area was much advanced by the comments of an anonymous referee of mine.

16. Rawls, *A Theory of Justice*, 72.

17. Rawls, *A Theory of Justice*, 72.

18. Rawls, *A Theory of Justice*, 74.

19. The thought that we are responsible for whatever we do and that we are not responsible for whatever happens to us is one I borrow from Thomas Nagel:

Nagel, T., 'Moral Luck', *Mortal Questions* (Cambridge: Cambridge University Press, 1979), 24–38. Nagel is the inspiration for the discussion that follows on from that distinction, but I do not claim to be presenting Nagel's views, still less to be attacking them.

Chapter 4: The social division of responsibility

1. There is some overlap between the distinctions I draw here and the distinction drawn by Norman Daniels between what he calls egalitarian *concerns*, where what is at issue is how things should be distributed, and the *target* of those concerns, where what is at issue is the measure or index of well-being we should favour in distributing the relevant things one way or another. See Daniels, N., 'Equality of What: Welfare, Resources, or Capabilities?', *Justice and Justification: Reflective Equilibrium in Theory and Practice* (Cambridge: Cambridge University Press, 1996), 208–31, 208. As is obvious, I have opted to separate questions about what should be distributed from questions about the index or measure of well-being we should adopt.

2. Robert Nozick's entitlement theory is one such example, standing opposed, as it does, to what Nozick calls 'end-result' and 'patterned' principles of allocation: Nozick, R., *Anarchy, State, and Utopia* (Basic Books: New York, 1974), 149–64.

3. Here I borrow from Thomas Nagel's 'Equality', *Mortal Questions*, 106–27, 111.

4. As I am using the notions of broad and narrow here, a theory is broad or narrow in terms of how far-reaching its implications are rather than in terms of the values it regards as ultimately important.

5. Rawls defends his choice of primary goods in chapter 2 of *A Theory of Justice* as well as in Lecture V of *Political Liberalism*. Dworkin articulates and defends his resource egalitarianism in a number of works, most prominently 'What is Equality? Part 1: Equality of Welfare'; 'What is Equality? Part 2: Equality of Resources', *Philosophy and Public Affairs*, 10 (1981), 283–345; and 'Foundations of Liberal Equality', S. McMurrin (ed.), *The Tanner Lectures on Human Values* (Salt Lake City: University of Utah Press, 1990), 1–119.

6. Thus we find Will Kymlicka, for instance, worrying that Rawls is unfaithful to the putatively Rawlsian principle that people should be compensated for shortfalls in the realm of 'unchosen inequalities' just as we find G. A. Cohen claiming of Ronald Dworkin that the latter's distributive prescriptions are not 'congruent with [his] own underlying motivation' in the matter of individual responsibility. See Kymlicka, W., *Contemporary Political Philosophy: An Introduction* (Clarendon Press: Oxford, 1990), 71; and Cohen, G. A., 'On the Currency of Egalitarian Justice', *Ethics*, 99 (1989), 906.

7. Brian Barry sketches a view of justice resembling the one I describe here, before going on to give it short shrift: Barry, 'Chance, Choice, and Justice', 142–58.

8. These constraints are articulated with admirable clarity by Daniels throughout his 'Equality of What . . .', and in particular on pp. 224–7.

9. Rawls, *Political Liberalism*, 182.

10. Rawls, *Political Liberalism*, 181.

11. A form of words deployed by Rawls throughout *Political Liberalism*.

12. Rawls, *Political Liberalism*, 182.

13. Rawls, *Political Liberalism*, 330.

14. Rawls, *Political Liberalism*, 180–1, n. 8.

15. A point well made by Daniels in his discussion of the distributive theories of Cohen and Arneson, 'Equality of What . . .', 218–23.

16. It has been suggested to me that this may be simplistic: preference revelation techniques employed by microeconomists go some way towards addressing the problem I describe.

17. Rawls's arguments under this heading have been subjected to detailed scrutiny by Scanlon, 'The Significance of Choice', 197–201; by Scheffler in his 'Responsibility, Reactive Attitudes, and Liberalism in Philosophy and Politics', 320–321; and by Schaller, W. E., 'Expensive Preferences and the Priority of Right: A Critique of Welfare-Egalitarianism', *The Journal of Political Philosophy*, 5:3 (1997), 254–73.

18. Rawls, *Political Liberalism*, 189.

19. Rawls, J., 'A Kantian Conception of Equality', R. M. Stewart (ed.), *Readings in Social and Political Philosophy* (New York: Oxford University Press, 1986), 187–95, 191.

20. Rawls, *Political Liberalism*, 185.

21. Rawls, *Political Liberalism*, 269.

22. Rawls, *Political Liberalism*, 183.

23. Rawls, *Political Liberalism*, 185.

24. Rawls, 'A Kantian Conception of Equality', 192.

25. Rawls, 'A Kantian Conception of Equality', 191.

26. Points I take from Schaller, 'Expensive Preferences . . .', 258–9.

27. The example of homosexuality was suggested to me by Raymond Plant but Brian Barry expresses similar doubts about Rawls's argument in his 'Chance, Choice, and Justice', 155.

Chapter 5: The egalitarian intuition

1. Nagel, *Equality and Partiality* (New York: Oxford University Press, 1991), 71.

2. Nagel, *Equality and Partiality*, 71–2.

3. Nagel, *Equality and Partiality*, 72.

4. Cohen, 'On the Currency . . .', 908.

5. Cohen, 'On the Currency . . .', 916.

6. Cohen, 'On the Currency . . .', 931.

7. Dworkin, 'What is Equality? Part 2 . . ', 293.

8. Dworkin, 'What is Equality? Part 2 . . ', 293.

9. Dworkin, 'What is Equality? Part 2 . . ', 296.

10. Of course, there is also an obvious sense in which it might indeed be your fault that there exists an inequality between us: if the options facing us are the same, you might be responsible for the fact that you elected not to follow me in pursuing the options that I pursued.

11. Nagel, *Equality and Partiality*, 71–2.

12. And, in so doing, adopt what Parfit calls the Pluralist View of egalitarianism, 'Equality or Priority?', 4.

13. The distinction between the intention behind, and the effect of, (re)distributing goods in different ways is one drawn also by Parfit, 'Equality or Priority?', 8.

14. Parfit, 'Equality or Priority?', 22, 26–7.

Chapter 6: Natural talents, luck, and the market

1. It might be objected here that being tall or fleet of foot do not happen to us so much as *constitute* us. I defer discussion of this, however, until later in the chapter.

2. Hayek, for one, is anxious to maintain the analytical link between distributions and distributors, although his primary concern is with the distribution of social goods rather than natural talents: Hayek, F. A., *Law, Legislation and Liberty, Volume II: The Mirage of Social Justice* (London: Routledge & Kegan Paul, 1976), 62–100.

3. Parfit discusses this point, and others relating to it, in his 'Equality or Priority?', 14–15.

4. Here, I am endebted to an anonymous referee of mine.

5. Susan Hurley, I know, ventures a similar but more sophisticated argument in an unpublished manuscript of hers dealing with these questions.

6. Rawls's views on procedural justice—pure and impure, perfect and imperfect— are spelled out in his *A Theory of Justice*, 86.

7. Gauthier, D., *Morals by Agreement* (Oxford: Clarendon Press, 1986), 220–1. Gauthier's views are subjected to scrutiny by Parfit in the latter's 'Equality or Priority?', 14.

8. Nozick makes his argument in *Anarchy, State, and Utopia*, 227; and Nagel in 'Equality', 119.

9. Notwithstanding the doubts I have already expressed as to whether it obscures matters rather than clarifies them to speak of a *distribution* of natural talents, I none the less use this form of words at various points in the discussion that follows.

10. Rawls, *A Theory of Justice*, 102.

11. Nagel, *Equality and Partiality*, 107.

12. Nagel, *Equality and Partiality*, 106.

13. Nagel, *Equality and Partiality*, 106.

14. Nagel, *Equality and Partiality*, 107.

15. Gray, J., *Beyond the New Right: Markets, Government, and the Common Environment* (London: Routledge, 1993), 87.

16. To which, I think, the reply might be that there is nothing in what Nagel, for instance, says—or, at least, nothing in what he says *qua* egalitarian rather than *qua* *liberal* egalitarian—that *rules* out redistributing body parts even if there is nothing that *demands* it.

17. Nagel's commitment to the principle of negative responsibility—the principle that there is not a morally fundamental distinction between what the state does and what it allows to happen—is one he advertises in *Equality and Partiality*, 99–101.

18. Norman Daniels makes a similar point, 'Equality of What? . . .', 210.

19. As a matter of Rawlsian exegesis, this claim is contentious. Parfit, for one, thinks that Rawls's account of distributive justice is, in part, motivated by the thought that natural inequalities as such are objectionable. See Parfit, 'Equality or Priority?', 10.

20. Nagel, *Equality and Partiality*, 99.

21. Nagel, *Equality and Partiality*, 100.

22. Nagel, *Equality and Partiality*, 101.

23. Nagel, *Equality and Partiality*, 114.

24. Rawls, *A Theory of Justice*, 311. Emphasis added.

25. Dworkin, 'Why Liberals Should Care about Equality', *A Matter of Principle* (London: Harvard University Press, 1985), 207. Emphasis added.

26. Dworkin, 'What is Equality? Part 2 . . .', 284.

27. Dworkin, 'Foundations of Liberal Equality', 36.

28. Dworkin, 'Foundations of Liberal Equality', 104.

29. Miller, D., 'Equality', G. Hunt (ed.), *Philosophy and Politics* (Cambridge: Cambridge University Press, 1990).

30. Dubious reasoning that is comprehensively exposed by Cohen, both in his analyses of libertarian—and, especially, Nozickian—thinking and of Dworkin's own distributive scheme. In respect of the latter, see Cohen, G. A., *Self-Ownership, Freedom, and Equality* (Cambridge: Cambridge University Press, 1995), 111, n. 32.

Chapter 7: Why work?

1. White, S., 'Liberal Equality, Exploitation and the Case for an Unconditional Basic Income', *Political Studies*, xlv (1997), 312–26. Although White's essay is intended primarily as a response to the arguments advanced by P. Van Parijs in the latter's *Real Freedom for All* (Oxford: Clarendon Press, 1995), my focus in what follows

is on the distinctive position adopted by White rather than on the success or otherwise with which he conducts his arguments in respect of Van Parijs. I should make clear that whilst White was generous enough to comment on an earlier version of this chapter, I do not pretend here to be incorporating those comments, still less to be offering a full account of what White has to say, generally, about questions of distributive justice.

2. White, 'Liberal Equality . . .', 318–19.

3. White, 'Liberal Equality . . .', 319.

4. Michael Lessnoff has suggested to me a powerful objection to bracketing promises and contracts together, namely, that contracts, unlike promises, include a recip-rocal element. A contract of sale is a contract to exchange benefits, whereas a promise that I will help you is not. If someone refuses to pay for a good he con-tracted to buy and duly received, he not merely breaks an undertaking but exploits his partner who has kept *his side* of the bargain.

5. The canonical statement of Rawls's fair play argument is to be found in Rawls, J. 'Legal Obligation and the Duty of Fair Play', S. Hook (ed.), *Law and Philosophy* (New York: New York University Press, 1964).

6. White, 'Liberal Equality . . .', 318.

7. There are two obvious lines of objection to this argument. One says that it does not establish that I *benefit* in any way from the persecution undertaken by my Red neighbour. If I do not benefit from his persecution, so the objection runs, then it is not clear why I should be required to reciprocate his conduct. The second line of objection instructs us to look beyond the immediate relation between my neighbour and me and to examine the broader social context within which rela-tions between Reds and Greens operate. Thus it might be claimed that the existence of a law demanding persecution attests to the fact that the society in question cannot be regarded as a scheme of social *cooperation* of the kind in and to which White assumes his reciprocal duties will apply. That is, part of what it means for a social scheme to be cooperative, on White's account, is that it bene-fits each and every member of that scheme. Of course, the issue then becomes that of how demanding one takes the relevant baseline or point of comparison to be.

8. As I have already indicated, this constraint is implicit in White's characterization of the background conditions against which his reciprocity principle operates.

9. Rawls, 'Legal Obligation and the Duty of Fair Play', 10.

10. Let me repeat that my aim here is to cast doubt on whether considerations of reciprocity have independent force in such cases, not to establish, once and for all, that they do not. At the very least, it seems to me an open question whether duties of reciprocity carry independent moral weight, which is not to assert that reciprocal duties are necessarily reducible to substantive justice nor to deny the existence of conditional duties altogether. My point is that even if reciprocity is a rule of justice it is, at best, a secondary rule of justice.

11. White, 'Liberal Equality . . .', 313.

12. White, 'Liberal Equality . . .', 317–18.

13. White, 'Liberal Equality . . .', 318.

14. White was good enough (in correspondence with me) to offer this clarification of his position, as it relates to the particular article in question.

15. White, 'Liberal Equality . . .', 317.

16. White, 'Liberal Equality . . .', 318. In this, there are certain similarities between White's reciprocity principle and the 'reciprocity thesis' described by Allen Buchanan: Buchanan, A., 'Justice as Reciprocity versus Subject-Centred Justice', *Philosophy and Public Affairs*, 19:3 (1990), 227–52. Buchanan divides what he calls 'the contribution variant' of 'justice as reciprocity' into 'self-interested reciprocity' and 'fair reciprocity'. White's own reciprocity principle appears to belong in the latter camp. Moreover, I think White's reciprocity principle places more emphasis than do the reciprocity principles analysed by Buchanan on the *willingness* of individuals to make a social contribution than on the fact of their doing so as a qualification for the receipt of social benefits. White's emphasis on willingness rather contribution is perhaps intended to counteract some of what Buchanan sees as the more 'inhumane' implications of contribution-based reciprocity principles: Buchanan, 'Justice as Reciprocity . . . , 232.

17. White, 'Liberal Equality . . .', 318.

18. The precise relation between some of these notions is unclear to me. In particular, I am not sure whether social cooperation, on White's view, is *necessarily* reciprocal and indeed whether reciprocal relations are *necessarily* cooperative. Nor is it clear where relations of exchange fit into the picture. Is a market system comprising billions of innocent exchanges a reciprocal system, a cooperative one, neither or both? I am pretty confident that how one answers these questions will have a bearing on the eventual form of the argument but I do not pursue these points here.

19. White, 'Liberal Equality . . .', 319–20.

20. White, 'Liberal Equality . . .', 319.

21. White, 'Liberal Equality . . .', 318.

22. White, 'Liberal Equality . . .', 318.

23. It might be countered here that the claim that productive labour is burdensome, if such a claim there be, is not an empirical claim at all and is not therefore open to empirical refutation. This non-empirical reading of the claim would be supported by my contention that the link between labour and burdensomeness appears as a stipulative one in White's argument. Against this, it seems clear that much of his case is intended to be based on a diagnosis of the defects of existing social arrangements. For White to ignore empirical considerations altogether in such a central part of his argument would be somewhat out of keeping with the tenor of the rest of the chapter.

24. In fairness to White, he acknowldges in his article and elsewhere the importance of pinpointing what contributive activity should be taken to be.

25. Sadurski, W., *Giving Desert its Due: Social Justice and Legal Theory* (Dordrecht: Reidel, 1985). For a discussion of Sadurski's work see chapter 6 of Campbell, *Justice*.

26. Miller, D., *Market, State, and Community: Theoretical Foundations of Market Socialism* (Oxford: Clarendon Press, 1989), 86.

27. Sadurski, *Giving Desert its Due*, 116.

28. Rawls, *A Theory of Justice*, 310.

29. Rawls, *A Theory of Justice*, 314.

30. There are two uncontroversial senses in which desert judgements may be said to be moral in character. First, to claim that X deserves b in virtue of c is to make a moral claim about X. It is to claim that X *ought* to receive b, 'the ought here being the familiar moral "ought"'. Second, desert judgements are moral judgements in the sense that they are predicated of moral agents. See Miller, *Market, State, and Community*, 158.

31. A point I take from Baker, J., *Arguing for Equality* (London: Verso, 1987), 54.

32. Rawls, *A Theory of Justice*, 310–11.

33. Rawls, *A Theory of Justice*, 115, 311–13.

34. Dworkin, 'Bakke's Case: Are Quotas Unfair?', *A Matter of Principle*, 299.

35. I have taken it that Dworkin's argument under this heading, whilst not explicitly invoking the language of desert *per se*, is indeed directed against desert theory.

36. I take this point from Janet Radcliffe-Richards, who made it during a series of seminars on equality which she ran at the University of Oxford in winter 1993.

37. This said, it should be conceded that desert theorists themselves have still to provide a convincing account of what makes some qualities relevant for the purposes of assessing occupational merit and others irrelevant. For a discussion of this point see section 5 of Miller's 'Deserving Jobs', *Philosophical Quarterly*, 42:167 (1992), 161–81.

38. Rawls, *A Theory of Justice*, 312–13.

39. Rawls, *A Theory of Justice*, 313.

40. Rawls, *A Theory of Justice*, 102.

BIBLIOGRAPHY

ARNESON, R., 'Equality and Equal Opportunity for Welfare', *Philosophical Studies*, 56 (1989), 77–93.

—— 'Liberalism, Distributive Subjectivism, and Equal Opportunity for Welfare', *Philosophy and Public Affairs*, 19:2 (1990), 158–94.

—— 'A Defense of Equal Opportunity for Welfare', *Philosophical Studies*, 62:2 (1991), 187–95.

BAKER, J., *Arguing for Equality* (London: Verso, 1987).

BARRY, B., *A Treatise on Social Justice, Volume I: Theories of Justice* (London: Harvester Wheatsheaf, 1989).

—— 'Chance, Choice, and Justice', *Liberty and Justice: Essays in Political Theory 2* (Oxford: Clarendon Press, 1991), 142–58.

—— *A Treatise on Social Justice, Volume II: Justice as Impartiality* (Oxford: Clarendon Press, 1995).

BUCHANAN, A., 'Justice as Reciprocity versus Subject-Centred Justice', *Philosophy and Public Affairs*, 19:3 (1990) 227–52.

CAMPBELL, T.D., 'Humanity before Justice', *British Journal of Political Science*, 4 (1974), 1–16.

—— *Justice* (London: Macmillan, 1988).

COHEN, G.A., *Karl Marx's Theory of History: A Defence* (Oxford: Clarendon Press, 1978).

—— 'On the Currency of Egalitarian Justice', *Ethics*, 99 (1989), 906–44.

—— 'Incentives, Inequality and Community', S. McMurrin (ed.), *The Tanner Lectures on Human Values, Volume XIII* (Salt Lake City: University of Utah Press, 1992), 261–329.

—— 'The Pareto Argument for Inequality', *Social Policy and Philosophy*, 12:1 (1995), 160–85.

—— *Self-Ownership, Freedom, and Equality* (Cambridge: Cambridge University Press, 1995).

DANIELS, N. (ed.), *Reading Rawls* (New York: Basic Books, 1975).

—— 'Equality of What: Welfare, Resources, or Capabilities?', *Justice and Justification: Reflective Equilibrium in Theory and Practice* (Cambridge: Cambridge University Press, 1996), 208–31.

DWORKIN, R.M., *Taking Rights Seriously* (London: Gerald Duckworth, 1977).

—— 'What is Equality?' Part 1: Equality of Welfare', *Philosophy and Public Affairs*, 10 (1981), 185–246.

—— 'What is Equality?' Part 2: Equality of Resources', *Philosophy and Public Affairs*, 10 (1981), 283–345.

—— 'Comment on Narveson: In Defence of Equality', *Social Philosophy and Policy*, 1-1 (1983), 24–40.

——— *A Matter of Principle* (London: Harvard University Press, 1985).

——— *Law's Empire* (London: Harvard University Press, 1986).

——— 'Foundations of Liberal Equality', S. McMurrin (ed.), *The Tanner Lectures on Human Values, Volume XI* (Salt Lake City: University of Utah Press, 1990), 1–119.

FRANKFURT, H., 'Equality as a Moral Idea', *Ethics*, 98 (1987), 21–43.

GAUTHIER, D., *Morals by Agreement* (Oxford: Clarendon Press, 1986).

GRAY, J., *Beyond the New Right: Markets, Government and the Common Environment* (London: Routledge, 1993).

GREEN, L., *The Authority of the State* (New York: Clarendon Press, 1988).

HART, H.L.A., *Punishment and Responsibility* (Oxford: Clarendon Press, 1968).

HAYEK, F.A., *Law, Legislation and Liberty, Volume II: The Mirage of Social Justice* (London: Routledge & Kegan Paul, 1976).

HONDERICH, T., *A Theory of Determinism* (Oxford: Clarendon Press, 1988).

——— *The Consequences of Determinism* (Oxford: Clarendon Press, 1988).

JONES, P., *Rights* (London: Macmillan, 1994).

KYMLICKA, W., *Liberalism, Community, and Culture* (Oxford: Oxford University Press, 1989).

——— *Contemporary Political Philosophy: An Introduction* (Oxford: Clarendon Press, 1990).

MILL, J.S., 'On Liberty', *Utilitarianism, Liberty and Representative Government* (London: Dent, 1968).

MILLER, D., *Social Justice* (Oxford: Clarendon Press, 1976).

——— *Market, State, and Community: Theoretical Foundations of Market Socialism* (Oxford: Clarendon Press, 1989).

——— 'Equality', G. Hunt (ed.), *Philosophy and Politics* (Cambridge: Cambridge University Press, 1990).

——— 'Deserving Jobs', *Philosophical Quarterly*, 42:167 (1992), 161–81.

——— 'Complex Equality', D. Miller and M. Walzer (eds.), *Pluralism, Justice, and Equality* (New York: Oxford University Press, 1995), 197–225.

NAGEL, T., 'Poverty and food: why charity is not enough', P.G. Brown and H. Shue (eds.) *Food Policy: The Responsibility of the United States in the Life and Death Choices* (New York: Free Press, 1977), 54–61.

——— *Mortal Questions* (Cambridge: Cambridge University Press, 1979).

——— *The View From Nowhere* (New York: Oxford University Press, 1986).

——— *Equality and Partiality* (New York: Oxford University Press, 1991).

——— *Other Minds: Critical Essays 1969–1994* (New York: Oxford University Press, 1995).

NORMAN, R., 'The Social Basis of Equality', *Ratio*, x:3 (1997), 238–52.

NOZICK, R., *Anarchy, State, and Utopia* (New York: Basic Books, 1974).

PARFIT, D., 'Equality or Priority?', *The Lindley Lecture* (Kansas: University of Kansas, 1995).

RAKOWSKI, E., *Equal Justice* (New York: Oxford University Press, 1991).

RAWLS, J., *Law and Philosophy* (New York: New York University Press, 1964).

——— *A Theory of Justice* (Cambridge, MA: Harvard University Press, 1971).

——— 'Kantian Constructivism in Moral Theory', *Journal of Philosophy*, 77 (1980), 515–72.

RAWLS, J., 'Social Unity and Primary Goods', A. Sen and B. Williams (eds.), *Utilitarianism and Beyond* (Cambridge: Cambridge University Press, 1982).

—— 'Justice as Fairness: Political not Metaphysical', *Philosophy and Public Affairs*, 14 (1985), 223–51.

—— 'A Kantian Conception of Equality', R.M. Stewart (ed.), *Readings in Social and Political Philosophy* (New York: Oxford University Press, 1986), 187–95.

—— *Political Liberalism* (New York: Columbia University Press, 1993).

RAZ, J., *The Morality of Freedom* (Oxford: Clarendon Press 1986).

SADURSKI, W., *Giving Desert its Due: Social Justice and Legal Theory* (Dordrecht: Reidel, 1985).

SCANLON, T.M., 'The Significance of Choice', S. McMurrin (ed.), *The Tanner Lectures on Human Values, Volume IX* (Salt Lake City: University of Utah Press, 1988), 149–216.

—— 'Moral Basis of Interpersonal Comparisons', J. Elster and J. Roemer (eds.), *Interpersonal Comparisons of Well-Being* (Cambridge: Cambridge University Press, 1991).

SCHALLER, W.E., 'Expensive Preferences and the Priority of Right: A Critique of Welfare-Egalitarianism', *The Journal of Political Philosophy*, 5:3 (1997), 254–73.

SCHEFFLER, S., 'Responsibility, Reactive Attitudes, and Liberalism in Philosophy and Politics', *Philosophy and Public Affairs*, 21:4 (1992), 299–323.

SCRUTON, R., *An Intelligent Person's Guide to Philosophy* (London: Duckworth, 1996).

SEN, A., 'Equality of What?', S. McMurrin (ed.), *The Tanner Lectures on Human Values, Volume I* (Salt Lake City: University of Utah Press, 1980).

—— *Inequality Reexamined* (Cambridge, MA: Harvard University Press, 1992).

SHER, G., *Desert* (Princeton: Princeton University Press, 1987).

SMITH, G.W., 'Social Liberty and Free Agency: Some Ambiguities in Mill's Conception of Freedom', John Gray and G.W. Smith (eds.), *J.S. Mill: On Liberty in Focus* (Routledge: London, 1991), 239–59.

STEINER, H., *An Essay on Rights* (Oxford: Blackwell, 1994).

STRAWSON, P.F., 'Freedom and Resentment', *Freedom and Resentment and Other Essays* (London: Methuen, 1974), 1–25.

WALDRON, J., 'Theoretical Foundations of Liberalism', *Philosophical Quarterly*, 37:147 (1987), 127–50.

WHITE, S., 'Liberal Equality, Exploitation, and the Case for an Unconditional Basic Income', *Political Studies*, XLV (1997), 312–26.

WILLIAMS, B., *Morality* (Cambridge: Cambridge University Press, 1972).

—— *Moral Luck: Philosophical Papers, 1973–1980* (Cambridge: Cambridge University Press, 1981).

—— *Ethics and the Limits of Philosophy* (London: Fontana, 1985).

—— *Shame and Necessity* (Berkeley: University of California Press, 1993).

WOLFF, J., 'Fairness, Respect, and the Egalitarian Ethos', *Philosophy and Public Affairs*, 27:2 (1998), 97–122.

INDEX